TREATMENT OF THE BORDERLINE ADOLESCENT: A DEVELOPMENTAL APPROACH

TREATMENT
OF THE BORDERLINE
ADOLESCENT:

A Developmental Approach

JAMES F. MASTERSON, M.D.

Professor Clinical Psychiatry
Cornell University Medical College

Head Adolescent Program (Payne Whitney Clinic)
The New York Hospital

"Sorrow may be fated, but to survive and grow is an achievement all its own."

R. COLES
Children of Crisis

BRUNNER/MAZEL
A member of the Taylor & Francis Group

Library of Congress Cataloging in Publication Data

Masterson, James F.
  Treatment of the borderline adolescent.

  Originally published: New York : Wiley-Interscience,
1972. (Wiley series on psychological disorders)
  "This volume . . . is the centerpiece of a trilogy
that begins with The psychiatric dilemma of adolescence
in 1967 and ends with From borderline adolescent to
functioning adult . . . in 1980"—Introd.
  Bibliography: p.
  Includes index.
  1. Borderline personality disorder. 2. Separation—
individuation. 3. Adolescent psychopathology. I. Title.

RJ506.B65M37 1985   616.89'022   85-4236
ISBN 0-87630-394-7

This book is written for those students of the human condition who can face the sad facts of reality neither dismayed nor despairing but resolved to bring about what change they can through psychotherapy—that art which blends the magic of Gods, the faith of priests, the craftsmanship of artists, and the logic and reason of scientists.

J. F. M.

Introduction to the 1985 Edition

This volume, originally published in 1972, is the centerpiece of a trilogy that begins with *The Psychiatric Dilemma of Adolescence* in 1967 and ends with *From Borderline Adolescent to Functioning Adult: The Test of Time* in 1980. It presents answers to questions raised in the first volume of the trilogy, questions such as Why do adolescents with a personality disorder not grow out of it? and What therapeutic interventions are necessary to treat these patients?

The book demonstrates why an understanding of the psychodynamics of separation-individuation is essential to both diagnosis and treatment of the borderline adolescent. It shows how the separation-individuation theory lays bare the underlying psychodynamic anatomy of the borderline syndrome and enhances the understanding of transference and resistance, so that it makes intensive psychotherapy not only possible, but the treatment of choice for many of these patients. If the patient receives the proper therapeutic support outlined in this book, he can and will work through much of the painful effect associated with the tie that binds.

The work presented here lays the foundation for the developmental, object-relations approach. With the exception of the concept of etiology, which was subsequently broadened in *Narcissistic and Borderline Disorders: An Integrated Developmental Approach* (1981), the findings have weathered the years almost unchanged. The core has remained intact, although there have been extensive elaborations.

We came to this work without preconceptions and dealt with the clinical evidence on its own merits, following wherever it led. We were gradually drawn deeper and deeper into psychoanalytic developmental theory to find the answers.

At the same time, the clinical work with the adolescents described in detail here taught us how to manage the unique character of adolescent psychopathology—particularly the almost universal use of the defense mechanism of acting out. In recent years, as I have seen supervisees struggling to understand and manage this most difficult of defense mechanisms, I have often wished they could have had clinical experience of the kind described here. It is my hope that this volume will provide an approximately comparable experience for the reader.

It seems to me that there is no better way to begin a study of the borderline personality disorder than with the borderline adolescent. The borderline adolescent's dramatic, flamboyant defenses, and the intense pressure he puts on the therapist for understanding and control, create an ideal learning crucible. Beyond that, a unique advantage of the trilogy is that it combines 30 years of clinical research to guide the reader in his study.

J.F.M.
March, 1985

Preface

The distraught and doting mother of a 2-year-old calls her pediatrician to complain that her toddler follows her around the house and will not leave her side. The angry, depressed, frightened mother of a 15-year-old calls the pediatrician in despair about her son's dropping out of school and taking drugs. These two children, examples of the Borderline Syndrome at different ages, suffer from the same developmental failure—a failure of separation-individuation.

This book demonstrates why an understanding of the psychodynamics of separation-individuation is essential to both diagnosis and treatment of the Borderline Adolescent. It shows how the separation-individuation theory lays bare the underlying psychodynamic anatomy of the Borderline Syndrome, and so enhances the understanding of transference and resistance that it makes intensive psychotherapy not only possible, but the treatment of choice for many of these patients. If the patient receives the proper therapeutic support—as outlined in this book—he can and will work through much of the painful affect associated with the tie that binds.

The basic conflict in the Borderline Syndrome is between a child's inherent developmental push for separation-individuation and the withdrawal of essential maternal supplies that this move entails. If he grows, his mother will cut off his supplies—but grow he must. Thus this tie that binds changes a normal developmental experience into one so fraught with intense feelings of abandonment that the child experiences it as a real rendezvous with death. To defend against these feelings the child clings to the mother, thus fails to develop through the stages of separation-individuation, to autonomy. He cannot loosen the tie. This conflict between growth and supplies produces the two diagnostic hallmarks of the Borderline Syndrome, that is, the abandonment depression and the narcissistic orally fixated ego structure.

The ideas presented oppose the traditional view that one must not interpret his core defenses to the Borderline patient for fear of precipitating a psychosis. It argues for a specific and definitive therapy that is possible only by working with these very defenses—the defenses against the abandonment depression. The goal of therapy, growth through the phases of separation-individuation to autonomy, cannot be reached until the abandonment depression engrafted to this process is relieved. Otherwise, treatment can be only supportive and palliative. The essence of the disorder is left untouched and the patient's adaptive capacity remains crippled.

The treatment must be both intensive and long-term as is illustrated by presenting it in two divisions: first as inpatient care and later as outpatient follow-up.

The material presented is taken from my ongoing clinical study of this disorder over the past 10 years. Hypotheses about therapy derived from these studies have been subjected to clinical test over the past 5 years and the results are reported here.

The skeleton is structured from the stories of the treatment of two adolescents, George and Anne. Parts of the stories of several dozen other adolescents are used to elaborate the basic theme.

JAMES F. MASTERSON

New York, New York
November 1971

Acknowledgments

First and foremost I thank the staff of the Adolescent Program (listed below) for their high standard of performance which virtually created a clinical laboratory for this study.

NURSING

HEAD NURSE:	Mrs. Barbara Nissley
ASSISTANT HEAD NURSE:	Miss Linnea Hammersten
GENERAL STAFF NURSES:	Miss Paula Workman
	Miss Susan Reycraft
	Miss Angie Kulishek
	Miss Lorraine Helms
	Miss Lynn Ostrow
	Mr. Andrew Leon
NURSES AIDES:	Mrs. Corrine Davis
	Mr. Garret Binneweg
	Mrs. Lettie Scurry
	Miss Irene Townsend
	Mrs. Elzia Lake

OCCUPATIONAL THERAPY

Mrs. Francine Herbitter

RECREATIONAL THERAPY

Miss Grace Newburg
Mr. Osborne Walsh

SCHOOL

Mr. William Good
Mr. Julius Schmidt
Mr. Julius Rich

SOCIAL WORK

Miss Grace Hyslop
Mrs. Barbara Gall

PSYCHOLOGY

Mrs. Edna Lerner

The psychotherapy was conducted by a number of residents under my supervision. I am particularly grateful to Drs. Robert MacMurray, Mary DiGangi, and Elmore Rigamer for their treatment efforts that occupy a large portion of the book, and to Drs. Suzanne Draghi, Douglas Elliott, and Anna Zagoloff. Mrs. Barbara Gall, who treated the parents, deserves much thanks for organizing her material so that I could include it. My two staff colleagues, Dr. William Lulow and Dr. Thomas Henley, have my thanks for reading and rendering an opinion on the manuscript.

I specially want to thank Dr. Peter Giovacchini of Chicago, Illinois— an acknowledged expert in the field of character disorders—who devoted much time to a careful and detailed review of the manuscript and whose suggestions as to both content and style improved the work. His theoretical expertise was particularly helpful as illustrated by the following which are but a few of his many contributions: the developmental perspective, the level of ego fixation, and the relationship of ego development to libidinal development.

I am also vastly indebted to Dr. Donald Rinsley, Topeka, Kansas. His published work taught me a great deal. Also, he willingly and generously shared his extensive knowledge with me, raising many critical questions that helped to clarify my thinking.

I am grateful to Dr. Eduardo Kalina of Buenos Aires, Argentina, for his excellent critical review of the manuscript.

The work would not have been possible without the consistent administrative support of Dr. William T. Lhamon, Chairman and Head of the Department of Psychiatry, Cornell University Medical College.

My chief residents during this period Drs. Rudolph Ehrensing, Robert MacMurray, Frank Hamilton, and John Ives contributed indirectly as did my two long-time friends and associates Drs. Willard Hendrickson and Daniel Offer.

I can never thank enough Miss Helen Goodell, Research Associate in Neurology, for being such a patient, tireless editorial companion to a writer's struggles. I offer my gratitude and thanks to my secretary, Miss Taube Honigstock, for her services through the dog days of two hot summers typing, retyping, and retyping.

Finally, I want to thank my wife Pat and my three children, J. F., Richard, and Nancy, for understanding the need for time of a man who would write.

J. F. M.

Contents

PART FOUR   OTHER THERAPEUTIC FACTORS

TREATMENT OF THE BORDERLINE ADOLESCENT:
A DEVELOPMENTAL APPROACH

Prologue*

Resurrection by L. C. M.

I shied from what I considered real, building a world of
my own . . . impregnable; I was unaware of the slowly decaying
castle, a part of which would ebb away with every sudden
storm.

Around the castle I had built a wall of sand,
within this, a wall of sturdy oak.
With grains of hate, I fortified the wall of sand,
yet I did not know that the blinding storm of tears
would dampen the sand, rotting the wood,

> until suddenly, in a flash of lightning,
> in a rumbling that shot and tore through the earth,
> I, in my hate, attempted to destroy it,
> ignorant of the consequences in my silent call for aid,

consciously rejecting all hands thrust in my direction.
I ran from my castle of dreams, attempted to escape from it—
the roaring of despair and the wind of self-pity
swept about me and I rushed to the wall . . . tried to scale it,
and fell back, exhausted . . .

> for my fingers could not grip
> and I slipped in the sand, moaning, crying in the howling
> wind, crawling to a corner to await my own destruction,
> caring no longer for myself, my world, those within it.

Through the foul air, through the whirling mist
that surrounded me, a figure approached. It did not beckon,
but waited for me . . . it did not force me; it was I who
had the choice. And I, with tears of self-hate in my eyes
and venom in my lungs, confusion in my brain,

* The first section of a poem, describing treatment, by a 15-year-old girl—a Borderline Syndrome; the remainder appears in the Epilogue.

1

found, although I resisted, could not conquer it,
and defeated, surrendered my mind.
Surrender was not enough for him—apathy was not the answer.
I spoke through cracked lips, parched from lack

of communication, I finally asked the question aloud,
slowly, meaningfully . . . "what is?",
for he took my hand and led me back to the world I had created,
and I a fugitive, feared to return.

PART ONE

The Borderline Adolescent

CHAPTER 1

The Need for Treatment

HISTORY

Two historical psychiatric scapegoats—the Adolescent and the Borderline Syndrome—are brought together in this volume. Their separate developments have shown some intriguing parallels.

Approximately 15 years ago our knowledge about adolescents and the Borderline Syndrome was woefully confused. The chronologic age of the adolescent as well as the traditional belief that his myriad symptomatology comprised a turmoil normal to adolescence served as formidable barriers to understanding [85, 86]. Similarly, the former diagnostic focus on descriptive symptomatology and the psychodynamic focus on oedipal conflicts left the Borderline Syndrome vague and ill defined. At that time, with good cause, neither the Adolescent nor the Borderline Syndrome received much attention in psychiatric textbooks. Inevitably, this led to poor therapeutic results along with continual frustration.

In the intervening years the picture has brightened. Long-term psychiatric follow-up studies of young patients through and beyond the adolescent years have helped to clarify those psychopathological elements and in turn have led to more definitive therapy [82, 86]. Similarly, long-term psychoanalytic study of the Borderline Syndrome has revealed that the essence of the disorder rests neither diagnostically in the descriptive symptomatology nor psychodynamically in conflicts at the oedipal level of development. The work presented here and in a number of papers [87–89] depended on these two developments. Both the Adolescent and the Borderline Syndrome are no longer used as psychiatric scapegoats.

REVIEW OF THE PSYCHIATRIC DILEMMA
OF ADOLESCENCE

A brief description of follow-up studies of adolescents reveals the background from which the present work on the Borderline Adolescent emerged.

5

In the early 1950s the notion was prevalent that adolescence was a time of such emotional turmoil that in a given patient it was difficult to decide whether he suffered from a psychiatric illness which required treatment or from so-called normal adolescent turmoil that would subside with further growth. This point of view, reflected in the diagnostic category of "adjustment reaction of adolescence" in the *APA Manual,* carried with it a potentially hazardous implication that treatment might be postponed and even be unnecessary, since the patient's problems were related to his current growth stage and would disappear with time.

To view the situation objectively, I followed 78 adolescent out-patients for 5 years, or at least chronologically past their adolescent years, and found that, contrary to such a belief, they did *not* grow out of their difficulties. Time was not on their side. By far the majority, particularly those with personality disorders, were not able to make even a functional adjustment but continued to show both symptoms and impairment of functioning. A smaller number of those with a personality disorder, and most of those with a character neurosis or psychoneurosis, although they managed to make a functional adjustment to their difficulties, found better ways of dealing with their conflicts in an ameliorative way rather than resolving them. Consequently, with conflicts still smoldering, never quenched, they remained vulnerable to stress.

These patients were then compared with a control group of healthy adolescents and marked differences were found between the two groups in symptoms, ways of functioning, and family relationships. Adolescent turmoil did not produce enough symptomatology in the healthy as to make them appear to be psychiatrically ill. These findings were later confirmed by Offer [93].

The findings suggested that the psychiatric significance of adolescent turmoil had been overestimated; that it was at most an incidental psychodynamic factor that had little effect on the onset, course, and outcome of adolescent psychiatric disorders. It was but a way station along a path of psychiatric illness which began in childhood and followed its own inexorable course; it was only temporarily colored by the developmental stage of adolescence. Adolescent turmoil exerted its effect primarily by exacerbating and coloring preexistent pathology.

A revision of theory was suggested as follows. The psychiatric effects of adolescent turmoil may be viewed as a product of the interaction between the turmoil and the personality structure of the adolescent. In the healthy, where there is considerable integration and flexibility sufficient to withstand the onslaught of adolescent trauma, the ensuing turmoil produces, at most, subclinical levels of anxiety and depression. In those with characterological pathology whose personalities are rigidly organized and inflexible, it precipitates an acute clinical breakdown, often with psychosomatic symptoms, which may subside as the patient grows older but which usually leaves a residue of pathologic character traits. Adolescent turmoil has its most chaotic effect in those adolescents suffering from schizophrenia and severe personality disorders characterized by a relative lack of ego structure and adaptability in response to stress. Thus the adult personality will also reflect these earlier disturbances.

The Diagnosis of Personality Disorder

The diagnostic category of personality disorder in the APA manual was extremely unsatisfactory. It implied that the basic difficulty of the adolescent patient stemmed from a personality defect which began early in childhood and was manifested in behavior rather than symptoms, and which was relatively refractory to therapy. This diagnostic category confused the issue by implying that the patient did not have subjective symptoms, when in fact he did; it also shed no light on the exact nature and evolution of the personality defect nor on its effects and consequences. Actually the APA diagnostic category was a sentence rather than a diagnosis, since it condemned the patient to an inevitably poor therapeutic result.

Nevertheless, since the APA classification was in wide use, we employed it for statistical reasons in our study. The findings obtained from patients in the category of Personality Disorder are reproduced here exactly as I described them at that time for three reasons: (1) These led me to the work presented in this volume. (2) They are excellent illustrations of the consequences of inadequate treatment or no treatment to adolescent patients in later life. (3) In the last chapter I reevaluate these cases from the new perspective of the Borderline Syndrome and the psychodynamics of separation-individuation.

Table 1 presents the roster of patients with a diagnosis of personality disorder by level of psychiatric impairment. A brief description of each impairment group with an appropriate case illustration follows.

Severe and Moderate Impairment

Severe   = 16
Moderate = 16
Total   = 32

The seven sociopaths who had had severe functional impairment at the approximate age of 16 continued to show severe functional impairment on follow-up 5 years later as judged by the following typical interim

Table 1. Patients with a Diagnosis of Personality Disorder

Level of Impair- ment[a]	Socio- path	Passive- Aggressive	Miscel- laneous	With Epilepsy	Total
Minimal	0	4	1	1	6
Mild	0	4	1	0	5
Moderate	3	9	2	2	16
Severe	7	3	4	2	16
Total	10	20	8	5	43

[a] As defined in *Diagnostic and Statistical Manual of Mental Disorders*, American Psychiatric Association, Washington, D.C., 1962.

reports: inability to hold a job, drinking, gambling, taking drugs, police arrests, conflicts in relationships with people, and recurrent bouts of anxiety and depression, some with paranoid trends. The three passive-aggressive patients who had shown severe functional impairment still had a multitude of symptoms on follow-up, including anxiety, depression, psychoneurotic and psychophysiologic complaints, and bodily symptoms, with marked inhibitions of emotional expression due to their passive-aggressive character structure (in school, at work, etc.). The nine moderately impaired passive-aggressive patients also suffered from anxiety, depression, and psychophysiologic complaints as well as from difficulties with initiative. They were barely able to finish school and to maintain themselves for short periods of employment, usually at jobs well below their potential. Two cases follow.

Severe Impairment: Example.   A 15½-year-old girl, with a childhood history of having been a "feeding problem" and of soiling, had chronic feelings of inferiority, temper tantrums, nail-biting, thumb-sucking, and asthma. Since adolescence she had experienced recurrent and alternating episodes of depression and elation. She was repetitively a truant from school and in great conflict with her family. She came to the clinic in the setting of a depression, following rejection by a boy because she repulsed his sexual advances, and an impulsive suicide attempt by swallowing 15 aspirin tablets and 5 sleeping pills. On examination, it was our opinion that this patient had no major affect or thinking disorder, but that she represented a personality disorder, either inadequate or sociopathic in type.

The follow-up interview 5½ years later, when the patient was 21, revealed that her interim course had been one of progressive deterioration. By age 18, she had attempted to attend college away from home but had become depressed, gained a lot of weight, felt rejected, and eventually returned home. At this time she engaged in sexual play with a male friend without excitement and was fearful of sexual intercourse. By age 21, the patient had given up school entirely, had left home, and had lived alone for 2 months. She had started to use narcotic drugs and had been arrested by the police for theft. She also had become involved in a sadomasochistic sexual relationship with an emotionally disturbed older man.

Moderate Impairment: Example. A 14-year-old boy, a psychopath, had complaints of anxiety, restlessness, concentration difficulty, school failures, obesity, rivalry with his sister, excessive concern about money, and conflict with an overprotective, overindulgent mother and a rejecting father.

When seen in a follow-up interview 6 years later, at age 20, he had been in college for 2 years but had failed several subjects. His inability to get up in the morning caused one failure, which he later circumvented by arranging afternoon classes. He suffered from procrastination and on the rare occasions when he studied, he experienced concentration difficulties and daydreaming. He was obese, impulsive, dependent, manipulative, and in conflict with his father. He was in constant need of money, which he spent impulsively. In the follow-up interview both the patient and his mother denied the presence of problems. Being away at school had minimized the tension involved in the conflict with his father, and by getting a job he had managed to augment his income to better satisfy his need for money.

Minimal and Mild Impairment

$$
\begin{array}{ll}
\text{Minimal} & = 6 \\
\text{Mild} & = 5 \\
\text{Total} & = 11
\end{array}
$$

These patients, although their functioning had improved, also continued to show overt symptoms. All but one finished high school, commonly requiring extra time to do so; two were in college, two women worked as secretaries, two men were in the armed services, and five men worked at miscellaneous jobs. They complained of recurrent anxiety and depression, headaches, insomnia, feelings of inadequacy, obesity; the women complained of dysmenorrhea; all revealed overconcern with other bodily feelings and functions. One patient had epilepsy.

Minimal Impairment: Example. A 16-year-old boy, when first seen was markedly depressed, failing in school, hostile toward and in open conflict with a cold and distant father, and in social difficulty with his peers, as he had been since childhood. He did not graduate from high school, left home at age 18, and "for lack of anything else to do" went into the army; while in the service he experienced a dramatic change when he joined the Baptist Church at age 19. He had a good relationship with the minister and changed from being passive and withdrawn to being active socially and intensely interested in the Baptist Church and religion, to the point of evangelizing. He disliked army work, hated authority figures, and exhibited strong sadistic trends in his humor. Although he dated girls, he avoided emotional commitment and had no heterosexual activity. In addition, he had withdrawn from both his mother and his father. He admitted to having anxiety, insomnia, and feelings of inadequacy and on examination showed prominent defenses of repression, reaction formation, intellectualization, and denial.

Resolution of Conflicts in Personality Disorder

The eight patients with personality disorder of the passive aggressive type who were mildly or minimally impaired were examined further in follow-up interviews to ascertain their resolution of conflicts over dependency, sex, and aggression. In seven patients there was clear evidence of dependency on and conflict with the mother that had lessened very little over the course of time. They handled this either by continuing to live at home, which possibly enabled them to function better than they otherwise would, or by withdrawal from the parents as well as the home. In those who remained at home, the conflict with the mother seemed to persist almost intact and unabated from early adolescence. For example, two girls, both 21, were obese and living at home. One showed passive rebellion toward and withdrawal from her mother, and the other had episodes of depression.

As to sexual adjustment, two others have had sexual intercourse. One, a girl 21 years old, later declined a marriage proposal; the other, a boy 22, had not allowed himself to become emotionally committed to a girl. Five had been emotionally involved to the point of "going steady," and five had dated without ever "going steady" or having sexual intercourse.

Aggression continued to present a problem that was handled by defenses such as avoidance, denial, repression, reaction formation and intellectualization, rebellious acting out, or passively by provocation with withdrawal. Almost all gave evidence of some pathologic character traits; they varied from being passive, submissive, overcompliant, lacking initiative, with other immature emotional expression, to being withdrawn, suspicious, and perfectionistic, with much repression and denial of emotion.

Example

The 16-year-old boy described (pp. 9–10) provides a most striking example of reaction formation in response to aggressive and sexual impulses. This patient evidently transferred his dependency needs to the Baptist minister and, through identification with him and the church, changed from a passive to an active orientation toward his environment, being highly motivated by his new religious standards. Although he functioned better, it was at the cost, rather than through a satisfactory resolution, of his aggressive and sexual impulses, and he developed a markedly rigid, defensive character structure. That his elaborate reaction-formations have made him vulnerable to future stress is a justifiable inference.

Treatment of Personality Disorder

Our own treatment results described below certainly did not improve this dismal outlook. Eighteen patients with personality disorder received treatment once a week up to at least a year; the mothers and fathers were also seen once a week by a social worker. Seven improved; eleven did not. Of the seven who did improve during treatment, five were later found to be moderately impaired, two mildly impaired. In other words, they improved under treatment but when seen 4 to 5 years later they were still having considerable difficulties.

Those who improved usually had established dependent relationships in which they easily ventilated their complaints of anxiety, depression, and environmental conflicts. In the course of treatment, anxiety and depression subsided, environmental conflicts became minimized, and the patient's functioning improved. However, such basic characterologic problems as passivity, dependency, and negativism, were usually inadequately dealt with so that although the patient had improved when he left treatment he ran into further difficulty. In those who did not respond there were a number of characteristics. Some therapists, threatened by the patient's acting out, responded either permissively or punitively thereby repeating the patient's problems with the parents. With other patients, despite the therapist's efforts, it was not possible to circumvent their resistance. In still others, their basic character defects were not effectively dealt with. Two illustrative cases are described below.

Example 1

A 13-year-old boy presented a history since age 10, when his father died, of intense conflict with his mother and brother, excessive lying, stealing, truancy, and failing in school. The patient was seen in treatment for about a year. He had a dependent relationship with his therapist, and his interviews consisted mostly of discussing current activities and airing a long series of complaints about the mother's rejection and nagging behavior, his anger and counter provocations, and his need to assert his masculinity. The therapist supported the patient's constructive activity and tried to redirect his anger. The mother's interviews consisted of repetitive hostile and rejecting complaints about the patient which yielded little to therapeutic intervention. In the course of treatment, however, the mother's rejecting behavior was somewhat modified, and the patient's functioning in school and behavior at home also improved.

When we saw this patient again, at 18, he had left high school, where he had failed in two subjects, and he was working in a supermarket. He complained of migraine headaches and reported that the conflict with the mother was still present but had decreased in intensity, because now he tended to withdraw and rebel passively. Rivalry with the brother continued as before. The patient's hostility was easily aroused and he frequently "blew up" at his job and suffered recurrent depressions. He spent a great deal of time sleeping and had withdrawn from his usual social life.

Example 2

A 17-year-old girl, treated for 1 year, established a dependent relationship with her therapist, spoke freely of her need for her mother's love, of anger at the mother's hostile rejection, of acting out her anger to provoke the mother, and of seeking satisfaction of her needs through dependent relationships with boys. She spoke, too, of being afraid of sexual feelings and therefore of dating homosexual boys. The mother, however, in treatment was so rejecting of the patient and so narcissistic and preoccupied with her own conflicts with her husband that it was not possible to make much progress with her attitudes toward her daughter. Nevertheless, the patient's depression improved by the end of the year. Although she readily verbalized her hostility over the frustration of her dependency needs and the acting out of this hostility, apparently no effort was made to help the patient gain control of or to define alternate ways of dealing with these feelings. When seen 6 years later, at 24, the patient showed continued difficulty with control of these impulses.

These findings left a decidedly gloomy impression. The diagnostic category of personality disorder was not very useful. There were enormous clinical differences between the healthy, the neurotic, and those with personality disorder. Not only were the latter clinically sicker, but also the parents were sicker; furthermore, the core of the illness began in early childhood, not in adolescence and was manifested in the ego structure, not simply in subjective symptoms. Even those patients who responded well with 1 year of psychotherapy did poorly later.

EVOLUTION OF THE BORDERLINE SYNDROME CONCEPT

Further reflection led to a number of questions that prompted the work reported in this book. (1) What exactly was the specific ego defect or defects in the personality disorders? (2) How did these manifest themselves? (3) What caused them? (4) Would the answer to these questions lead to more specific diagnosis and more effective psychotherapy? The first and most important step toward answering such questions was a clearer definition of the Borderline Syndrome, the concept of the depression due to abandonment and the narcissistic-orally fixated ego structure.

METHOD

The method was clinical research or careful observation of clinical material and the construction of clinical hypotheses that were tested by treatment. This was conducted through a microscopic study of the patient and the family in intensive psychoanalytically oriented psychotherapy. Out of the testing of various hypotheses, the clear concept of the abandonment depression and the oral fixation emerged.

I felt that an inpatient rather than an outpatient setting for study and for psychotherapy would be more productive since adolescents in general and those with a personality disorder in particular express their ego defects in their behavior. The behavior would be under careful observation 24 hours a day and could be intimately related to the contents and shifts of affect in therapeutic interviews. In addition, abandonment depression remained repressed and was not directly available for observation until the therapy could make inroads into the patient's defenses. Furthermore, it soon became clear that effective treatment of a Borderline Adolescent requires as a precondition the control of behavior which can be much more quickly and efficiently accomplished in an inpatient setting. Later, as the therapeutic techniques were better understood, they then were modified and applied to outpatients. (See Chapter 19).

From 1966 to 1968 I conducted this study of the Borderline by supervising a second-year resident who was in direct charge of the patient. One-step removal from the actual therapeutic situation resulted in clear and more objective observations of the patient as well as of the therapist's countertransference. The resident took process or word-for-word notes, and the nurses recorded their detailed observations of the patient's behavior round the clock.

The resident interviewed the patient from three to five times a week and a psychiatric social worker interviewed each parent once a week also recording these interviews verbatim. In addition, the patient participated in group therapy twice a week. Unfortunately, this latter experience could not be incorporated here.

The resident and social worker met with me in a 1½-hour seminar once a week at which time the verbatim recordings were scrutinized. At the conclusion of each session the salient points in the material of the preceding week were reviewed and I dictated a summary. The seminars, approximately 34 a year, were held weekly from September until June. At the end of each year the weekly summaries, as well as the individual notes, were again reviewed.

By 1968, the treatment was sufficiently effective to be further tested by applying it to an entire service. I took charge of the inpatient service for adolescents whose treatment I specifically designed along the lines of the ideas previously developed in treatment of individual patients. This gave me an opportunity to apply our concepts more widely and effectively since I now had authoritative control over all treatment decisions. The results are presented in this book.

METHOD OF PRESENTATION

Although, ideally, I would have preferred to use one or two cases for all the evidence—that is, clinical picture, psychological testing, psychotherapy, treatment of parents, and follow-up—this was not possible. All the evidence was not produced in sequence by a methodology entirely devised and worked out in advance. In the early patients I focused on one aspect of the clinical problem at a time—usually the most urgent—then developed therapeutic hypotheses, tested them until one was successful, and went on to the next problem. For example, the two cases whose therapy is presented at length were two of the earliest treated, and since the treatment has changed very little, it seemed appropriate to present them.

The need for follow-up treatment became obvious much later in the study; thus I have presented the follow-up treatment of one of these later patients. In addition, as our knowledge and confidence grew, the ideas derived from inpatients were reflected in my own outpatient work presented in Chapter 18. Continuity has been maintained by using two early cases to illustrate the entire inpatient treatment. The later cases present some of the many variations on the general theme.

The bulk of the material is presented from the clinical point of view and is the result of observations either by myself or my staff; the exceptions are the theoretical Chapters 2 and 7 and the psychological testing in the appendix.

The book therefore is not meant to be a strict report of research. I have drawn extensively from my own background experience with many patients; those chosen best illustrate a point, either in comparison or in contrast.

TREATMENT

The book makes a plea for the delineation and treatment of the abandonment depression and narcissistic oral fixation that have prevented the patient's growth to the developmental stage of autonomy. Failure to attack these fundamental causes of the patient's difficulties leaves him in a situation where the price exacted by the unresolved emotional conflict increases exponentially during the course of time. The boy who has not separated from his mother cannot later face the challenges or tasks that life opens to him, that is, he cannot express himself in a chosen field of work, cannot love a woman, and when finally married, is a failure as a father. Similarly the girl who is yoked to her past by a separation failure can neither adequately love a man nor mother a child.

The passage of time presents these unfortunates with inevitable life tasks and thereby faces them with truly a Hobson's choice: to avoid the challenge of growth, marriage, and parenthood with the consequent loneliness and suffering that this entails or to take on the challenge though emotionally ill-equipped. Should they opt for the latter they receive the additional dividend of becoming an appalled and helpless eye witness to the repetition of their own unresolved problems in their children. (See Chapters 6 and 7.) It is neither fate nor the gods (as the ancient Greeks would have us believe) that dictate this pathway to a living equivalent of Dante's Inferno, but rather arrested separation-individuation.

A social analogy may emphasize the necessity of a more decisive and specific approach. American society in its efforts to deal with the civil rights problem and the war in Vietnam has tended to approach both with a short-term "patch-up" view. In both instances the problem was viewed as one of limited scope, with hopes that temporizing efforts—only later recognized as inadequate—would patch up the conflicts. However, the "patch-up" efforts resulted in the persistence of smoldering explosive conflicts despite the gradual escalation of effort.

Efforts to "patch-up" the Borderline Adolescent result in the abandonment depression continuing to smolder until it either causes further breakdown, or until the defenses against it are transformed into pathologic character traits. What had been fluid becomes fixed. What had been ego-alien, caused suffering, and therefore, produced motivation for change, becomes egosyntonic, reduces anxiety, and constitutes a resistance to treatment. A corollary of this process is that much of the patient's potential to derive emotional satisfaction through the expression of his feelings in reality is lost by being drained into maintaining the pathologic character traits. At the same time, the character takes on a rigidity that makes the person less able to cope with future stress. These latter eventualities constitute the final and most persuasive argument for the specific psychotherapy outlined in this book.

The therapeutic process presented here is a wearying and traumatic one for therapist as well as for family. The resistance to separation of both parent and adolescent is intense. The therapist must be patient, tolerant, vigilant, and persistent. He must make the necessary confrontations to enable both parents and patient to give up their resistance and seek a more lasting solution.

Once he has unmasked the family's neurotic compromises, numerous emotions are unleashed which throw the family members into emotional disarray but at the same time prepare them for the necessary change. The therapist must have a well-defined, embracing therapeutic goal, as indeed, any one who has a limited therapeutic goal cannot commit himself sufficiently either to make the necessary confrontations or to deal with the unleashed emotional forces. As a result he often never gets the facts necessary to understand the problem. The successful therapist must have courage and persistence to ferret out the necessary facts, no matter how turbulent the process may be.

In the beginning the therapy assumes the aura of a battle. One could compare the underlying family symbiosis to a boil or "abscess" that has caused drastic limitation of communication in the family to avoid the pain of separation-individuation. As the therapist probes for the symbiotic ties and the abandonment depression both the adolescent and the parents resist to avoid separation anxiety and depression. The therapist, the most objective person in the group, is the only one who can guide the family to the center of the problem. As he gets closer and closer the resistance of patient and parents becomes frantic. When he does reach the "abscess" and lays bare the symbiosis and depression, the family reexperiences their original pain and suffering.

The resulting emotional catharsis drains the "abscess," relieves the anxiety and depression and frees the family to repair the damage. The emotional climate of the treatment undergoes a marked change as the aura of battle is replaced by a joint therapeutic consensus.

These patients' stories reveal in a clinical metaphor the ancient struggle of mankind against fate—his tragedy as well as his triumph. They tell of human beings condemned by birth and subsequent accidents of fate to be victims rather than masters of their own fortune; they are emotionally attacked and impaled before they have developed the resources and weapons with which to do battle.

They cannot seek for they are blind; they cannot fight for they have no weapons. Unable to face their fate, they make of it a virtue. Their chains become a halo; their way of life in all its human misery is defended as their pathway to salvation.

The therapist must not allow his professional judgment to be swayed by his perception of the tragic human elements in his patient's life. He should use these perceptions to strengthen his professional motivation and discipline to provide what help he can.

The sad fact of the matter is that the adolescent with a Borderline Syndrome has a severe emotional illness with little prospect of future life satisfaction unless there is decisive therapeutic intervention. This book is a beginning effort at such a decisive intervention. The treatment outlined here though arduous and prolonged, often necessarily stretching into years, offers the Borderline Adolescent his one sure escape from his predestined course. The results already promise much for the future.

Let the reader now share the adolescent's lonely and painful struggle up through the levels of Dante's Inferno toward a new day that will witness not only survival but also even the mastering of life's blows.

I first review the observations and theories of others that have helped me evolve my theory for treatment of the Borderline Adolescent. To begin, I discuss certain fundamental theoretical orientations that stress developmental factors that are particularly pertinent to our understanding of the psychopathology of the Borderline patient.

CHAPTER 2

A Developmental Theory: A Separation-Individuation Failure

The customary practice of presenting the clinical picture first has been reversed (1) to emphasize the thrust of the entire book; namely, that the role of separation-individuation is the key to understanding the adolescent Borderline Syndrome, and (2) to assist the reader to "read between the lines" of the clinical picture—presented in the next chapter. Neither the abandonment depression nor the narcissistic oral fixation—the two diagnostic hallmarks of the Borderline Syndrome—spring readily to the examiner's view. The former is concealed by the patient's defense mechanisms (splitting, denial, etc.), which mask his feelings of abandonment and the latter is concealed by his chronologic age, which belies the infantile state of his character.

The theory of the role of the separation-individuation phase in the Borderline adolescent presented in this chapter is my own responsibility. I found myself turning more and more to psychoanalytic theory to understand the clinical manifestations of the Borderline adolescent. For example, my efforts to understand one patient's feeling that when his therapist took a vacation, the therapist was literally disappearing forever led to a study of the issue of object constancy. (See p. 30.) An understanding of the development and function of object constancy in the child sheds great light on the meaning of the adolescent patient's statement, "I will never see you again," that is, object constancy had failed to develop in this patient. The theory of the role of separation-individuation evolved from endless repetitions of this type of interaction. The better I understood the theory, the better I understood the patient; the better I understood the patient, the better treatment became.

In the construction of this theory, however, I have drawn heavily on the work of others, for example, Spitz's [127–131] studies of the first year of life, Bowlby's [10–14] studies of the reaction of children to separation from the mother by hospitalization at the separation-individuation phase of development (i.e., 18 months), Rinsley's [107–115] important work on the psychodynamics and intensive treatment of the hospitalized adolescent, and finally Mahler's [77–84] most important studies of the role of separation-individuation in the ego development of normal children.

Spitz's, Mahler's, and Bowlby's studies, based on carefully planned direct observation of crucial phases of development rather than on reconstructions from adult analyses (Spitz [127] and Mahler [78] studying normal, and Bowlby [12] the pathological) are an index of the progress of psychoanalytic research.

I indicate in the following the most important role that this work played in my thinking by expressing my understanding of it.

The heart of the theory is that separation for the Borderline patient does not evolve as a normal developmental experience but on the contrary entails such intense feelings of abandonment that it is experienced as truly a rendezvous with death. To defend against these feelings, the Borderline patient clings to the maternal figure, thus fails to progress through the normal developmental stages of separation-individuation to autonomy.

As a background for understanding the developmental antecedents of the Borderline Syndrome let us turn first to the theory of the role of symbiosis and separation-individuation in normal growth and development.

ROLE OF SEPARATION-INDIVIDUATION IN NORMAL EGO DEVELOPMENT

The concept of separation-individuation as a normal phase of the mother-child relationship is relatively recent and has emerged as an outgrowth of the study of ego psychology and increased interest in mothering patterns. This theory has evolved through the work of many people, but most important are Benedek [3–6], Jacobson [56], Spitz [127], and Mahler [78] who studied by direct observation the separation-individuation process of normal children. It is beyond the scope of this book to give a comprehensive discussion of this vast topic and for further detail the reader is referred to their work. However, a short outline provides the background essential to understanding the role of separation-individuation in the Borderline adolescent.

Stage of Symbiosis

In normal development the separation-individuation stage is immediately preceded by the symbiotic stage. Symbiosis can be defined as an interdependent relationship in which the combined energies of both partners are necessary for the existence of each. Apart from each other, each member appears to "perish."

The child's image of himself and of his mother in this phase is of one symbiotic unit. The importance of the symbiotic phase, which usually spans ages 3 months to 18 months, to the normal development of ego structure can hardly be overemphasized. For example, Spitz [127] suggests that it is the mother who mediates every perception, every action, every insight, and every knowledge. The emotional climate of the mother interacts with that of the infant in an ever stimulating mutual experience that propels the infant into ever new and more involved experiences and responses. The quality of the mothering, the character, gifts, and talents of the mother, her ability to pick up clues and signals from her child, and her imagination in this complex interrelationship during the first year of the symbiosis seems to be the fertile soil in which ego development takes place.

Mahler [78] states that the child's dim awareness of the mother as a "need" satisfying object marks the beginning of the symbiotic phase in which the infant behaves and functions as though he and his mother were a single omnipotent system, a dual unity within one common boundary.

Mahler [78] then emphasizes that the mother because of the absence of an inner organizer in the human infant must be able to serve as a buffer against inner and outer stimuli, gradually organizing them for the infant and orienting him to the inner versus the outer world to boundary formation and sensory perception. Thus in the symbiotic stage, which continues through approximately the eighteenth month, the mother performs many of the ego functions the child will later learn to perform himself.

Separation-Individuation Stage—18 to 36 Months

The symbiotic stage so crucial to ego development should soon attenuate and be succeeded by the separation-individuation stage which is equally crucial to development. Mahler suggests that this phase begins around 18 months and parallels the development of the child's capacity to walk and therefore physically separate himself from the mother. Mahler further suggests that the 2-year-old child soon experiences his separateness in many other ways, enjoying his independence in exercising mastery with great tenacity. Accompanying these events the infant's sense of individual entity and identity—the image of the self as an object—develops, mediated by bodily sensation and perception. The child now undergoes an intrapsychic separation and begins to perceive his own ego as being entirely separate from the mother's.

Rinsley [107] has outlined some of the most important accomplishments of this event as follows: there is an end to object splitting and the development of a capacity to relate to objects as wholes. (See object splitting p. 24.) Aggression becomes separated from positive or affectionate feelings, and energy is made available to the patient's ego for further growth and development. The self and object representations have become more progressively differentiated as the child's perceptual apparatus matures and these perceptions of the self and object then become associated with either positive or negative feelings. For example, the child's sense of a worthwhile or positive self-image springs in part from the child's introjections during this phase of the mother's positive attitude toward him.

Three forces, (1) the infant's unfolding individuality, (2) the mother's encouragement and support, that is, continuation of "supplies," and (3) the mastery of new ego functions (see below), press the child on his developmental pathway through the stages of separation-individuation toward autonomy.

Mahler [78] states that from the end of the first year on the average toddler seems to become so preoccupied with practicing his newly developed skills that he does not seem to mind his mother's short departures from the familiar playroom. He does not clamor for his mother's attention and bodily closeness during this practicing period. Some infants behave as though they were drunk with their newly discovered ability to walk in space and widen their acquaintance with large segments of reality. However, the infant does toddle up to his mother once in a while for "libidinal refueling" but his behavior seems to indicate that for the most part he takes his mother's emotional presence for granted.

Mahler further states that as soon as free locomotion is mastered, the toddler only returns to the mother to seek proximal communication with her. This behavior leaves no doubt that the representations of his self and that of the mother are now well on their way to differentiation. As the toddler masters the ability to move from and to the mother the balance dramatically shifts within the mother-toddler interaction from activity on the part of the mother to activity on the part of the child. Mahler concludes that the mother as the catalyst of the individuation process must be able to read the toddler's primary-process language. She emphasizes the resiliency with which the child's autonomy unfolds from within his own ego if he feels a fair degree of emotional acceptance and a fair degree of what she calls "communicative matching" on the mother's part.

In the course of this separation, the child assumes into his immature ego through the mechanism of introjection those ego functions that the mother had performed for him—and his ego structure becomes endowed with essential new functions: secure ego boundaries against both inner and outer stimuli; strengthening of repression that makes more affect available for sublimation; improved reality perception; frustration tolerance; and impulse control. He begins to substitute the reality principle for the pleasure principle. His feelings about his own now separate self-representation as being worthwhile or positive spring in part from the introjection during this phase of the mother's positive attitudes toward him. This new sense of self and these new functions can be viewed as benefits of the achievement of separation and autonomy. Clearly, the mastering of this phase is a key part of the foundation upon which the rest of ego structure is built.

ROLE OF SEPARATION-INDIVIDUATION IN THE BORDERLINE SYNDROME

The theory described below is based on evidence from our adolescent patients that shows that in the Borderline the above events do not take place. The mother of the Borderline adolescent suffers from a Borderline Syndrome herself.

Having been unable to separate from her own mother she fosters the symbiotic union with her child thus encouraging the continuance of his dependency to maintain her own emotional equilibrium. She is threatened by and unable to deal with the infant's emerging individuality.

She depersonalizes the child, cannot see him as he is but rather projects upon him the image of one of her own parents or of a sibling, or she perceives him as a perpetual infant or an object and uses him to defend herself against her own feelings of abandonment. Consequently, even in the symbiotic stage she is unable to respond to his unfolding individuality and he early learns to disregard certain of his own potentials to preserve his source of supplies (approval) from the mother. The mother clings to the child to prevent separation, discouraging moves toward individuation by withdrawing her support.

Emergence of Feelings of Abandonment

Therefore, between the ages of 1½ and 3 a conflict develops in the child between his own developmental push for individuation and autonomy and the withdrawal of the mother's emotional supplies that this growth would entail. He needs her approval to develop ego structure and grow; however, if he grows the supplies are withdrawn. These are the first seeds of his feelings of abandonment (see Chapter 4), which have such far reaching consequences.

Unable to tolerate the awareness of these feelings he handles them by ego splitting [29, 30, 133] and denial [52] defense mechanisms and turns his back on his own unfolding individuality since it now threatens his support. Although separated he continues to cling to the mother to defend himself against the return of feelings of abandonment into awareness. The clinging, ego splitting, and denial are further reinforced by various defense mechanisms which later in his life determine the form of the clinical picture: acting out, reaction formation, obsessive-compulsive mechanisms, projection, denial, isolation, detachment, and withdrawal of affect.

The abandonment feelings then recede into the unconscious where they lie submerged like an abscess, their overwhelming but hidden force observable only through the tenacity and strength of the defense mechanisms used to keep them in check. These defenses, however, effectively block the patient's developmental movement through the stages of separation-individuation to autonomy. He suffers from a developmental arrest. He is caught, so to speak, in midstream, enroute between two stages of development. Unlike the autistic or infantile psychotic child, the child with the Borderline Syndrome has separated from the symbiotic stage and has become fixated in one of the subphases of the separation-individuation stage —possibly the rapprochement stage (15 to 22 months) where the mother's sharing becomes a vital catalyst to the individuation process.

To understand the disastrous consequences of these events for the development of the child's ego structure we must shift to another framework, that is, Freud's psychosexual continuum, which has common meeting points with the one we have been discussing. Freud spoke of two phases, the autoerotic and the narcissistic [31] phases that precede the oral phase of development. Symbiosis is a narcissistic phase and separation-individuation is ushered in by orality. It is likely that the developmental arrest of the Borderline occurs either in the narcissistic or early oral phase. The earlier the arrest occurs the more likely the patient's clinical picture will resemble the psychotic, and the later this occurs the more likely the clinical picture will resemble the neurotic. In either case the developmental arrest produces severe defects in ego functioning. There is a persistence of the defenses of ego and object splitting, a failure to achieve object constancy [26, 64, 67] and the development of a negative self-image.

Narcissistic-Oral Fixation

Rinsley [107, 108] suggests the characteristics of this ego structure— he uses the term "weak ego"—are as follows: failure of normal repression; persistence of primitive mechanisms of defense with reliance on splitting, projection, introjection, regression, and denial; impairment of ego's synthetic function; lack of "basic trust"; failure of sublimation of "raw" instinctual impulses. In addition there are fluid ego boundaries, that is, a difficult differentiation between inner and outer stimuli; poor reality perception; poor frustration tolerance; and poor impulse control.

Object Splitting

One crucial dividend of a successful separation-individuation experience is a prerequisite for later interpersonal relations—both intimate and social; this is the capacity to relate to others as individual whole objects*, that is, to see them as a whole, both good and bad, gratifying and frustrating, and to have this relationship persist despite frustration at the hands of the object. This key characteristic so essential for later satisfying interpersonal relationships does not develop in the Borderline; instead there is a persistence of the primitive defense of object splitting (paranoid position of Klein [64–67]). In other words, relating to objects as parts, either totally gratifying or totally frustrating, rather than as wholes.

The child's intense oral dependency and need for affection and approval from his mother to build ego structure and grow are so absolute and his rage and frustration at the deprivation of these very supplies on the part of the mother so great that he fears these feelings may destroy her and himself. To deal with his fear and to preserve the feeling of receiving supplies, the infant splits the whole object of the mother into two parts, that is, a good and bad mother.

On the groundwork of the various kinds of physical care he did receive as an infant—being kept warm and fed—the growing child constructs a fantasy, an illusion of being cared for, loved, fed, and receiving supplies from the good and gratifying mother. He projects as the other half of the image, the bad, the frustrating and depriving mother who induces such rage, on other people. The images of the bad and good mother are never integrated as one object, a manner of relating that persists throughout his later life. He does not relate to people as one whole object but as if they were either good, that is, gratifying, or bad, that is, frustrating. Both sides of this split are equally unrealistic. In other words, he does not achieve the depressive position described by Klein [64–67].

This state of affairs is one of the factors responsible in the family for the well-known phenomenon of "scapegoating." The child complies with the mother's unconscious to preserve his fantasy of being fed as well as to avoid the threat of abandonment. He remains unaware of the mother's deprivation or of his rage at her. These are projected on others. Later in life he will also relate to people in a similar manner thereby contributing to a persistence rather than a cessation of the "scapegoating."

* Objects here refers to the child's introjected image of his mother.

Snow White and the Seven Dwarfs and *Cinderella.* These are parables of object splitting as a defense against abandonment.

In early infancy all humans probably use the defense of object splitting. This helps explain one of the many factors that have contributed to the success of the two fairy tales, *Snow White and the Seven Dwarfs,* and *Cinderella;* I was led to these two stories by my Borderline patients descriptions of their own mothers. The similarities were so striking that I thought an analysis of the stories here would help to clarify the meaning of object splitting.

These stories portray in dramatic form abandonment and the defenses against it: object splitting, denial, projection of hostility, and rescue fantasies. On the narrative level these are stories of a girl's conflict with a hostile stepmother. On the psychodynamic level they are stories of the girl's defenses of object splitting to deal with her hostile feelings toward her depriving mother.

SNOW WHITE AND THE SEVEN DWARFS

Dramatis Personae

THE MOTHER

The image of the good mother is split and preserved by the dramatic device of relating that although she wanted (i.e., loved) the child very much, the good mother died shortly after birth. The blood mother loves the child. The same theme is noted in Cinderella.

FATHER

The father literally plays no role. Both stories describe the relationship between a girl and her stepmother. For example in *Snow White* the father is mentioned in one line: "after the year had passed the King married a second time." This reflects exactly the role the fathers of our Borderline patients play (see Chapter 5)—a distant, passive, almost nonexistent role.

THE QUEEN

The object splitting is reinforced by the image of the bad stepmother; that is, she is no blood relation. No effort is spared to make the Queen the very personification of evil with solely hostile motivations—a perfect projection for the rage at the bad mother, this queen is *all bad.* For example, the queen is introduced as follows: "His new wife who is now Queen is very beautiful but haughty and proud and vain. Indeed, her only

wish in life is to be the fairest in the land." Her narcissism is further illustrated by her addresses to the mirror on the wall.

The stepmother's narcissism and vanity is dwelt upon. For example,
after she hears that Snow White is more beautiful than she, she "became
alarmed and turned green and yellow with envy and whenever she saw
Snow White after that her heart turned upside down within her—that was
how much she hated the innocent child for her beauty. These envious feelings grew like weeds in the heart of the Queen until she had no peace by
day or by night":—this illustrates not only the Queen's rage but also the
central focus it played in the Queen's own emotional equilibrium. The oral
quality of her wishes and rage are indicated when the Queen eats with
"great relish what she thinks is Snow White's heart."

The Queen's "badness" is elaborated: "You will not be surprised I am
sure when I tell you this wicked creature was skilled in the art of witch-
craft." Later her sorcery is referred to as "wicked witchery." The degree
to which her jealousy and envy rankled is suggested in the following:
"After Snow White had taken the poisoned apple and was presumably
dead the mirror said to the Queen, 'so now thou art the fairest in the
land.'" The author then continues: "Now there was peace at last in the
heart of the Queen, that is, as much peace that ever could be found in a
heart full of envy and hate." This description of the Queen provides a
perfect example of object splitting with the good mother image preserved
by having the mother who wanted the child die and the very essence of
evil projected upon the bad mother, that is, the Queen.

This portrait of the Queen shows a striking resemblance to the Borderline patients' descriptions of their mothers. For Snow White's beauty substitute the patient's individuality and/or femininity. The narcissism, envy,
rage, and orality of our patients' mothers are almost identical to that of
the Queen.

SNOW WHITE

The evil of the Queen is contrasted with the innocence and trust of
Snow White. Early in the story she is described as an innocent child. Her
innocence and trust is later emphasized when she does not see that the
Queen is trying to deceive her. This portrayal of Snow White as innocent
and trusting in its denial of any rage on her part is the perfect complement
to the projection of this rage on the bad mother or Queen.

THE DWARFS

The dwarfs also serve as the perfect counterparts to the evil Queen who
abandons Snow White. They seem to represent a rescue fantasy to banish

the abandonment experience. They are small, jolly, kind, genial, and loving, and from their first contact with Snow White, they love her and want to make a home for her. For example, they say to her, "If you will keep everything tidy and homelike you can stay with us and you should want for nothing in the world"; that is, Snow White has been rescued from abandonment by the dwarfs.

THE PRINCE

Snow White sleeps, perhaps through her years of latency, and she awakens to become a woman (princess), again because of her object splitting not through identification with the mother, but at the behest of a man, the prince charming. Another rescue fantasy—the man who will rescue her from the trap with the mother.

THE STORY

The real mother dies shortly after birth of her child and the new self-centered, beautiful Queen is angry and envious of Snow White's beauty (for beauty, read individuality). This so disturbs the Queen that to restore her own equilibrium (the reason why our mothers cling to their children), the Queen abandons Snow White to be killed. Incidentally, several patients have expressed the feeling that the only way they could please their mothers was to kill themselves. However, Snow White is saved or rescued from abandonment and finds a home with the Seven Dwarfs who are kind and loving, the exact opposite of the Queen. Still angry and frustrated, the persistent stepmother (just like the persistence of our patients' mothers) makes several additional efforts to kill Snow White. First by strangling— which brings to mind the asthma-like symptoms of some of our patients— and second by poisoning—which brings to mind some of the G.I. symptoms patients develop in abandonment states. Incidentally, as the splitting starts to resolve in psychotherapy and the bad mother begins to emerge, the patients' dreams frequently contain this very theme; that is, if the patient expresses her angry feelings the mother will kill her (see Chapter 4). Each time Snow White is rescued by the dwarfs. The last time when the dwarfs fail Snow White sleeps throughout the years and is awakened by one of the prince's helpmates and lives happily ever after. The Queen, however, is condemned to dance out the rest of her life wearing red hot shoes as punishment for her anger and evil.

Thus we have portrayed the essential conflict with the mother—the fear of abandonment with defenses of object splitting, denial, projection of anger, and rescue fantasies.

CINDERELLA [96]

Dramatis Personae

MOTHER

In this story again the image of the good mother is preserved through her death. The blood mother, not present, had loved Cinderella.

FATHER

Cinderella's father, although he gets better treatment (four lines) than Snow White's father (one line), still plays literally no role in her life. "Once upon a time there was a nobleman of France who took a second wife after the death of his first. He did it for the sake of his little daughter so that she would have a mother. Then he left for a journey that would take him a whole year. He believed that his daughter would be well cared for and happy while he was away." The loss of the father is glossed over and rationalized. So many of our patients are so embroiled in the intense conflict with the mother that in the beginning of therapy their conscious view of a distant father shows striking similarity to the way the author describes Cinderella. Although their father is never around, it doesn't seem to bother them. Of course the anger at the father is repressed and does come out later in therapy. However, occasionally the father becomes a target for the *negative* image of the mother and the initial anger is expressed toward him.

STEPMOTHER

The stepmother's role here parallels that of the Queen in *Snow White*. She was a mean, proud woman who cared only for her own two ugly daughters.

SISTERS

In this story in contrast to *Snow White,* the envy and jealousy are further split off and conveyed not by the stepmother but by the sisters with the complicity of the mother however. "Their mother agreed with the sisters that they had best put Cinderella to work in the kitchen."

GOOD FAIRY

The Good Fairy is the good mother reincarnated to banish Cinderella's feelings of abandonment by magically fulfilling her wishes.

PRINCE

Again the man, not the father, rescues her from her state of abandonment.

CINDERELLA

Great emphasis is placed, as in *Snow White,* on Cinderella's kindness and lack of negative emotion. For example, "Cinderella had nothing at all but her own kind heart." The sisters knew that Cinderella had excellent taste and was too kindhearted to let them leave looking anything but their best. At the end of the story Cinderella's kind-heartedness is emphasized again. "She was too kind-hearted to leave her sisters lonely while she had so much joy." Not long after Cinderella married her sisters to noblemen of the court and all lived happily for a long, long, time. Cinderella had no anger. No wonder; it was all projected on the stepmother and sisters.

THE STORY

Cinderella's mother dies after childbirth; the father remarries a proud, mean woman and Cinderella's abandonment begins. The two sisters "had everything (love) and Cinderella had nothing (was abandoned)." For example, "the sisters had their own rooms furnished with the finest things money could buy. There were silken sheets and satin covers on the beds and velvet curtains at the windows. Early morning they ate breakfast in bed and they never got up until 11 or 12 o'clock. Each had seven dresses. In their jewel boxes there were so many rings and bracelets and necklaces that it took them hours to decide which one to wear. They even had a bird in a cage to sing to them and a round, plump puppy to play with." Is the author trying to illustrate that through material things the sisters "had emotional supplies and Cinderella had none?" Many patients' families substituted things for love.

Cinderella's abandonment is in stark contrast to the "plushness" of her stepsisters' life situation. "Cinderella slept in the attic with the mice who kept her company but did not keep her warm. She often crept back to the kitchen to sleep the rest of the night by the fire. The fire was warm but toward morning the wind slipped down the chimney and blew cinders all over her. She had no dress to change to. She was always dusty and dirty as an old shoe. Her sisters called her Cindertail or if they were in a good mood Cinderella. All day long she washed dishes and scrubbed floors and swept and dusted and ran errands. She ironed their dresses and sewed lace on their petticoats and turned up the hems of their skirts. If they were hungry she ran to the store for candy. They never gave her a bite of it. When they went on picnics she packed their lunches and brought them a rug to sit on. They never asked her to go along or said they were sorry she had to stay behind."

There are few better descriptions of the family scapegoat—a role which all our patients play. This technique for expressing the feelings of abandonment, that is, dirty clothes, no warmth, days of endless drudgery, endless scapegoating, is almost identical to that shown by our patients in some of their compositions (see Chapter 4).

Cinderella's state of abandonment reaches its height when she sees her sisters going to the party: "Cinderella felt so sad at having to stay at home that she could not keep back her tears. She ran to the kitchen, sat down by the fire and cried and cried. So pitifully did Cinderella cry that the mice could not comfort her, the fire burned its hardest to warm her but it could not." Her abandonment depression was now beyond repair and at this point her dilemma is resolved by the creation of a fantasy, the Fairy Godmother who then outfits her to go to the party wanting her to be home by midnight. Cinderella's having to return at midnight brings to mind the great sense of impermanence that our patients have about anything that is going well. It seems as if they are perched on a razor's edge; although temporarily enjoying themselves, they expect to be plunged back into their feelings of abandonment.

On her second visit Cinderella gets so "involved" with the Prince that she forgets about the time and suffers the punishment. The story ends with the Prince fulfilling the rescue fantasy.

The fear of abandonment and the defenses of object splitting, denial, projection of anger, and the rescue fantasies are portrayed almost as well as in *Snow White*.

We turn now to consider the third important issue, object constancy.

Object Constancy

Object constancy, equally fateful for later interpersonal relations, also is a fundamental consequence of successful separation-individuation. This concept had origins in both general psychology [98–100] and psychoanalysis. Those interested in a complete discussion are referred to the excellent article by Fraiberg [27]. The term as it is commonly used refers to the capacity to maintain object relatedness irrespective of frustration or satisfaction. The relationship has relative autonomy from the fluctuations of need states. The emotional investment of the mother remains stable regardless of fluctuation of the infant's need states or externally imposed frustration. This quality is associated with, and some believe dependent on, the capacity to evoke a stable consistent memory image or mental representation of the mother whether she is there or not. The achievement of this capacity has been variously placed depending on the observer: for example, Spitz [127] places it at 8 months. Mahler [78], however, places it around 25 months, specifically linking the attainment with the emergence of a stable mental representation that enables the child to tolerate separation from the mother. The further importance of object constancy is illustrated by the fact that it is a prerequisite for that process so vital to the repair of an object loss—that is, mourning. If one cannot evoke mental images of the lost object, how can one resolve all the painful feelings caused by this loss to form new object relations? If one cannot mourn, he becomes fatally vulnerable to object loss.

The Borderline patient fails to achieve object constancy. This has far reaching clinical significance. (1) He does not relate to objects, that is, persons as wholes but as parts as already described. (2) The relationship does not persist through frustration but tends to fluctuate widely with the need states. (3) He is unable to evoke the image of the person when he is not present. When the person is not physically present the Borderline patient feels, he has literally disappeared and is not going to return; (4) he cannot mourn. Any object loss or separation becomes a disastrous calamity. This can be seen clearly in the transference relationship during the therapist's vacation period; because the patient does not feel that the doctor will return, he sets his defensive operations in motion well in advance to protect himself. Some styles of defense are emotionally withdrawing from the interviews in advance, actually physically leaving the doctor before he can leave the patient, complete emotional detachment, acting out by starting an affair, carrying through a previously tentative marriage possibility, and trying to provoke the therapist by acting out, for example, coming late for appointments.

Negative Introjection

A final undesirable consequence is that the mother's negative attitudes toward the child are introjected unconsciously by the child and become associated with his own fragmentary self-image. This introjection of the mother's attitudes into the psyche of the child creates an intrapsychic conflict out of what had been an environmental conflict. At every move toward individuation and away from symbiosis the patient feels guilt because of this introjected attitude, that is, guilt at the unpardonable step of leaving or wishing to leave the mother. His own superego remonstrates him for these wishes. This guilt, like a fifth column behind his own lines, erodes his capacity to continue the move towards individuation. The guilt is further intensified by the homicidal rage and desire for revenge provoked by the deprivation. Thus the introjection creates in the intrapsychic sphere the conflict that originated in the environment between the child and his mother.

Prepuberty—A Second Separation-Individuation Phase

Having outlined the consequences of the separation-individuation problem for the Borderline ego structure, that is, abandonment depression and oral narcissistic fixation, let us now see what happens later in development.

Splitting, denial, and other defense mechanisms enable the child to contain his feelings of abandonment and to function until prepuberty—approximately ages 10 to 12—when a second marked developmental maturation of the ego occurs. This growth spurt, manifested by a thrust toward activity combined with a turn toward reality, is similar in scope to the maturation of the ego that occurred in the separation-individuation phase. This maturation together with the need to separate further from the mother produces a recapitulation of the separation-individuation phase of development, that is, a second separation-individuation phase.

Deutsch [19, 20] suggests that prepuberty is a phase in which sexual instincts are the weakest and development of the ego is most intense, and that the phase is characterized by this thrust of activity and turning toward growth and independence; also it is an intensive process of adaptation to reality and mastery of the environment. The adolescent is caught between the past and the future, between childhood and adulthood, just as the infant is caught between a symbiotic relationship and autonomy. She emphasizes that the struggle for independence in this period is strongly reminiscent of the processes that take place approximately between the ages 1½ and 3 years, that is, the transition from the symbiotic stage to autonomy. She gives an example of the girl in prepuberty who, full of hatred and rage, wants to tear herself away from her mother's influence but at the same time frequently reveals an intensified, anxious urge to remain under the maternal protection. She concludes that prepuberty repeats the preoedipal or the separation-individuation phase not only in the struggle for liberation from the mother—the central point of the girl's psychological life at this time—but also in other respects too.

There is debate in the psychoanalytic literature as to whether this second separation-individuation stage occurs. For example, Peter Blos [8] disagreeing with Deutsch explains the same phenomenon as follows: "The girl's 'thrust of activity' constitutes an attempt to master actively what she has experienced passively while in the care of the nurturing mother; instead of taking the preoedipal mother as love object, the girl identifies temporarily with her active phallic image."

Although Blos' view is interesting, he is describing specific dynamic constellations which do not necessarily invalidate Deutsch's formulation. I suspect that the lack of further psychoanalytic verification of Deutsch's view may be due to the fact that this area has received so little study. I found her report helpful when attempting to understand why the Borderline Syndrome in adolescents so often makes its clinical appearance during prepuberty. For example, it often appears during the change from local elementary school to the larger amalgamated junior high school.

Precipitating Stresses

The theory described by Deutsch [19, 20] seemed to fit the pieces of the puzzle together. It suggests that all adolescents go through a second separation-individuation phase in prepuberty due to the maturational spurt of the ego. In some, this alone precipitates a clinical Borderline Syndrome while in others this combined with an actual separation experience brings on the syndrome.

These precipitating factors, (1) the second separation-individuation phase itself, or (2) the phase combined with an actual environmental separation, reinforce the feelings of abandonment and produce a clinical syndrome via the need for intensification of the defenses.

The clinical manifestations will depend on the patient's unique style of defenses against his feelings of abandonment as outlined in Chapter 3.

Further Defenses Against Separation

How the adolescent, clinging to the maternal figure, experiences and deals with separation can be illustrated by Bowlby's study of infants age 18 months who were separated from the succoring maternal figure [10–14]. The relationship of Bowlby's observations to the Borderline adolescent, first brought to my attention by Rinsley [107, 108], indicates their excellence and clinical usefulness. I do not agree, however, with the broad theoretical inferences that Bowlby draws from these observations.

Bowlby, studying infantile mourning, described the mourning process as a complex sequence of psychological processes and their overt manifestations, beginning with craving, angry efforts at recovery, appeals for help, then proceeding through apathy and disorganization of behavior, and finally ending with some form of reorganization. He suggested that mourning may take one of several different courses: those which enable the individual ultimately to relate to new objects and find satisfaction in them are commonly judged to be healthy; those which fail in this outcome are pathological.

If the separation is not successful, Bowlby describes the infant as going through three phases, protest and wish for reunion, *despair,* and detachment.

Protest and Wish for Reunion

He states that this phase may last for a few hours to a week or more during which time the child appears acutely distressed at having lost its mother and seeks to recapture her by the full exercise of his limited resources. His behaviour suggests strong expectations and wishes that she will return. Meantime, he is apt to reject all alternative figures who offer to do things for him although some children will cling desperately to a nurse.

Despair

In this second phase the infant's preoccupation with his missing mother is still evident, although his behaviour suggests increasing hopelessness, the acts of physical movement diminish to come to an end, and he may cry monotonously or intermittently. He is withdrawn and inactive, makes no demands on the environment, and appears to be in a state of deep mourning.

Detachment

Because the child shows more interest in his surroundings, the phase of Detachment which sooner or later succeeds protest and despair is often welcomed as a sign of recovery. He no longer rejects the nurses, but accepts their care, food, the toys they bring; he may even smile and be sociable. When his mother visits, however, it can be seen that all is not well for there is a striking absence of the behavior characteristic of the strong attachment to the mother normal at this age. So far from greeting his mother he may seem hardly to know her; so far from clinging to her he may remain remote and apathetic; instead of tears there is a resistless turning away; he seems to have lost all interest in her.

Should his hospital stay be prolonged and should he, as is usual, have the experience of becoming transiently attached to a series of nurses, each of whom leaves, thus again and again repeating for him the original experience of loss of his mother, in time he will act as though neither mothering nor contact with humans has much significance for him. After the upset of losing several mother figures to whom in turn he has given some trust and affection, he will gradually commit himself less and less to succeeding figures and in time will stop altogether taking the risks of attaching himself to anyone. Instead he will become increasingly self-centered and, instead of directing his desires and feelings towards people, become preoccupied with material things such as sweets, toys, and food. A child living in a hospital or institution who has reached this state will no longer be upset when nurses change or leave. He will cease to show feelings when his parents come and go on visiting days; and it may cause them pain when they realize that, although he has an avid interest in the presents they bring, he has little interest in them as special people. We have described this as the phase of detachment.

When Borderline adolescents go through the experience of separation which they have been defending themselves against all their lives they seem to react just as Bowlby's infants. The adolescent feels the separation as an abandonment, a loss of a part of himself which brings with it unique and intense fears of death. He initially defends himself against these feelings by clinging to the lost object, that is, expressing the wish for reunion.

The power of this wish for reunion, no small matter by itself, can be extraordinarily influenced or strengthened by environmental experiences such as recurrent illnesses when the mother must care for him, or efforts of the mother to restore reunion whenever any minor separation occurs. When the clinging fails to achieve its aim the patient next passes into a depression which, however, contains such intense feelings of rage, despair, and hopelessness that he further defends himself against this state by acting out, or by other styles of defense, that is, obsessive-compulsive, schizoid, which in turn protect him against feeling the despair and remembering the abandonment.

Although the cause of the rage is the abandonment, the content of the rage is not only the abandonment but also many of the deprivations experienced in the symbiotic relationship.

Finally, those patients for whom there is no relief enter a condition such as that characterized by Bowlby as detachment with its progressive constriction of the ego and deepening inability to be influenced or to be involved in a relationship—it is too painful.

The clinical picture portrays the repetition in adolescence of an infantile drama—the abandonment depression engrafted to the separation-individuation process with a resultant halting of further ego development.

In other words, the patient develops an abandonment depression; his ego structure remains orally fixated; his object relations transpire at an oral level; and his most basic fears are of engulfment or abandonment. His most basic problems have to do with the primitive sense of identity and separateness, as well as of mastery and control of impulses.

ETIOLOGY

Why do these patients fail to go through a normal developmental experience of separation-individuation? The etiology of their disorder poses a version of the nature-nurture problem. I have presented a hypothesis that the Borderline Syndrome is a result of the feelings of abandonment which are in turn created by the mother's withdrawal of supplies when the patient attempts to separate and individuate. The patient's need to defend himself against his feelings of abandonment produces the developmental arrest and the clinical picture. The evidence for this view comes from three sources:

1. When the patient's defenses are interrupted in psychotherapy, he relives the abandonment depression with appropriate affect and appropriate recall of the traumatic separation experience that later in life revived the feelings of abandonment. (See Chapter 4.)

2. Direct observation of the mother's behavior in joint interviews, as the patient under the influence of psychotherapy attempts to separate and individuate, reveals the mother's counter attempts to frustrate her child by withdrawal of supplies. (See Chapter 11.)

3. Other possibilities that must be considered are (1) the patient has a constitutionally inadequate potential for autonomy, and (2) there is a bad "fit" between mother and child, perhaps due to conflicting temperments as described by Chess [17].

It is difficult to understand the "inadequate potential for autonomy" argument. If maternal supplies are vital for growth, and these supplies are withdrawn, is this not a sufficient explanation for the arrested growth? How can one determine the potential for autonomy until the supplies necessary for its unfolding are present? I submit that this point of view smacks strongly of the old "poor protoplasm" argument resurrected and dressed in a new disguise. At the moment it is impossible to say which factor or what combination of factors is the root cause of the disorder. However, I will clearly document the clinical evidence for the developmental forces in the ensuing chapters.

CHAPTER 3

The Clinical Picture

THE BORDERLINE SYNDROME—A BRIEF REVIEW

This chapter indicates the main trends in the emergence of the Borderline Syndrome, particularly as these relate to the Borderline adolescent, and offers further justification for the concept of the abandonment depression.

The diagnosis of Borderline Syndrome has had a long and unmerited bad reputation in psychiatry. It has rarely been described in psychiatric textbooks and has been frequently attacked as a misnomer in both the psychiatric and psychoanalytic literature [44, 106, 147].

The term, originally applied to patients who had evidence of both a neurosis and a psychosis, seemed to convey more of the uncertainty and indecision of the psychiatrist than the condition of the patient. Knight [68] observed a number of years ago that "most often these patients were called severe obsessive-compulsive cases; sometimes an intractable phobia was the outstanding symptom; occasionally an apparent major hysterical symptom or an anorexia nervosa dominated the clinical picture; and at times there was a question of the degree of depression, or of the extent of paranoid trends, or of the severity of the acting out."

A plethora of labels appeared, varying by the diagnostic style of each psychiatrist, suggesting that the diagnosis might be schizophrenia. For example, some labels were incipient schizophrenia, latent schizophrenia, ambulatory schizophrenia, transient schizophrenia, pseudoneurotic schizophrenia, and chronic undifferentiated schizophrenia. Others favored labels such as chronic severe personality disorder, chronic severe character disorder, narcissistic character disorder. The official APA nomenclature included these patients under the diagnosis of personality disorder.

This confusion—in retrospect a reflection of the diagnostic emphasis on descriptive symptomatology as opposed to an emphasis on psychodynamics and developmental considerations—persisted, and the ambiguities of the disorder continued to trouble the psychiatrist as he began to see more patients with this clinical picture.

In the last 20 years as interest in ego psychology grew this disorder became more of a focus of psychoanalytic study [1, 7, 9, 15, 16, 18, 21–23, 25, 28, 32–46, 49–51, 54–63, 69–76, 90–92, 94, 97, 102, 105, 116, 119–124, 126, 132, 134, 141–144, 146]. Much of the confusion cleared and a consensus developed that the basic psychopathology was not the presenting symptoms but a specific and stable form of pathologic ego structure, that is, a developmental arrest.

Kernberg [56] emphasized that the presenting symptoms did not differentiate the syndrome. He stated that many symptoms could be present in different combinations, that is, "anxiety, polymorphic perverse sexuality, schizoid or hypomanic prepsychotic personalities, impulse neuroses and in addition, infantile, narcissistic and antisocial character disorders and many polysymptomatic problems such as phobias, obsessions, conversions, dissociation, hypochondriasis and paranoia."

Speaking of the adult Borderline, Knight made the important point that despite severe damage to ego functions the patients' adaptation to the demands of the environment for conventional behavior were adequate, superficial object relations were intact, and habitual performances were unimpaired, that is, the patient was sicker than he looked [68].

However, despite transient psychotic episodes under severe stress and despite symptoms such as depression, withdrawal, and schizoid adjustment, the Borderline Syndrome was not an incipient or early schizophrenia.

Giovacchini [15, 37–43] of the Chicago Psychoanalytic Study Group observed that these cases distribute themselves, according to the severity and complexity of their disturbances, along a spectrum from the more severe psychoneurotic to the most disturbed "Borderline" case, which closely resembles the overt psychotic. At the healthier end of the spectrum are the patients with narcissistic defenses, giving them an appearance of more or less normality. In the center of the spectrum are the bulk of the cases, which are less stable, less successful, more erratic, and more actively disturbed. They tend to act out more, trying to combat their emptiness with alcohol, excessive sexual indulgence, or another kind of excitement. However, they do manage to preserve considerable successful adaptation. Closest on the spectrum to the psychotics are the most disturbed patients who show considerable paranoid ideation, marked feelings of void, very tenuous object relations, and the most marginal adjustment. In spite of their serious pathology, what seems to characterize the bulk of the Borderline patients, they resist psychotic illness.

A corresponding general consensus developed as to the psychodynamics of the Syndrome as outlined also by Giovacchini from the Chicago Psychoanalytic Study Group. He stated that the dynamic basis of the clinical picture was a developmental arrest resulting in excessive narcissism beyond that found in the normal or neurotic adolescent, deficiencies in crucial ego functions, such as the perceptual and executive, and fixation. The ego defects deprive the patients of techniques for mastery that they need to deal with their internal and external world. The narcissistic, magical, and omnipotent fantasies erected by these patients to contend with these defects and to protect themselves from the painful memory traces of a traumatic infancy and childhood are of little help in coping with the realities of the adult world. In spite of their unadaptive value, these fantasies are cherished by the patients who even live their lives around them, perhaps in an effort at belated mastery.

Kernberg [56] added that although the Borderline as contrasted with the schizophrenic had differentiated ego boundaries and good reality testing, he could not synthesize positive and negative introjects and identifications. As a result he resorted to the defense of object splitting to preserve the good self- and object images and the external good objects from the bad.

Ekstein and Wallerstein [24] described their concept of the ego defect in children. They postulated an ego mechanism of control that could be roughly compared in its function to that of a thermostat. A reliable thermostat can maintain a somewhat even temperature in a room despite climatic changes. This is analogous to the ego state of the neurotic, which fluctuates minimally and is subject to relative control by the individual. An unreliable thermostat, on the other hand, can lead to unpredictable and inappropriate temperature changes and figuratively represents the unpredictable regulatory and controlling devices in the Borderline.

Ekstein and Wallerstein stated that it seemed characteristic for the Borderline that ego-state fluctuations occurred many times throughout their day, occasionally with control, but that a large part of their waking life bore strong similarity to the sleep-dream life of their neurotic contemporaries in the lack of control exerted by the dreamer.

The same authors illustrated the intensity of this disorder by saying that the neurotic patient conceives of his problems as leading to dangerous or unhappy consequences, but the possible solutions he envisions have some real anchorage and are less overwhelmingly catastrophic than for patients in the Borderline group who seem to face absolute dilemmas that admit of no solution. If we think of the neurotic dilemma in terms of the excursions of a pendulum, can we say that the excursions of the pendulum in the psychological world of the Borderline patient cover an infinitely wider amplitude than in the neurotic?

In 1968 Grinker et al. [48] gave clinical verification to the concept of the Borderline Syndrome through study of the ego functions as manifested in the behavior of 51 Borderline adults. Behavior was observed, described, and rated through traits extracted from an egopsychology framework. They found the clinical characteristics of the Borderline Syndrome to be not only consistent when subjected to cluster analysis but also realistic clinically. They described the essential clinical characteristics as a defect in affectional relationships, an absence of indications of self-identity, and depressive loneliness, and anger as the main or only effect. Within this gestalt the patients could be divided into four groups representing different positions. Members of Group I gave up attempts at relationships but at the same time overtly, in behavior and affect, reacted negatively and angrily toward other people and to their environments. Persons in Group II were inconsistent, with movement toward others for relations followed by acted out repulsion and movement away into isolation where they were lonely. This movement corresponded with the fact that these people were both angry and depressed but at different times. Patients in Group III seemed to have given up their search for identity and defended themselves from their reactions to an empty world. They did not have the angry reactions characteristic of Group I. Instead they passively awaited cues from others and behaved in complementarity—"as if [19]." In no other group were the defenses as clearly or consistently observable as in Group III. Subjects in Group IV searched for a lost symbiotic relation with a mother figure which they did not achieve, and they then lapsed into what may be called an anaclitic depression.

A PSYCHODYNAMIC CLASSIFICATION OF
BORDERLINE PATIENTS

Grinker's clinical classification is an important contribution to the verification of the concept of the Borderline Syndrome. We can now broaden this classification by applying the theory of separation-individuation in Chapter II. It seems to me, as outlined below, each of Grinker's four clinical groups has made a character trait or life style out of a defense against the abandonment depression involved in a faulty separation-individuation; uniting the psychodynamics with the clinical picture gives a broader based classification of the Borderline patient.

Thus to amplify in this way Grinker's classification, those in Group I appear much like the infants, described by Bowlby [10–14] as being in the stage of detachment. They have no interest in people; they show no feelings. They are self-centered, care primarily for things, and are mainly angry. They have given up hope of forming a meaningful relationship with another and instead have developed a character style of detachment whose function is to defend them against the abandonment depression related to involvement and loss. The pervasiveness of their affect of anger is a reflection of the generalization of their anger at the original separation from the mother to anger at involvement with all people. Group II contains the patient who is inconsistent, moving toward others, and, being repelled by them, becomes either lonely, depressed, or angry. These patients are similar to Bowlby's infants in the stage of protest and wish for reunion. They are acutely distressed and pursue the wish for reunion with great vigor, only to be equally blocked by their own fear of attachment should their pursuit be successful. To protect against this fear they then withdraw and feel lonely and depressed. Group III contains the "as if" patient who completely represses his feelings and individuality and relates by imitation the earliest form and precursor of introjection. These patients have given up their search for identity. They do not get angry. They passively await cues from others and behave in complimentarity. The "as if" patient [19, 20, 140] has defended himself against the anger, depression, and pain of loss, that is, abandonment, by repressing completely the move toward individuality by giving up hope of any gratification from involvement or expression and has settled for infantile imitation as a life character style. Group IV patients also reflect Bowlby's first and second stages—protest and wish for reunion then depression. They pursue reunion overtly and when pursuit fails they fall into an abandonment depression.

Rinsley, working with hospitalized Borderline and schizophrenic adolescents, made many contributions to the understanding of the psychodynamics, clinical manifestations, and intensive psychotherapy of the Borderline adolescent. For example, he observed the relationship of Bowlby's studies to the Borderline adolescent; he described the characteristic features of the "weak ego," the benefits of separation for ego development, the resistance of parents and patient to separation by hospitalization, and the "phasic" character of the treatment. He was one of the first to study and advocate the use of intensive analytically oriented psychotherapy for these patients.

All of this work has brought the Borderline Syndrome into clearer focus. Its clinical characteristics have been described and verified in adolescents and adults and its underlying psychodynamic structure has been outlined. In Chapter 2 a theory as to the cause of the developmental arrest was suggested. Let us now apply these concepts to the clinical picture of the Borderline adolescent.

THE CLINICAL PICTURE OF THE
BORDERLINE ADOLESCENT

Understanding the role of separation-individuation enables us to predict the components of the clinical picture: the overt manifestations will consist of the patient's particular style of defenses against his feelings of abandonment which are handled by splitting and denial. These defenses not only determine the form of the present illness but also reflect the style of the patient's character. These defenses, occurring in many different combinations, are as varied as the number of patients one sees but there is usually a predominance of one or two defenses which assists in further categorizing the clinical picture.

The clinical picture I have seen most commonly is also the one that causes the most diagnostic confusion; the adolescent whose defense is aggressive acting out. I concentrate on the acting out clinical picture in the discussion of diagnosis in this chapter as well as in the report of treatment in Chapters 7–13. However, examples are given of the following additional clinical types: passive-aggressive acting out, obsessive-compulsive, schizoid, anorexia nervosa, and flight.

Five factors in the clinical picture outlined below aid in making the diagnosis and are discussed in the ensuing pages.

1. The present illness—the patient's defenses against the abandonment depression.
2. The precipitating stress—the environmental separation experience.
3. The past history—evidence of narcissistic oral fixation.
4. Type of parents—parents with a Borderline Syndrome. Their character structure and capacity to parent.
5. Type of family communication—deeds or acts, not words.

DIAGNOSIS

The diagnosis should be made at two levels—the presenting symptomatic episode (even though the history may be 4 or 5 years in duration), and the underlying character structure within which this symptomatic episode is taking place. Some of the difficulties encountered both in obtaining the clinical facts necessary for the diagnosis and in conceptually ordering these facts into a comprehensible whole are discussed below.

Present Illness

The key to the diagnosis is not the subjective symptoms which the patient will report, but his acting out behavior which is obvious to all but which he is very reluctant to report. The adolescent will not tell you he is depressed; he wishes to avoid the whole affair. Not only will he deny, avoid, and evade it, but also he probably will "holler bloody murder" if you confront him with it too soon.

Much of the evidence therefore must be obtained from the reports of the parents, who, suffering from a Borderline Syndrome themselves, are not good observers. They may be unaware of their adolescent's behavior because of guilt or denial on their part, or they may have been unconsciously provoking this behavior to obtain vicarious satisfaction. Therefore, very often the diagnosis must be made on the basis of evidence supplied by unqualified observers. In the face of this situation, the examiner must realize that the story he has obtained from patient and parents is probably at best only the top of the iceberg of the patient's total behavior. The therapist must press for facts from the patient in as much detail as possible since most of the history and details of behavior are submerged in the dark sea of resistance and denial. It may not be till many months later that the true story will be uncovered when control of the adolescent's acting out brings his depression to the surface, and when the parents having worked through their guilt, are able to reveal the true facts.

The Patient's Defense against the Abandonment Depression

Having pressed the issue, what kinds of acting out are found? It may begin with mild boredom, restlessness, difficulty in concentrating in school, hypochondriasis, or even excessive activity (physical and sexual). Finally, more flagrant forms of acting out appear—antisocial behavior, stealing, drinking, use of drugs such as marijuana, LSD, methedrine, heroin, glue sniffing, promiscuity, running away, having car accidents, and behaving like a hippie, for example, having long hair, wearing sloppy dress, and keeping hippie companions. These companions form an excellent target upon which the parents can project their guilt about their own role in their adolescent's difficulties. They will say that their adolescent has been enticed away by bad companions, not driven by conflicts at home.

Another common form of acting out (based on object-splitting as described in Chapter 2) is the use of a sexual relationship to substitute for reunion with the maternal figure, that is, clinging, dependent relationships with older males or females.

Hopefully having now obtained the clinical history of acting out, there are a number of issues which the examiner should keep in mind in making the diagnosis. Acting out may serve many functions—for example, it may be a defense against psychosis in those who are schizophrenic, or against anxiety in those who are neurotic. In these Borderline Syndrome patients it is none of these, but specifically a defense against feeling depressed and remembering the desperation, abandonment, and helplessness associated with the pain of separation from the parent.

Precipitating Stress—The Environmental Separation Experience

The separation experience itself, although sometimes blatant and obvious, is more often hidden and must be winnowed out of a great deal of chaff by selective questions. For example, actual separations such as in death or divorce are obvious but often it can involve subtle occurrences such as an older sibling going away to college, a grandparent, a governess, or maid becoming ill, or merely some change in the focus of the symbiotic partner's behavior—for example, George's mother who became involved in an affair, or another who became depressed or had to attend a sick sibling. It is important to keep in mind that neither the patient nor the parent have any awareness of the profound significance of the separation experience; the examiner must ferret this out by himself.

The Past History of Underlying Character Structure: Narcissistic-Oral Fixation

The difficulties in obtaining the clinical facts necessary for the diagnosis of the oral fixation in the underlying character structure are similar to those encountered for the presenting symptomatic episode. The parents, almost universally suffering from Borderline Syndromes themselves, are most often quite unaware of the fact that the patient has failed to achieve the usual developmental milestones. The mother has unconsciously received gratification from the fact that her child remains "tied to her apron strings," even though she fails to give the kind of mothering he needs to achieve autonomy. Therefore, again, the doctor must pursue the developmental history on his own, looking for signs of prolonged dependency and passivity, developmental defects in ego structure such as poor frustration tolerance, poor impulse control, and reality perception, which give rise to a host of symptomatic expressions from very early in life; these range from disciplinary problems at home and in school, difficulties in developing social skills with peers, and to such symptoms as enuresis, headaches, and gastric upsets.

Particular attention should be paid to the possibility of traumatic experiences during the separation-individuation stage, that is, 18 months to 3 years. For example, the birth of another sibling who falls ill and requires the mother's attention, or the maternal grandmother dying and precipitating a depression in the mother may be important. In addition an early history of clinging, following the mother after learning to walk, separation anxiety at first going to school, or childhood phobias should be looked for. Attention should also be paid to the prepuberal period, ages 10 to 12, for symptomatic evidence of increased anxiety or for separation experiences. The mother's and patient's collaboration in regressive, dependent modes of relating is one of the most difficult clues to unearth because of their mutual defensiveness. Once an accurate developmental history has been obtained, the clinician must look for a difference between developmental level and chronological age.

Parents' Character Structure and Capacity to Parent

The parents have Borderline Syndromes (Chapters 5, 6, and 10) and suffer as much from a lack of parenting as do their adolescents. Consequently, having been inadequately mothered and fathered they have great difficulty performing the tasks of a mother and a father.

The fathers are for the most part passive men, who are dominated by but who maintain great distance from their wives. They relinquish their paternal prerogatives in exchange for complete freedom to immerse themselves in their work.

The mothers are demanding and controlling women who need and maintain vigorously the symbiotic tie with their child. They do not object to the father's distancing as long as he permits them complete control over the child. This unconscious bargain often surfaces for the first time around the decision as to whether to undertake treatment—the father leaving the decision to the mother.

The parents' affect-hunger drives them to perceive the child not as he is but rather as a parent, peer, or object [2, 43, 115, 145]. The child's emotional needs for supplies to effect separation and individuation go unmet. The child does receive supplies and nurture for those needs that are not related to separation and also receives them when his behavior meets the parents' narcissistic needs, that is, when his achievements gratify a wish of the parent that life had frustrated such as the mother who had wanted to be a pianist rather than a housewife. It is the crucial area of separation-individuation that spotlights the parents' inadequate parenting.

When the abandonment finally occurs and the acting out begins, the parents' permissive-punitive response only furthers the adolescent's sense of abandonment and throws him back on the anarchy of his own impulses.

Type of Family Communication

Behavior as a Plea for Help

Adolescents have a reputation of being unmotivated toward treatment. This myth was recently exploded in a paper by Rogers [117]. She points that "these youngsters needed to reject treatment in order to be able to accept it eventually."

The initial refusal, springing as it did from conflicts over passivity versus activity, was only a first and needed step toward eventual acceptance of treatment. It was impressive, she noted, how deeply interested they were subsequently in treatment.

Curiously our borderline patients, rather than even appearing unmotivated, as are Dr. Rogers' group, are actually desperate for help although they are not able to verbalize this desperation.

They express it by an act—a plea for help—which expresses exactly and poignantly the trapped crying out for succor and aid. The act that brings the patient to treatment usually occurs at the end of a long series of gradually escalated acts whose goal is somehow to break through the seeming vacuum of unawareness, even of indifference, created by the parents' inability to see the adolescent as the child he is. The adolescent is drowning in his struggle in this stormy sea and unable to swim; he cries out for help as he is about to go down for the third and perhaps last time.

The long history of pleas for help in the form of acts by these adolescents is dramatic testimony to the strength of the parents' resistance. To each the parents respond with apparent unawareness which then leads to an even more flagrant and dramatic act on the part of the patient, until intervention finally occurs—and even then the intervention often is still not at the behest of the parents, but rather some outside figure such as a friend, a school teacher, or even the police or a wise judge.

The parents' resistance influences the initial contact with the doctor. They often "doctor shop" not in the ordinary sense of the term—to find the "best" doctor—but to find one who will give some "treatment" without really getting into the issue of separation from the adolescent. Consequently it behooves the doctor to be very cautious in his initial comments to the parents lest he raise their anxiety so much that they sense his therapeutic intent to foster separation-individuation and go elsewhere.

However, the doctor's behavior toward the adolescent must be quite different. It is clearly of the utmost importance that the clinician sense and respond to the underlying distress and alarm that the adolescent is not able to verbalize. This response is as much a true rescue operation as the lifeguard who dashes into the water with a life preserver. The doctor's response becomes the life preserver that assists the adolescent in keeping afloat long enough for more definitive measures to be taken; in other words, until the therapy begins to help him in his struggles.

A question arises here: why a soundless act rather than a simple verbal request for help? These families, both parents and adolescent, have Borderline Syndromes, and the significant, if not all the meaningful communication between them, occurs in the form of acts and not words. Feelings are communicated by doing and not by saying. It is small wonder that when the adolescent is in danger he turns to this most familiar vehicle to express his distress.

Two cases from my practice illustrate this phenomenon. It was 2:00 a.m. in the morning when Mr. Johnson was awakened by a phone call from his former wife; they had been divorced for the last 4 years. He was dismayed to hear that their 17-year-old son, a senior at a New England Prep School, had been arrested for entering houses and stealing. He put down the phone, tried to clear the cobwebs of sleep from his brain, and puzzled as to why this had happened and how?

Peter returned from Christmas vacation, bored, apathetic and disinterested in his work although he had been previously a good student. He gave initial warnings of his future activities in two well written English themes that described breaking into houses and stealing. When this plea was disregarded, he unconsciously intensified the plea by proceeding to carry out his plan. Each night when the others in the dormitory were asleep, he would slip out and enter a different house just for the satisfaction and thrill of doing it. This was followed by a second phase. He began stealing objects from the houses—usually small objects such as jewelry and candlesticks. This kept up for several months until an alarm was spread about the neighborhood and policemen were posted.

Then one night, after all his previous efforts to obtain the necessary help had failed, Peter walked directly past a policeman into a house; he was finally apprehended and brought down to the police station. He freely admitted his guilt and took the officer back to his dormitory where he had carefully wrapped and stored all the things he had stolen in his footlocker.

Later the source of his distress was found to be as follows. His mother and father had been divorced when he was 12, the year he went away to prep school. He usually spent most of his time with his mother, but this year when he had come home for Christmas vacation, he got into a fight with his mother; she threw him out and told him to spend the vacation with his father. The father, then living with his current mistress, had no room for Peter so he put him up in a hotel room for the vacation. Peter, abandoned, alone, and depressed, spent the whole vacation sitting in his room reading and watching television. Little wonder that he later found an inappropriate but effective vehicle to express his plight and to obtain the necessary help.

The second case is Mike, age 15, in the tenth grade. He had been at swords point with his controlling, domineering, and possessive mother since the onset of his adolescence. She permitted him little freedom and required that he report his every move, not associate with certain friends, and account for all his free time. Under the guise of maternal protection she was vigorously fighting her son's individuation. He was equally disappointed in and angry at his passive inadequate father who gave him no support against the unfair and humiliating demands of the mother.

As his resultant depression deepened, his previously high grades began to go down and he withdrew from the family. They reacted with sublime unawareness of his unhappiness and pressured him more to perform.

When he began to fail in school, no more perceptive response on the part of his parents occurred. Still unsuccessful in his silent cries for help, he began to be truant from school, again receiving only punishment and orders to do better.

After about 6 months to a year of this, one night in desperation after a fight with his mother, Michael drank for the first time. He consumed half a quart of gin in half an hour, passed out, and was picked up by the police and brought to the police station.

The parents again ignored their son's plea and were hurt and ashamed that their son would so humiliate them in front of the community. Finally, all other measures having been exhausted, Michael ran away from home. Astonishingly enough, even this failed to penetrate the steel of the parents' defenses, and it was his guidance counselor who recommended that he come for treatment.

Comments

These patients are not only strongly motivated, they *are desperate for help.* It is of the utmost importance that the therapist not look for verbal assurance of motivation, but that he appropriately "read" the message in the patient's behavior and respond to the level of desperation. Failure to do so repeats for the patient the same disappointment that he has experienced at his parents' inability to read the message, and probably will cause him to drop out of treatment.

THE STYLES OF DEFENSE

Let us turn now to clinical examples of the various styles of defense against the abandonment depression.

George and Anne's case histories are described below. Their treatment is presented in Chapters 8 to 12. These two are followed by briefer examples of other styles of defense.

Acting Out Defense

Patient George Graves

The Problem.   Mr. Graves was not completely surprised to receive a phone call from the police chief that his son George, age 17, had been arrested for stealing; he and Mrs. Graves had long been worried about George's behavior. For at least 5 years George had been an increasingly serious problem at home and in school; he rebelled against rules of any sort, and stole, drank, and smoked marijuana. Neither discipline nor punishment had had any effect.

History of Present Illness.   George had always had a rather close but turbulent relationship with his mother. When he was 12 she became involved in an extramarital affair, and because she was preoccupied with this romance, she withdrew from him. George felt abandoned, became angry and rebellious at home. He was arrested for breaking and entering a store and forced to work to pay $50 worth of damage. His school marks declined, his defiance at home increased, and he was taken to see a child psychiatrist. Although the psychiatrist recommended treatment the parents did not follow his advice when George's behavior improved over the summer—an all too frequent occurrence in these cases.

At age 13, in the eighth grade, George's marks continued to be poor, and he went on sprees of stealing records, sun glasses, and clothes, without being caught. He then began to withdraw socially, stayed in his room, and refused to see his friends, at which point his parents (at the end of the eighth grade) again took him to see yet another psychiatrist. This time the patient reluctantly accepted the treatment recommended. He saw the psychiatrist three times a week for the next 3 years. George later reported that he talked very little in these interviews, leaving most of the talking to the psychiatrist whose attitude of indulgence and permissiveness compounded his problems. George manipulated the psychiatrist to "get his way" and when he succeeded he held the doctor in contempt.

The psychiatrist had no contact with the parents and gave them no assistance in dealing with George's behavior. Nevertheless, over the next year his stealing diminished, being confined to only the things he fancied, such as sun glasses and candy.

In the second year of treatment, the psychiatrist, in line with his lenient approach suggested a different, more permissive school for the ninth grade and less discipline at home. The results of these suggestions were disastrous. With removal of the discipline George's room rapidly became untidy; he missed meals and watched television late into the night. At the new school, his grades were poor and his attendance worse. He would leave his attendance record on his parents' dresser or would run into his mother in town on days he was supposed to be in school—the mother said nothing. George was not withdrawing less, but unfortunately he began to mix with an increasingly antisocial crowd with whom he would steal, smoke pot, and take barbiturates. In addition, he would leave marijuana and seconal around the house, and occasionally stumble in drunk and vomit in the bathroom.

Although this behavior was obviously a mute "plea for help," the parents remained blind and deaf to the plea, thus unwittingly furthering their son's feelings of rejection and loss of control. Surprisingly, during part of this period, because he was a natural athlete, he did well in athletics and on the football and basketball teams.

Two weeks before admission to the hospital, he was apprehended by the police in a stolen automobile. When the police searched him they found the keys to another car in his pocket. He volunteered that he had stolen these, too, and gave the address of the owner of the car to which they belonged. He was arrested and taken to the police court.

In a seemingly endless series of manipulations, the father's lawyer helped to get the patient free with a curfew as the only punishment. The patient, undaunted and determined in his efforts to get help, responded by breaking the curfew, drinking heavily, and breaking into a bungalow to steal some blankets and a wallet. He was again caught without a struggle by the police who finally suggested hospitalization.

George's history illustrates dramatically what so often happens to the adolescent who acts out flagrantly. His parents and often his psychiatrist handle the behavior permissively, thereby missing its true meaning and rejecting his mute plea for control. This throws him back on his own meager capacities and plunges him into lonely despair.

Past History.   George, the eldest of four boys, was favored by being born to an upper middle class family. However, his first life trauma came at 9 months of age when he developed irritability and constant diarrhea which was diagnosed as celiac syndrome. His mother was instructed to give him special foods and frequent feedings. She recalled giving him a great deal of attention—from 9 months to 2½ years, when the diarrhea subsided—more than her subsequent children or her friends' children received. He was described as a tense stubborn child who "got his way or else." When George was 2½ he experienced his second trauma when his brother was born and he was sent to live with his paternal grandparents for 3 to 4 weeks while the mother was busy with the new baby.

On his return his mother felt that he had not been properly cared for as he had a diaper rash, was constantly crying, and had had a relapse in toilet training; all of this in retrospect suggests that he experienced for the first time an abandonment at the birth of his brother. In addition, throughout these early years, the mother had great difficulty in controlling George's behavior.

When he was 5, life dealt its third blow. His father's business collapsed, and George and his family were forced to live with the paternal in-laws in a setting of conflict; incredibly at the same time his second brother was born and his mother developed pyelonephritis which caused her "to let things go" for a year. George suffered from lax discipline and sparse attention.

When he started school at 6, his first grade teacher noted that he was anxious and tense. His marks in school were poor and teachers claimed this was due to emotional stress evidenced by his restlessness in class and occasional stuttering which started at about age 6 and continues to the present whenever he is anxious. He sucked his thumb until age 9 and at about age 6 or 7 he began stealing gum and candy, much of which the parents overlooked.

Patient Anne

Present Illness. Fate struck Anne, a 16-year-old adopted girl a particularly cruel blow at the age of 10 when the maid who had taken care of her died and her mother became chronically ill with porphyria. The mother and father had a very distant relationship, the father spending most of his time at work so that the patient was left alone to care for the mother.

Anne, always a problem, responded by acting worse both at home and at school. At home she was rebellious, stayed up most of the night, and slept during the day. In school she resented the teachers and dressed inappropriately.

As she entered her teens, she started to smoke marijuana. At age 14, she, like George, was also taken to see a psychiatrist who said she was hopeless and recommended that she be committed to a state hospital. Her parents refused to do this but took her out of the public school system after clashes with teachers, and sent her to a private boarding school. After 1 year there, at age 15, she was suspended for violating a number of rules, including visiting a boy in his room. At this time she had her first sexual intercourse; she soon feared she was pregnant and had fantasies of running away, taking the baby with her and working to support it. Fortunately this event did not come to pass. After being suspended she returned to the local high school where she remained for only 7 weeks before dropping out. She was taken to see another psychiatrist, started treatment, and again, like George, she would not talk about herself. The psychiatrist sought more information by means of amytal interviews which were also unproductive. Several months before admission, her behavior got worse; she began leaving the house to take long walks during the middle of the night and dated boys who took heroin. Finally her doctor insisted that she be hospitalized. She was sedated and placed in the hospital against her will.

Past History.   Anne began life with the handicap of having an unwed mother about whom little was known except her age—15 years old. Anne suffered early a second reversal when she was adopted at the age of 6 weeks by a couple presumably because they were unable to have a child due to the father's sterility—but probably in an attempt to preserve an already shaky marriage. Surely, this was an ominous beginning for a new life.

According to her adopted mother, she was a difficult baby, crying constantly, and banging her head during the first year of life. A Negro maid, Louise, was hired to care for her. The mother says "the three of us took turns rocking her to sleep. She was a feeding problem. She didn't like anything, she spit everything out unless Louise cooked it for her."

She had difficulties in school beginning in the first grade and disobeyed teachers continually. At 5 she was told she was adopted and that she was the chosen one for her parents.

Her mother says she had so much difficulty in school that "I would be in school in answer to the teacher's complaints more than she would." The mother tried to discipline her by spanking her or depriving her of things she wanted, but "Anne would scream so that I couldn't stand it." During the first 6 years Louise was the only one who could handle her. Louise was overindulgent, did everything for her, and took sides with her against the parents. The mother frequently felt angry at the maid, yet acknowledged inability to manage Anne without the maid's help. When Anne was 8½ the maid left. The patient looked forward to her infrequent visits. Then when Anne was 10, fate stepped in again and suddenly and unexplainably Louise stopped visiting.

Other Types of Defense

Obsessive-Compulsive and Schizoid Defenses

Bill, age 15, a model student at school, had begun at about age 9 to have outbursts of anger and aggressiveness at home usually when his father, a successful Broadway producer, was away and he was left with his permissive indulgent mother on whom he made excessive demands. In the beginning his tantrums were mild, occurred about once every several months, and did not involve destructive behavior. By age 11 or 12, however, he began to smash his own possessions, for example, a telescope that he valued highly. These would later be replaced by the parents. On occasion if Bill had an outburst when the father was at home the father would expel him from the house for the night forcing him to sleep in the garage or at a friend's house.

The conflict with the mother and father exemplified by the outbursts gradually escalated. Then 6 months before Bill's admission to the hospital the father again left home for a period of a month. The patient's anger increased to a point where he began to threaten his young brother and talk about killing the mother. In one of these outbursts of anger accidentally he did fracture his mother's finger. The poignant thing about this story is that this patient's behavior again was a plea for help. The mother's lack of firmness and the father's inconsistency forced the patient to escalate his plea. Having received no help he finally turned from destroying his own property to destroying the property of others, such as the phone on the wall or his father's possessions.

Despite this history of acting out the patient's basic defenses were obsessive, schizoid, and paranoid. For example, on examination his facial expression had the quality of a Greek mask—a superficial smile with almost no emotion underneath. The defense of intellectualization was manifested by his obsessive interest in spending large amounts of time on science projects—at which his performance was excellent, although his meticulous attention to detail consumed endless hours. The schizoid quality of his character was illustrated by the fact that although he was a good student and had no behavior problems in school, he either became the class clown to get attention or had no friends at all. He had fantasies of retreating to the North Pole where he would have no contact with humans and could become like a machine—a task at which he seemed to have almost succeeded. He idolized "Dr. Spock" of the television show, "Star Trek," because "Dr. Spock" was devoid of human feelings. His clinging and paranoid defenses became quickly apparent after admission to the hospital where he adopted the same clinging demanding relationship with a nurse that he had had with his mother; socially he could not relate with his peers because he was constantly preoccupied with a fear that they might attack him. The minimal role of acting out as a defense was confirmed by the fact that his aggressive behavior never became a problem during his entire hospital stay.

Passive-Aggressive Acting out Defense

Ben, a 16-year-old tenth grader, gave a history of passive-aggressive response in conflict with his parents from early life. Until age 2 he clung to his mother, followed her around, and cried hysterically whenever she left him. Otherwise his early development was reported to be without incident and he showed no separation anxiety when starting school. Following a bout of infectious hepatitis at age 7, however, which caused him to be kept in bed at home for a number of months, Ben, previously a good student, became an "underachiever." Perhaps the physical illness which threw him back into the arms of his mother promoted an emotional regression to the clinging symbiotic bind of his first 2 years from which he was later unable to emerge. He felt strange in class, did little homework, daydreamed, and was preoccupied with staring out the window. He dreaded bringing home his progressively bad report cards although he only received a brief 15-minute lecture from his mother.

At age 5, his mother, a piano teacher, began to give him piano lessons which he enjoyed—"they were the high point of my day." Was it the lessons or the symbiosis he enjoyed? At age 10 in the fifth grade—perhaps spurred on by an inner maturational spurt—he became rebellious toward his mother and the piano and gave up practicing. In the sixth grade he had psychotherapy once a week for 6 months, stopping because he felt no change. At age 11 he began to teach himself to play the electric guitar and played in a dance band. He almost failed the seventh grade and he resumed playing the piano on his own in the eighth grade.

By the summer of the ninth grade, at age 14, depressed and apathetic, he began experimenting with drugs: he used LSD, mescaline, and marijuana daily. These drugs did away with his "bad feelings" and allowed him to get closer to people. His course over the next two years prior to hospitalization was progressively downhill. His passive-aggressive behavior increased and caused him to be expelled from several different schools. He started psychotherapy which was of no help because he failed to attend or participate. Ingestion of drugs continued unabated. His behavior deteriorated further so that for a number of months prior to admission he would spend more than half the day in bed and got up just before his parents came home (they both worked) to go out and acquire his drugs.

His physical appearance broadcast his state. He was of average height with extremely long hair, had braces on his teeth, and wore glasses. He appeared almost catatonic; his affect was flat; he was withdrawn, almost mute and extremely passive. He talked in a distressingly slow manner as if retarded. The extent of his passivity became readily apparent shortly after admission. In interviews he would only speak when asked questions, and on the floor he remained aloof from his peers. He only attended activities upon direction and he then quickly demonstrated his passive resistance by oversleeping; he was unable to control his oversleeping until after prolonged psychotherapy.

Further Styles of Defenses

The type of defense the patient employs against the abandonment depression probably depends on many factors. An important one, illustrated below, is identification with the defenses of the parent.

Flight

An adopted 14-year-old seventh-grade girl after becoming bored and unhappy and getting poor grades, ran off to Greenwich Village—where she smoked pot everyday. She stated that she felt "free for the first time in my life—being taken care of by hippies." She adopted a pseudonym, Stefanie, which in contrast to dull, childish Alice, symbolized a mature, well-liked, sexy, swinging, and hippyish girl. Her father's reaction to the first time she ran away was to break down and cry, saying "look what you have done to your mother and me." The mother, on the other hand, calmly questioned Alice about her still intact virginity and then took her to a gynecologist for a check-up. Alice ran away a second time, joined a group of "teenyboppers" under her new name, Stefanie; she again smoked pot and related grandiose stories about herself.

When she returned home, the father said, "If you ever try that again I'll stick a knife through your heart." The mother, however, accused her of being promiscuous; she rejected her denial and forced the patient to submit to a second gynecological examination which revealed an intact hymen.

The father was a passive man who deferred everything to his wife and had never spanked the patient. The mother was strict, punitive, and prone to outbursts of temper, but beneath this facade she was permissive with her daughter, actually encouraging the patient's acting out, perhaps to fulfill her own unconscious promiscuous fantasies.

The patient was caught between stimulation on the part of the mother to act out promiscuous fantasies, and terrible threats of punishment from the father. Her only recourse was flight. One might expect that the type of defense she would choose against depression would be to act out in promiscuity, but fear of retaliation by her father caused her to run away instead.

Anorexia Nervosa. Another style of defense against depression is illustrated by a 16-year-old girl whose parents were divorced and whose mother had anorexia nervosa. Already somewhat withdrawn in this unhappy situation, following the father's remarriage, the patient became even more withdrawn, moody, and irritable. She then threw herself into studying. In other words, she used obsessive studying as a defense against her rage at being abandoned, both by her sick mother and her remarried father.

To make matters worse, soon after her father's remarriage, the brother to whom she was very close left home to spend all summer in camp. At this point when she heard that her father was going to divorce his second wife, the patient's defense broke down; she started a self-imposed diet and developed anorexia nervosa. In other words, she chose the mother's style of defense against her rage.

Heterosexual Clinging

A third style of defense against depression is illustrated by Martha, who, 1 year prior to admission to the hospital at the age of 14, entered a new school where she became increasingly unhappy and frustrated. She felt unable to communicate with her parents about her anxieties and missed her older sister who had left for her freshman year in college.

She turned first to her work to deal with her difficulties but soon thereafter began dating a 27-year-old man whom she saw quite frequently; she went to concerts and museums with him and visited his apartment. Finally, she began having an affair with him. She never invited him to her home, nor discussed him with either of her parents, except to say that she was dating him. As a child she had always been extremely close to her mother, but during the past few years her mother had become colder, withdrawn, business-like, and unapproachable as she gave more time to her job.

The mother was an aggressive and domineering woman who had successfully supported the family by earning $20,000 a year as an office manager. She had been in a chronic depression for many years because of the tension between herself and her husband. There were frequent open fights between them.

The father was reportedly a producer who had been unable to support the family, and who was basically passive and withdrawn in his relationships at home. The mother considered her husband helpless, weak, and self-centered, but both the mother and the father appeared to have unconscious fantasies of promiscuity.

The patient, feeling abandoned by her mother's withdrawal, and her sister's going away to college, developed a depression and acted out both her parents' unconscious sexual fantasies to relieve the depression.

MANKIND AND FATE

The histories of these patients—those presented are more representative than unique—reveal the unbearable emotional burdens that accidents of fate subject these youngsters to, at a time in their lives when they are too young and their ego structure too fragile to cope.

Their stories read like Greek tragedies; the patient reels blindly from trauma to trauma. Perhaps the key question might be, not why are they so sick, but, how did they survive (if one can call it survival) as well as they did? Life is unjust and everyone must contend with life events over which he has no control, but surely the experiences which these patients had, so early in life, remind one of the ancient Greek motto, "whom the gods would destroy, they first deprive of their senses."

For example, George developed the bowel problem at the age of 9 months, which brought him into a unique dependency relationship with his mother; this however was suddenly broken with the birth of his brother and George's being sent to the grandparents where he was apparently neglected. Then again, at age 5, his father's business collapsed, precipitating his mother and father into great discords and dissension. The second brother was born and his mother developed pyelonephritis. Finally, when he was 12 years old, his mother entered into an extramarital affair and withdrew from him.

Fate dealt its final blow when he was taken to see a psychiatrist who, oblivious to the real roots of the problem, instituted a kind of treatment that was doomed to fail.

Our second case, Anne, is even more poignant; fate struck its blow at the moment of conception when she was brought into the world by an unwed mother with whom she could not stay. On top of this, she was adopted by a couple—not for her own sake, but probably to preserve their marriage—who were themselves, like George's father and mother, very poor candidates for parents.

Anne managed for the few years of life to gain some support from a maid, but again fate stepped in when she was 10, and not only did the maid die, but her only other frail source of support, the mother, became chronically ill. Again, as with George, to complete the tragedy, she went to see a psychiatrist who did not understand the roots of her problem. Viewed through this prism, it is not very hard to share some of George's and Anne's bitterness about the nature of life, and to ascribe this bitterness not to their pathology but to the extraordinary concatenation of unfortunate events that fate decreed for them.

The next chapter approaches the source of this bitterness—the feelings of abandonment—by way of the patients' description of their feelings as well as from themes they have written to express better the intensity and depth of these feelings.

CHAPTER 4

Feelings of Abandonment—The Six Horsemen of the Apocalypse

The six psychiatric horsemen of the Apocalypse—depression, anger, fear, guilt, helplessness, and emptiness and void—vie in their emotional sway and destructiveness with the social upheaval and destructiveness of the original four horsemen—famine, war, flood, and pestilence. Technical words are too abstract to convey the intensity and immediacy of these feelings and therefore the primacy they hold over the patient's entire life. The patient's functioning in the world, his relationship with people, and even some of his physiologic functions are subordinated to the defense against these feelings.

It is small wonder that Bowlby [10–14] reverted to animal world concepts of ethology and evolution to conceptualize what appears to be the patient's most primitive order of business. This chapter outlines the origins and the components of these feelings and conveys their motivational power by reporting patients' descriptions in interviews and presenting patients' compositions written for school.

It is important to distinguish the feelings of abandonment or intrapsychic experience from an actual physical separation and abandonment in the patients' environmental experience. The term "abandonment feelings" refers to the intrapsychic experience of the patient, that is, to what he feels about the environmental experience of separation. Whether the environmental experience results in "feelings of abandonment" depends on the psyche of the patient, not on the experience itself. The abandonment feelings evolve from multifactorial intrapsychic reactions, namely the "six horsemen"; the separation experience is only a precipitating influence.

COMPONENTS OF ABANDONMENT FEELINGS

The abandonment feelings comprise not one feeling but a complex of six constituent feelings: depression, anger and rage, fear, guilt, passivity and

58

helplessness, emptiness and void. The intensity and degree of each of these component feelings will vary with the unique developmental traumas of each individual. However, each component will be present to some degree in every patient.

Depression

The depression has qualities similar to that emotion described by Spitz as Anaclitic Depression: feelings that spring from the loss or the threat of loss either of part of the self or of supplies that the patient believes vital for survival. Patients often think of this in physical terms comparable to losing an arm or both legs, or being deprived of vital substances such as oxygen, plasma, or blood. This aspect of the depression illustrates best how it differs in quality from the usual adult depression whose dynamics are predicated upon the presence of a sadistically cruel superego that persecutes the ego until it breaks down [127].

The manner in which the depression emerges in therapy is itself a statement of its motivational power. In the first or testing phase of therapy the patient may complain of boredom or a vague sense of numbness or depression but his affect will appear quite bland and he will not seem to be suffering from a very intense feeling; this is a reflection of the fact that he is now well defended against the abandonment feelings. As the defenses are successively interrupted the depression becomes more intense, repressed memories emerge, and the patient quite obviously is suffering. The patient intensifies his struggle to maintain his defenses but as the doctor interprets them the patient gradually slides into the bottom of his depression where lies, almost always, suicidal despair and belief that it will never be possible to receive the necessary supplies. At this point the patient is a genuine suicidal risk and there is no longer any doubt in the observer's mind about the motivational power of the patient's depression.

Rage

The intensity of the patient's anger and rage and the rate of the emergence of these emotions in psychotherapy parallel that of the depression. The more depressed the patient becomes the angrier he becomes. The content of the rage is first more general and very often projected upon contemporary situations. As memory of his feelings returns, the rage becomes more and more focused on the relationship with the mother. Finally at the bottom of the trough, parallel to the suicidal despair, are homicidal fantasies and impulses directed at the mother. Thus the rage parallels and is a companion to the depression throughout the stages of psychotherapy.

Fear

A third component is the fear of being abandoned which may be expressed as fear of being helpless, or of supplies being cut off, of facing death, or of being killed. Two psychosomatic accompaniments of this fear that I have observed when patients were in an abandonment panic were asthma and peptic ulcer. It is possible to theorize that these symptoms are an expression of the patient's separation fear. The former is a fear of death if supplies are cut off and the latter a hungering for the lost supplies. The panic itself can dominate the clinical picture to the point that it conceals both the underlying depression and rage.

The degree to which fear participates in the clinical picture seems to be related to the degree to which the mother used the threat of abandonment as a disciplinary technique. All these patients were mesmerized by the recent novel *The Godfather* [104]. Although I realize that, as a best seller, this book appealed to many people without a Borderline Syndrome, nevertheless, the degree to which these patients were attracted by the book was most striking. The book, describing the Mafia's use of terror and fear of death to discipline and enforce compliance, portrayed in concrete terms the theme which had dominated the patients' early lives. If one complies, one receives rewards. If one does not, one is actually killed. The patients live with an almost constant fear of abandonment, waiting for the "Sword of Damocles" to fall. Recalling childhood memories they express such feelings about their childhood as: it was "like living in a permanent funeral as if I might soon be buried." Also in their themes they refer to their childhood in terms of prisons, concentration camps, and disciplinary schools.

The threat of abandonment apparently had been used as a disciplinary technique to inhibit the patient's self-assertion or expression of anger and to enforce compliance. Therefore, as the depression and rage emerge in psychotherapy, the fear of being abandoned for expressing these feelings rises in tandem, sometimes reaching panic proportions.

Guilt

Guilt is the "fifth column" behind the front line of the patient's defenses. This guilt, springing from introjection of the mother's attitude toward the patient, now becomes the patient's attitude toward himself. Since the mother greeted the expression of his self-assertion and his wish to separate and individuate with disapproval and withdrawal, the patient begins to feel guilty about that whole part of himself which seeks separation and individuation, that is, his thoughts, wishes, feelings, and actions. Consequently to avoid guilt feelings he suppresses moves in this direction and resorts to a chronic state of clinging and demanding, and thereby sabotages as by a "fifth column" his own autonomy. This aspect of the guilt is seen most clearly in treatment after the environmental conflict with the mother has been more or less resolved when an intense intrapsychic battle comes to the fore between the patient's wish to individuate and the guilt that this entails.

Passivity and Helplessness

The mother withdraws her approval when the patient attempts to assert himself since she views his self-assertion toward individuation as a threatened "loss" of her child. Therefore the patient associates the fear of abandonment with his own capacity for assertion. When faced with a conflict, he becomes overwhelmed with feelings of passivity and helplessness since the only tool that might give him mastery, self-assertion, brings with it the fear of loss of his mother's love, of abandonment.

Emptiness and Void

The sense of void is best described as one of terrifying inner emptiness or numbness; it springs partially from introjection of the mother's negative attitudes that leaves the patient devoid, or empty, of positive supportive introjects.

Defenses against the Void—"Taking Care of Business"

This concept of void together with the activities that "fill the void" demonstrates a link between these patients and drug addicts and alcoholics, and also illustrates the motivational power of these feelings.

The addict uses a phrase "taking care of business" to refer to those activities involved in obtaining and taking heroin. For example, these include getting the money, obtaining the drug, avoiding the police, getting back home, taking the heroin, and experiencing the high after the injection. His total daily activity is devoted to "taking care of business." His motivation is so strong that he devotes his entire life to "business." Nevertheless, heroin addicts are comparable to our patients in that heroin is used as a "supply" to fill the void, to fill the emptiness caused by the abandonment depression. The Borderline adolescents described in this book, who act out and steal, who take drugs short of heroin are acting from the same motivation—using the drugs as emotional supplies to protect themselves against the inner void associated with the abandonment depression.

Furthermore, it is not an unusual clinical experience to find patients who commit suicide or become psychotic rather than experience these feelings. Whether these defenses are those of the character disorder such as acting out of the psychotic such as delusion and withdrawal from reality, or of the neurotic, such as obsessions and compulsions, they all serve to fill the void and avoid the feelings of abandonment.

Neurotic Defenses

1. *Oral.* Eating, drinking, smoking, chewing gum, alcoholism.

2. *Physiological.* The primacy of the need to defend against the feelings of abandonment as indicated by the fact that both bodily functions and sexual gratification are subordinated to this need. For example, on one physiological level the bowel movement can be associated with loss, and constipation suffered to avoid feelings of loss. On another physiological level, ejaculation with orgasm may also be associated with void and the pleasure of sexual arousal may be foregone to retain the semen to fill the void.

3. *Money.* Money is a prime symbol for "emotional supplies." When the patient spends it on himself it brings the satisfaction of receiving supplies while when spent on others, he has a feeling of deprivation and loss. One patient reported a fantasy where she could spend the rest of her days in a department store buying things for herself; she said she never felt better than when engaged in such activity.

4. *Clinging.* All Borderline patients except those who are detached use excessive clinging not only to persons as already indicated but also to places and things: a familiar piece of clothing, an art object, furniture, a room, an apartment or home, a neighborhood, a place of work, or a daily ritual or routine. The function of these clinging rituals or schedules is not to facilitate work but to avoid the fear associated with more independence.

Recapitulation

To recapitulate, there are six components to the feelings of abandonment: depression, anger, fear, guilt, passivity and helplessness, and emptiness and void. As the defenses against these feelings are worked through in psychotherapy they all emerge in parallel, precipitating the patient into the pit of his abandonment depression with feelings of suicidal despair, homicidal rage, panic about being abandoned, passivity and helplessness, and terrifying inner emptiness and void. Small wonder that the patient's defenses are so tenacious.

New let us turn to our patients' reports of these feelings as they emerged in psychotherapy.

DEPRESSION

One sixteen-year-old boy in an acute symptomatic state, unable to sleep and with headaches, nausea and diarrhea was able to describe his feelings. "I'm going down hill. It scares me. I feel paranoid, I don't want to see anyone. When I go to class I feel lonely, desolate, detached, alone on a brown place with no color, nobody around."

"I feel like I'm dying. I feel powerless sinking under 5000 pounds of self hate. I feel like a rotten tree with total despair inside. Hopeless, drained, no strength, I can't do it. Badly wounded, deeply hurt as though I'm being squashed, no way out. My own emptiness frightens me, if hemlock was sitting here I'd drink it."

RAGE AND FEAR

The role of fear is suggested by another example, a female patient. As this girl's defenses were worked through she became aware of her rage at her mother and expressed some of it in the interviews, albeit intellectually at first. The evening after she had expressed her rage with full affect she had a vivid nightmare in which she was pursued by the Mafia who wished to kill her. This led to such feelings of panic that she was unable to sleep and the next day she told me: "If I don't block out the feelings about my mother, I get depressed, self-depreciatory and think everybody hates me and I hate myself. I have these ridiculous fantasies that nobody likes me, I'm even sure that you think I'm a hopeless case and don't like me. I recognize that's ridiculous but can't do anything about it."

Over a period of weeks as the patient got closer and closer to verbalizing her rage at the mother she became more panicky and had repetitive nightmares of being attacked, tortured, murdered.

A similar example, a 17-year-old girl, entered treatment because of a depression after graduating from high school. When I confronted her with the fact that she tended to tailor herself to fit her mother's needs, and did not express her true feelings, she became very anxious in the interview. After the interview she had an acute attack of dyspnea in the subway, and afraid that her larynx was going to close off and she would choke to death, she left the subway and took a taxi home. At home she became even more frightened, had more difficulty in breathing, and was afraid she would suffocate to death. She called her father whose reassurance quelled her symptoms. That night she had a nightmare about a girl being bombed and killed. In her free associations to the dream she recalled other dreams of being shot and killed. She then said that she was afraid that her mother did not really care about her and was going to leave her, being without her mother would be like dying. When around her mother she often was afraid to breathe and held her breath: "I'm afraid if I leave her I'll die. Although her love is suffocating."

RAGE

The following example, Jean, illustrates the extent of the patient's homicidal rage and her battle against it.

After Jean's suicide attempt she felt enraged at her therapist, the hospital, her parents, and for the first time at her sister Sue. She stated: "I just couldn't take it—that I was alone and there was nobody to lean on—I just hate myself and don't want to live that much." Again she related these feelings to the time of her sister Ruth's birth. Then she became panicky while thinking of Sue and her mother—feeling alone, frightened—as if she was outside in the winter cold, tired or dead, and was alone, as if the whole world had died. "When she had Ruth I was about five, I can't remember her telling me ahead of time but when she did have Ruth she didn't look pregnant. When I told my teacher she didn't believe me. It was strange—you had to take care of it. I wasn't really that gung ho on the idea—seems like she was at the hospital for an awfully long time. I was really mad—she could come home with Ruth. For awhile she had to stay in bed. I didn't know very much about it. But at night I missed her so I'd cry [pause]. Oh, when my mother had Ruth I had my own room but someone would have to share a room so since I had a large room I had to share a room with Joan. A couple of nights turned into 8 years. At first I didn't mind the idea but after a couple of weeks we'd fight about stupid things. It was my mother's idea. It started off like Joan didn't like to sleep in the dark and it was supposed to be temporary. One time we had a fight and divided the room in half—we even put up a blockade. You can't pick on a 1-year-old so we'd gang up and bust Joan. I'm still closer to Sue than Joan. Now we really don't fight. About 2 years ago she moved out and I was so happy. In a way it was a big plan to get us together—why did I get this little sister shoved on me? I had an intruder."

She expressed her desire to be a child again and the hopelessness of her returning. Although she remained depressed her suicidal impulses abated as she talked about her jealousy and anger. She began to recall childhood homicidal urges directed toward her mother and these frightened her. She remembered childhood dreams and sticking pins into and hanging a doll which was an effigy of her mother. As she touched on this she would find ways of taking the blame on herself. Over the next several weeks she gradually began to express openly anger and resentment toward her mother but with minimal affect. She became less depressed as this centered on more recent events. She related her fear of expressing anger to fear of destroying her parents and to unbearable feelings of guilt. It seems this was reinforced by being told on various occasions that she was the cause of her parents' marital difficulties and that she would cause her father to have a heart attack or her mother to have a nervous breakdown. As her guilt was relieved she gradually became increasingly angry with her therapist. She displayed considerable affect but when she related this to earlier feelings her affect diminished. She became increasingly resistant to discussing early material, stating: "I don't like to be pushed and I don't like to be cornered."

This culminated in two violent sessions in early April in which she repeatedly screamed her hate for her therapist at the top of her voice. Following this she continued to project her anger but now more clearly as a specific defense to avoid early memories and feelings about her mother. In addition, she would attempt to withdraw—"I'm not in the mood for a session today. I want to go to sleep if you want to know the truth."

She also began to talk about her positive feelings for her father and how frightening these were. Following this she again sought out contact with one of the adolescent boys on the floor. Although she initially attempted to deny any connection between her feelings and this behavior, as she acknowledged it she began to project her anger toward her therapist. When this was interpreted, she became sullen and withdrawn. One evening she was restricted and while in her room, she smashed some personal objects. She stated: "I was angry cause I wasn't her little kid and because I was crying and she wouldn't come and hold me. She wasn't around." She also expressed resentment that her mother was not a wife to her father and that he turned to his daughters for attention. However, she continued to profess her love for her mother. It became increasingly clear that she felt her mother treated everyone as objects to be discarded when no longer gratifying. When Ruth was born, "she got a new toy to play with . . . (the old toy) got left in the toy box. I just don't feel like anybody's around. Just being scared there's nobody around."

FEELINGS OF ABANDONMENT AS REVEALED BY PATIENTS' COMPOSITIONS

Let us now turn to another vehicle of disclosure—the patients' compositions. Although the direction for writing the compositions did not specify the content, the compositions were loaded with feelings of abandonment. In the first story note the coldness and bleakness of the Arctic (the patient is Bill who wished to withdraw to the Arctic to get away from human contact). The death of the brother, mother, and father is expressed and finally the patient himself embraces death out of loneliness and fear.

50 East, 70 North, by Bill

I was a young boy of seven traveling with my parents through Central Greenland searching for my brother's downed plane.

We were traveling on one sled with six dogs for 50° 20′ E., 70° 23′ N. The authorities presumed the occupants of the plane dead, but we had to find out for ourselves.

My mother was now head of the two man party, for my father was killed by a polar bear who invaded the camp one night.

Mother was not as confident as father in the traveling in the snow. She lost her way many times and did not take good care of herself in the cold. She spent most of her time and effort on me.

Due to her lack of care she soon became very ill. The temperature and wind got to her. Frost bite affected her face and arms. Weakness affected her muscles. I told her all the time, "Go back mom, go back. Look at Dad. It's not worth it." But she ignored me.

We settled for the night by a huge block of ice to protect us from the biting wind.

She was very weak that night. I lit the fire and helped her eat. I lay down next to her and put my head next to her side. Her arm was behind my neck and over upon my chest. I took both my hands and clasped the freezing limb and went to sleep.

I woke up two hours before dawn. The hand I had clasped was cold. I unwrapped myself and tried to wake mother. She did not wake. Her face was red with cold, but blue with death. Chills went down my back. Tears rolled down my eyes, and froze before they reached my mouth. I flung myself on her breast and wrapped my arms around her and started to cry.

I rolled over on my back next to her and stared up at the soft stars in the beautifully serene night. It appeared as if they were receding from me. I felt extreme loneliness and fear. I calmly opened my jacket and felt the cold air rush over my body as I closed my eyes.

Rich, by Bill

This second composition of Bill's reminds one very much of *The Heart is a Lonely Hunter*, by Carson McCullers. Rich had no parents, suffered much from feelings of loneliness and emptiness, and could not communicate just as the protagonist in that book was unable to communicate. His loneliness springing from the feelings of abandonment and inability to communicate are beautifully expressed. Rich's experiences also bring Cinderella to mind.

Poor Rich, living in his own little stone cold world. A lonely, unwanted person was he. He spent all of his time in a park near the South side of the city. Rich was always there living inside of his own little psychotic world. Rain, snow, sleet, he was there in that small little park.

To this day he still sits by the gates to the park, watching the people day and night coming and going. He felt a longing to be one of them but he was different.

Yes Rich was different. He had no parents, at least he could not remember any. He only remembers that one day when he became a man, before that his memory fails. All through his life he suffered much due to his handicaps. He could not communicate to anyone and was never accepted, but was just looked at and usually that look became a stare, an unbelievable stare.

Nights were the worst of all. During the day he watched people doing what normal people do. Singing, dancing, dining, talking and just enjoying life. But he couldn't move from that cement binding that held him to his destined place. In the day people were around him and he could pretend he was one of those happy people. But at night his fantasies died. No people were present. The park was dark, desolate, cold and lonely. And did he feel lonely. He felt like crying every night, but some unexplainable force held him back. It was as if a force was in him saying "don't cry, don't give in to this world."

He many times thought of suicide but it would not work, for he was immortal. The immortal, lonely, rejected and unwanted of the world. He stood for those unfortunate souls who existed on that wretched planet called earth. He stood for those immortal souls who have always existed and always will.

That forlorn face, that immovable solitude, those torn ragged clothes. Yes, he was an outcast, and could not cry out for his lips felt like cement, too heavy to move. But one day he did cry out, although nobody heard him. And he said to this world, "I hate it, I hate it, I hate being a statue."

12 Bar Blues, by Nancy

"12 Bar Blues" emphasizes hopelessness, downtroddenness, loneliness, and abandonment. The patient portrays her character as seeking alcohol to deal with his feelings, and then upon realizing that this "decadent and ambiguous state of being" would be his death, he settles into a black hole devoid of any one thing that could possibly offer warmth or comfort—a beautiful description of the void.

Jake, moving somewhere between a walk and a jog, passed down the main street of Monterey going toward home. The street was almost deserted, save for a few stray drunks from the night past. And the sun was just beginning to spread its phantasmal fingers over the horizon, flashing tantalizing rich colors.

Jake slouched farther into his jacket as a chilly ocean breeze bit. He eyed the old canneries (now shops or restaurants), with their scaling wood and rusting machines. He felt a sudden throbbing and a painful flood of memories rushed back. Memories of the Row twenty years previous when jobs came easy and the town was prosperous. Then they went, the canneries ceased their racket and the town left too. He shuddered as a wave of depression broke over him.

Jake broke into a trot and the hotel came into view. A decade ago it was pure white clapboard with vermillion shutters. Now the clapboard was rotting and the shutters were hanging on their hinges, rattling in the wind. He bounded up the rickety steps and apologized to the old cook for his lateness (or earliness, depending on how you view the matter). Then Jake sprinted up the stairs, two at a time with derisive laughter trailing behind.

He stood in the center of the cramped, shabby room, ambivalent as to what to do, sleep or go out? After some thought he decided upon the latter and sauntered down to the street.

It was now close to six in the morning and if he was to find any work it would be now. Jake knew a shortcut to the docks and made for it, through a vacant lot and a short stretch of woods. The lot was scattered with decrepit tires, rusted tin cans, old boots and discarded appliances. He gingerly picked his way through the lot and stepped into the woods. It was dark and cool with the Cyprus trees casting gnarled, broken shadows.

A feeling settled down on Jake. A feeling that perhaps he may not be able to find work at the docks. He would get evicted like so many times before and would have to sleep in the woods or someplace.

The docks were awake now, crawling with life. Fishermen, dogs, and small boys carrying their masts and sails, dragging behind tough nets and poles. They all had something to do, some duty and they were going about it in swarms.

Jake hit the docks, meandering about with his nose out, hoping for some stray conversation that would indicate a hand was needed. Nothing. He could not catch even a single ray of hope. Asking about, "Do ya need any help?" "No, sorry, Jake. There's nothin' here today." Always he received the same answer. They all knew what he was doing at the docks but couldn't help him out.

Jake rambled back to the Row, thinking his unemployment inevitable and flouting everyone he ran into. Turning down a side street, he shuffled into Gildo's Bar and plunked down on a battered stool with a pint of Four Roses. He withdrew into a corner booth to sulk and drink his way to happiness. A slow numbness was working its way from his toes up and his head was soaring.

Like many of the men in Gildo's he had once worked in the canneries. And like many of them he had once had a wife but she left him when the sardines did and there was no work. A long time had passed and Jake had fallen into a dissipated pattern of living.

By late afternoon Jake was completely bombed. He had drunk all morning and afternoon and was on his way home. The remaining portion of his funds was long ago swallowed and he plunged downward.

Jake staggered in the door and up to his room. After dousing his head in the wash bowl he spread-eagled on the bed for the night.

At dawn he awoke with a spasmatic headache, slowly realizing his predicament. He saw that his decadent and ambiguous state of being would be his death. His disappointment was due to his lack of employment and only that. And all he really needed was to work. But work was merely a word and he settled into a black hole void of any one thing that could possibly offer warmth and comfort.

The sun was peeking over the black horizon stretching its fingers and gathering into its benevolent soul all that was good and kind. The dock was waking also, soon the buzz and hum of activity would start. Jake just then realized, tomorrow would be as yesterday and today. And the Row would breathe on forever with or without him.

Guilt, by Nancy

"Guilt" describes with intuitive insight the use of a heterosexual relationship to deal with the fear of being abandoned.

Ross and Jessica met while at their summer cottages in Massachusetts.

It was a relaxed summer for the newly graduated business man, Ross. He took full advantage of all the relaxations around this summer escape. One of these was lying on the beach sun bathing. That is how he met Jessica. Jessica had just turned twenty and loved tanning her nicely proportioned womanly body of which she was very well aware. Ross soon became aware of her appearance also and was immediately attracted to her.

By chance one day Ross got an opportunity to speak to Jessica. This talk sprang from a mutual liking of sea shells. He had long been infatuated by Jessica, and now leaped at this opportunity with open arms. He was living in a New York City apartment by himself with his only activity being his job. Ross was really pretty lonely and he wanted to love somebody. Jessica was this somebody. When he talked to her that day she was better than he had dreamed and his heart felt like a feather fluttering in his chest.

Apparently Jessica felt the same way because the rest of the summer they spent all their time together. When the summer ended and Ross found out Jessica lived in the City also the happiness continued.

Ross felt little loneliness as his affair with Jessica went on. His love for her grew stronger. Jessica had just turned twenty one when she decided to live with him.

Jessica lived with Ross for just about a year until the youthful exciting feeling of living with a man died off. Through a lot of fear and a bit of doubt she told him her feelings and left.

Ross's long fear of loneliness became real and he looked for another escape. Ross became terribly sad and increasingly more so each day. This sadness took over his abilities to function. He lost his job and moved to the lower east side. All his income amounted to just enough for him to stay alive. He never spoke to anyone and rarely came out of his apartment. His eyes became sad and he grew a beard. His whole appearance became like he felt.

Jessica got in touch with one of his relatives three years after her departure. When she found out his situation she felt guilt cloud her mind and decided to return to him. When she found him, he seemed to be the happiest person in the world until after about five minutes when he told her to leave.

The Tumor, by Nancy

This composition is also similar to the theme of *The Heart is a Lonely Hunter*—death all alone with a complete inability to communicate.

"That's all I remember doctor." That day is still hazy in my mind. All I remember is the game, and walking across the square. I must have gotten some blow on my head. I was so dazed, I just told the coach that it was nothing and I could go to the hotel. About an hour later I started to get dizzy and all. "Well, what did the test show?"

"Well . . . (he meditates for a brief second) you have a tumor Jake . . ."

"Of course you can operate and remove it!"

"Jake, I am sorry. It can not be removed, it's in an inoperable part of the brain." The words bit into him. Jake was a brute, mesomorphic type: Just an animal, majored in 1,000 credits of football in college . . . Joe crewcut.

"How long do I have?"

"It's very hard to say. Two, six months, maybe a year or two. It's very hard to say at this time."

"Oh my God! (the knife was starting to cut.) Death! Two, six, life gone
. . . where . . . What will I do (Complete incoherency here. Now shouting.) The pain . . . the pain . . ."

"There will be none, headaches toward the end. At that time I will give you something for it. Meanwhile I am putting you on tranquilizers and sleeping medication."

"Is that all? I am going to die, and you give me this crap?"

"That's all, I will send you the bill."

Jake left the office completely shaken, incoherent, and without any resolve. He was completely lost. He did not know where he was going, nor did he know what he was doing. He was nearly killed three times when he crossed the street. He meandered in and out of bars, only to pick up a witch and go to her apartment for food.

He arrived at his shabby apartment at two in the morning. He gulped down the doctor's medication and fell into bed fully dressed. He woke up finding himself hanging in a bee-hive; back to sleep.

Jake woke up suddenly. He was suddenly startled to find out that he was completely paralyzed, not only that, but he was blind. After a few seconds, he realized that he was also deaf. He wanted to scream, but the physical capability had left him. Instead his mind screamed. But that was no good. His mind was perfectly intact. He was in a prone position on his bed. There was no telephone. He had no real friends. Nobody would come for him. Panic struck him when he realized that he would die of starvation, and it might take weeks; meanwhile he would have to lie on his bed and do nothing but think. He kept wishing that he were dead. But he remained on that bed paralyzed, blind, and deaf, for two months before he did die.

Felicia's Hurt, by Nancy

The final story, "Felicia's Hurt," smacks very much of *Cinderella.* Her mother is dead; she lives in an orphanage (i.e., with stepsisters). Mrs. Sparrowheart (the evil Queen in *Snow White* or the stepmother in *Cinderella*) is angry, rejecting and punitive.

As the girls walked nervously back to the orphanage she observed with amazement the world around.

She could see the gently rolling hills off in the distance, that looked as if they had been painted there to match the mothering sky. Beside her a river danced with delight to the whistling of wind through the trees.

The girl observing and loving every minute of the scenery, realized that she was back at the orphanage, and, was also late.

"Why do all good things have to come to an end?" she thought depressingly to herself.

Felicia has been living at the orphanage for two years now. Her parents were killed in a car accident, and none of her relations could be so bothered.

She has big blue eyes that appear to tell the story of her unhappy life in one glance, and now if you were to look in her eyes you would find the sea rushing forth in rage, for she knew Mrs. Sparrowheart would be extremely angry with her.

Hesitating to open the door . . . finally the door was opened and there stood Mrs. Sparrowheart. Mrs. Sparrowheart was a small woman with gray hair, faded blue eyes and a stern forehead. She glanced at the child. Felicia stood before Mrs. Sparrowheart trembling.

"Well Felicia what do you have to say for yourself?" Mrs. Sparrowheart asked with repressed anger. "Nothing, you mean to tell me that you are late and that you have nothing to say for yourself," yelled Mrs. Sparrowheart with anger pouring forth anew. "Yes, yes You have the nerve to come to me and have nothing to say after you've been late."

By this time Felicia broke down in loud hard sobs, with apologies coming forth by the dozen.

"Quit crying like an infant. You're the only child in this orphanage that gives me so much trouble. Well I'm fed up with the whole thing. I cannot and will not keep you here any longer. Either one of your relatives comes and gets you or I'll have to send you somewhere else. I can't be so bothered with shameful little beasts such as you. Go to your room and there will be no dinner."

Felicia helpless and shaken with unbearable sobs slowly started to ascend the stairs.

The stairs were long and winding and of course Felicia's room was in the attic.

While ascending the stairs the hurt she felt was intensified by the thought that no one could be bothered with her. She wondered if Mrs. Sparrowheart really meant what she said. She hoped not.

Felicia reached her room. She turned the knob and went in. With heart sunk and eyes flooded with tears she flung herself onto the bed.

"Why do I always have to be the one, why can't anyone else have to be hurt, why me?" Felicia thought this and more while sobbing bitterly into her pillow.

After a while she fell asleep to be awakened the next morning by Mrs. Sparrowheart.

"Felicia, Felicia, get up child, have you no sense of time. Get up."
"Wha, what time is it?" asked Felicia trying to fight the sleep still on her.
"It is now 8:00 and you've missed breakfast," Mrs. Sparrowheart exclaimed angrily. "I cannot and will not put up with this any longer."

"You're leaving today for another orphanage that knows how to deal with kids like you. Now get dressed and pack your things—you're leaving at 10:00."

Felicia put on her slippers and bathrobe, gathered her toothpaste, washcloth and clothes to be worn that day and started toward the bathroom door. At the door she turned as if to speak only to be cut off by Mrs. Sparrowheart who quite impatiently told Felicia "Go on, I'll attend to the room."

While packing, Felicia's heart throbbed with pain. She felt a terrible sense of loss. How she longed for her mother and father. Mrs. Sparrowheart came in the room in quite a rush interrupting Felicia's thoughts.

"It's now ten and the man that is to drive you is here waiting. Is everything packed?" "Yes-yes" replied Felicia trying hard not to choke on her tears. "Well then, come on." Felicia walked down the stairs very quietly beside Mrs. Sparrowheart so as not to get her angry with her before she left.

They reached the landing, Felicia was introduced to the man, goodbyes were said, the man put the luggage into the car and they were off.

Felicia with tears in her eyes turned and looked at the orphanage as it faded away.

She didn't know why but for some reason she felt she was again being left by someone or something she loved.

As the orphanage faded out for good Felicia turned to the driver and asked, "Why do all good things have to come to an end?"

The patients' descriptions of the intensity of their feelings of abandonment give strong testimony as to why these feelings play such a key role in the organization of the personality; why their avoidance becomes such an urgent affair; why taking care of business becomes so vital that the rest of their lives pale in comparison to this urgent task.

The introduction of the Borderline Adolescent is now concluded. The next task taken up in Chapters 5 and 6 is to define the parental role in the Syndrome.

CHAPTER 5

The Parents: An Overview

Freud, developing his theories in an essentially patriarchal culture, located the core of emotional difficulties in the oedipal period and related them to castration anxiety. This emphasis on the father and the oedipal period so important to the development of psychoanalysis and to the furthering of the understanding of emotional illness in general, also threw a smokescreen over the core of the difficulties of the Borderline patient [137].

The families of these patients are matriarchal not patriarchal. The dominant figure is the mother and the core of the difficulties lies not in the oedipal period related to castration but in the oral period, in problems related to the mothering process and separation-individuation from the symbiotic relationship with the mother.

When we examined the mothers of our patients we found that they suffered from the same difficulties in their early life as did their children. They also developed the Borderline Syndrome. Having a Borderline mother of their own, they remained locked in a symbiotic relationship from which they had been unable to separate. Their character structure remained orally fixated and they were unable to form relationships on other than a symbiotic level. The mothers clung to their own children to defend themselves against their own feelings of abandonment. This symbiosis with the infant so important in the first year of life was continued pathologically way beyond the first year when locomotion and movement toward autonomy and a separate identity normally should have brought about its dissolution.

For the mother, separation was an abandonment and history repeated itself as she was unable to tolerate separation from her own son or daughter anymore than as an infant and growing child she was able to separate from her own mother [7, 43, 115, 145]. The mother's clinging then prevented the normal growth of her child toward maturity and self-differentiation.

The fathers of these patients do not play their historic role as head of the family and therefore they fail to provide an adequate masculine figure with which the boy child can identify in developing his masculinity and to which the girl can relate in developing her femininity. The father's essential part as a second love object which helps to break the mother-child symbiosis is defective or absent. Therefore the child is blocked from taking advantage of another avenue for dissolution of the mother-child symbiosis.

The father, also having a Borderline Syndrome, crippled by failure to solve his own developmental difficulties, is unable to respond to the mature demands of fatherhood which more often he sees as a threat to his dependent relationship with his wife rather than as an opportunity for satisfaction. Indeed, his own immaturity prevents him from sensing and enjoying that satisfaction. Nevertheless, he must meet his responsibilities in some fashion. He attempts to solve this dilemma by giving lip service to the formalities of fatherhood, while underneath he emotionally withdraws into passivity and/or distancing to contain his anger and frustration. At the same time his passivity furthers his wife's frustration and anger and his lack of support lends fire to her need to maintain the symbiotic relationship with the child. Thus the father, hamstrung in his capacity to love, cannot give his wife the love she hungers for, and she turns even more for fulfillment to her child.

The complex interweaving of emotions between parents and adolescent comprising the psychopathological link between the generations is presented in the next two chapters. This chapter 5 stakes out the general boundaries of the problem by giving brief clinical vignettes of the four pairs of parents of the patients whose follow-up is reported in chs XIV, XV, XVI. It then penetrates the subject matter more deeply by presenting in greater detail the background history and the parental behavior of the parents of George Graves as a prelude to Chapter 10, which ties in the casework treatment of these two parents with that of their son. Chapter 6 describes the intensive psychotherapy of a Borderline mother. It describes both the defensive function of clinging for the mother and its destructive effects on her daughter's efforts to separate and individuate.

One often hears of a tendency on the part of the psychiatrist to "blame" the parents for the patient's problems. An antidote to this hazard and an extension of professional acumen is to perceive the parents not as the wilfull instigators of their children's difficulties but rather as individuals themselves, caught up in their own struggles to cope with their own developmental problems—the Achilles heel of this is the job of being a parent, that is, taking care of a child.

It is important to bear in mind while reading the thesis presented in

the ensuing pages that I am focusing on one parameter of parental functioning, that is, the relationship of parental approval to separation-individuation because it is the crucial parameter for the Borderline patient.
There are other parameters—such as the child's identification with the
sublimation of the parents—that are equally important for ego development but are not discussed here. These would require a book in itself.
Suffice it to say that the Borderline parent can perform many other parental
functions that do not impinge on separation-individuation.

The parents' difficulty in parenting stems from the fact that they have
Borderline Syndromes themselves. They suffered as much deprivation from
their parents as they unwittingly inflict on their own adolescent; having
been unable to separate from their own parents they are unable to permit,
let alone encourage, their adolescents to separate from them. The degree
of individuation they permit their child is probably directly related to the
degree of individuation that they themselves achieved as children. They
inevitably seem to repeat with their children the identical behavior they
were subjected to by their own parents despite their own intense conscious
wish to spare their children this fate. The requirements of parental responsibility and care-taking strike at the Achilles heel of these Borderline
adults and present a poignant kind of challenge which they do not have
the resources to meet.

It is striking to note in the cases that follow the parents' inability to
perceive the child as a child in his own right with his own unique growth
needs as Giovacchini [15, 37–43] has suggested: "As parents, these
patients recapitulate with their children the difficulties they had in resolving their symbiotic phase during childhood—they cannot allow the child
to structuralize to a stage of relative separateness."

The parents without exception project their own fantasies on the child
and perceive him as a person from their own past. For example, Nancy's
father sees her as his mother and must "distance himself" from her as he
did from his own mother. Nancy's mother, on the other hand, sees her
child either as herself or her own mother. Despite her strong conscious
wishes to avoid treating Nancy as her mother did her, she manages to
repeat the relationship in identical detail, this time in the role of mother
rather than daughter.

Grace's mother sees her as a sister and as a mother. Grace's father sees
her as a mother or as an idealized female. Bill's mother sees him as a
companion, a peer, or a parent, and his father sees him as a rival or a
brother. Helen's mother sees all of her daughters as one symbiotic mass
object and the father "distances himself" from the entire dependent family.

PARENTS OF NANCY

Mother

Nancy's mother was a rigid, angry, depressed, moralistic woman. At times her ideas were quite paranoid; this tended to isolate her from her peers. She was masochistic and played the role of the martyr. The mother's strengths lay in her obsessive-compulsive defenses, and her basic, conscious commitment to do what was right for herself and her family once that was made clear to her. She was a bright and talented woman, quite capable of finding other interests once her children were grown.

Past History

Nancy's maternal grandmother was described as a depressed, angry, highly inconsistent woman who acted out much of her resentment and frustration against her daughter. Her behavior alternated between being physically violent and abusive and being physically ill and withdrawn. She also was moralistic and rigid in setting limits for Nancy's mother. For example, although there was no real basis for her suspicions she constantly accused Nancy's mother of smoking, checking her breath every time she returned from school.

She was also inconsistent; for example, she insisted that Nancy's mother have dancing lessons but forbade her from going to teenage dances. Nancy's mother complied with her mother's restrictions with some awareness of anger toward and fear of her, but with little awareness of her fear of her own loss of control. The grandmother apparently became more depressed and increasingly more critical during her daughter's adolescence. Nancy's mother feels, on the other hand, that she had a good and close relationship with her father, obviously idealizing him, denying the anger and resentment she must have felt toward him for not protecting her against her mother's rage.

Relationship with Patient

Nancy's mother had difficulty in setting limits to Nancy's behavior from early childhood. She had determined to be quite the opposite from her own mother, to control her anger and to behave in a rational manner. However, in fact it seems that she ignored Nancy's behavior until it became intolerable to her and she then turned from indifferent permissiveness to excessive punitive measures. She would withdraw from Nancy feeling guilty and frightened, thus effectively reproducing her own mother's behavior. Nancy's mother's control of her ambivalent feelings toward

Nancy lessened with the increased stress of family moves and Nancy's developing adolescence. The mother then began to enlist the support of her husband to help control Nancy (i.e., herself), and to protect her from her daughter (i.e., mother). At one point—a living image of her own mother—she went to the school and emptied Nancy's purse in front of her peers to see if she had cigarettes. She also obtained Nancy's locker combination and rummaged through her locker looking for cigarettes or drugs. Increasingly Nancy's mother viewed her as her enemy and rival and felt attacked by her no matter what she said or did.

Treatment Problems

The initial problem in working with Nancy's mother centered around her attitudes toward the social worker who she felt was hostile, critical, and judgmental. However, she was able to work through this sufficiently to request help following her daughter's hospitalization. The other major problem was the neurotic agreement with her husband that they both idealize each other and support each other's use of Nancy as a target for their projections.

Father

Nancy's father, a distant, detached, successful businessman, spent most of his time away from the family.

Past History

Nancy's grandfather died when her father was 10 years old under somewhat mysterious circumstances. His mother told him at one point that his father had been murdered. His mother, overinvolved with her only child, demanded high performance from him. When he wanted to go away to college, she wished to go and live with him, but finally yielded to his entreaties and stayed home. He felt her motto was always: "You do your part, I'll do mine, but I will always do mine better than you." From age 10 he managed to be out of the home working, using this distance to manage the relationship with the mother and at the same time feeling very guilty about it.

Relationship with Patient

The father's relationship with Nancy was similarly characterized by distance and lack of involvement. In family arguments he took his wife's side against his daughter out of fear of her disapproval as well as out of anger toward Nancy—an anger that he projected on her from his own mother. For example, at one point he joined his wife in the locker search at Nancy's school. His tremendous need to control Nancy was illustrated by his setting up a will which would leave her an income for life if she behaved according to certain standards and one dollar if she did not. Only after prolonged treatment was he able to change the will.

Parents' Marriage

In the marriage the partners seemed to regard each other as good parent figures, accepting each other's behavior unquestioningly. In relation to Nancy there was a mutual acceptance of each other's tendencies to be less and less involved with her problems and needs, which facilitated much of Nancy's acting out prior to hospitalization. The neurotic agreement seemed also to include the father's "distancing himself" from the mother: the children taking up the vacuum this left in his relationship with the mother.

Treatment Problems with the Father

The main task in working with Nancy's father was to break through some of his projections and help him to see his role in the family more realistically. He made many attempts to "distance himself" through business trips and also to comply and manipulate rather than become involved, and each attempt could be effectively interpreted to him.

PARENTS OF GRACE

Mother

Grace's mother was a rigid, angry, suspicious woman, whose main defenses were denial, projection, and displacement. She initially felt criticized by the social worker whenever she disagreed with her and was unable to make use of any interpretation.

Grace's mother's assets were her intelligence, attractiveness, seductiveness, and charm, and her conscious commitment to do what was best for her child. In addition, although there were serious marital problems, the mother and father seemed to be basically committed to each other and to have sufficient interests to maintain a small group of friends.

Past History

Her mother died when she was 6, at which point her father, an alcoholic, left her and her sister with a maternal aunt and a housekeeper who was very religious, cold, and distant. The aunt, who was the breadwinner, alternated between infantilizing her and her sister and withdrawing from them. For example, although the aunt was out of the home much of the time, she still insisted upon brushing their teeth and washing their faces and hair until the age of 17.

Grace's mother developed an excessively close relationship with her older sister which took on a somewhat erotic quality during adolescence; Grace's mother waited up for the sister after dates to discuss sexual experiences. Grace's mother recalls being particularly distressed when this sister attempted to exclude her from her circle of friends. This relationship was abruptly terminated for a long period when at age 18 the sister became ill with tuberculosis. Even now Grace's mother has the feeling of being "exiled" from her sister who lives in the West. She seems always to have looked for a replacement for this relationship, finding it at various times with friends, but failing to establish it with Grace. Nevertheless, she clearly had hoped that Grace would be a permanent replacement. Three years ago she established a very close sibling-like relationship with her 22-year-old godchild which took on the character of her relationship with her absent older sister. The establishment of this new relationship coincides with the beginning of her difficulties with Grace.

Relationship with Patient

Although Grace's mother was aware of wanting to use Grace to replace the older sister, she did not realize this was inappropriate. She verbalized a fantasy of an increasingly involved relationship with Grace with a brief interruption during adolescence after which Grace would return to her with even more devotion. As Grace did begin to move away, the mother alternated between trying to force an involvement with her and her activities and withdrawing from her—encouraging Grace to take her own place as caretaker of her younger brother. The mother's withdrawal seemed to be an expression of her anger toward Grace for beginning to move away and at the same time an effort to force Grace into a more parenting role.

Father

Grace's father was an angry, petulant, narcissistic, and controlling man. He worked as an advertising executive.

Past History

His mother was a controlling, domineering, seductive woman who insisted that he socialize with her and her friends throughout his adolescence. His mother divorced his father when the son was 8 and remarried a cold and apparently somewhat cruel man. The son was very frightened of his new stepfather who maintained his control over him primarily by withholding money and threatening to disinherit him.

Relationship with Patient

The father saw Grace alternately as an object of art with whom he was seductive and possessive, and as his hostile, controlling mother. He spoke of her as a fashion model, invited her frequently to be with him and his business partners, and at times took her on trips with him alone in place of his wife. At other times he either flew into a rage at her or withdrew from her.

Marriage of the Parents

The marriage had a sibling-like quality, the wife being the dominant person. Their alliance was around mutual likes and interests, mutual sexual problems, and a mutual dependence. The main threat to the marriage was Grace's development. The parents became competitive for the possession of this child, each for their own neurotic reasons. Also her developing sexuality brought into focus their own sexual problems. Their strengths lay in their obsessive-compulsive defenses and their conscious commitment to do what was best for their children.

PARENTS OF BILL

Mother

Past History

Bill's mother described her mother as a distant, cold, aloof, aggressive business woman, who spent most of her time in her hat shop and left the greater part of the mothering to the father. When she did get involved with her daughter she was often infantilizing, critical, or inappropriate. For example, she prepared elaborate teas for her daughter's casual dates. One of Bill's mother's strongest memories was her mother's response to her after 2 years of separation during the war when she was 13—her mother burst into tears because she was overweight. Her father was apparently overpowered by his wife and was seen by his daughter as weak and ineffectual; he was certainly infantile but also harsh and critical. The daughter recalls his being severely berated by his wife for bringing cookies home for her and his being so distressed by his wife's criticism that he began to cry; at this point her mother slapped him.

Relationship with Patient

The mother viewed Bill as her companion, her peer, and sometimes her parent. She was infantilizing, seductive, and unable to set realistic disciplinary limits. She looked to Bill to give her direction. When they drove to the doctor's office she continually asked him the way to go, but as Bill began to throw parts of the car out the window she did nothing to stop him. At another time on Bill's insistence his mother drove the car over the sidewalk to get around another car. When he had homework to do, she took over his paper route at no little inconvenience to herself.

In the family there was great confusion of roles, the father often taking the role of the eldest son. Much of the behavior was also inappropriate. For example, at one point the mother became enraged at Bill for taunting his younger brother, and to express this rage she flung her bowl of soup on her new tablecloth.

Treatment Problems

The basic problem in working with Bill's mother was her tremendous disorganization and diffuseness, and her intense mothering relationship with her husband. She was also a masochistic, martyred woman with underlying feelings of extreme loneliness and emptiness. The focus of work with her was around basic reality testing. There was some beginning crystallization of her own feeling of identity and increased sense of self-worth as she felt she was becoming a "person in my own right."

Father

Past History

Bill's father was the youngest of four children; his parents were much older than the average parent when he was born. Because his father was unable to maintain employment, the family moved many times and suffered economic hardships. He recalls never having a suit of his own. His father was a quiet man who periodically burst into rages. Bill's father's relationship with his own mother was more like that of a sibling. His older brother was a severely delinquent boy who was sent away from the family at age 14 to military school because of his uncontrollable behavior. However, when the rest of the family had soup, this brother was given a steak, his mother explaining "the bad dog gets the bone."

Relationship with Patient

Although Bill's father was talented and humorous, his behavior in the family was extremely infantile. He saw Bill as a rival for his wife's attention. He would express his anger either by withdrawing from him into his work or exploding at him in a bizarre and uncontrollable manner. For example, when he became angry about Bill's manners at the table he snatched up the tablecloth spilling all the food. At other times he threw water in Bill's face or ordered him out of the house. The father then became one of the children, demanding his wife's full time and attention. He often had her wait outside his office door for hours while he worked late into the night, the children being left at home alone. The mother complied with this role, displacing her anger and resentment onto the children. Although the father did well financially, he could not spend his money on himself or his family. The mother would not openly complain but would dress in extremely shabby clothes advertising in martyr-like fashion her husband's penurious behavior.

Family Interaction

The parents' keen sense of humor was often used to cover feelings and to express anger. For example, Bill's brother came home from school one afternoon fearful that he would be arrested by the police who were apparently looking for a boy who sold firecrackers in the school yard the day before. The parents became highly amused by his paranoid ideas and facetiously explained the laws in great detail, volunteering to be a witness at his trial, rather than responding with any degree of sympathy for the boy's fear.

PARENTS OF HELEN

Mother

Past History

Helen's grandmother died of breast cancer when her mother was about 12 years of age; the grandfather remarried 1 year later. Helen's mother denied any feeling at the time of her mother's death as well as when recounting the story. She also denied any problems in her relationship with her mother or stepmother. There was a general shadowiness about her background. Helen's mother herself had had two mastectomies, 4 years apart, at the same age that her own mother developed breast cancer.

Relationship with Patient

Helen's mother had tremendous problems in differentiating herself from any one child as well as in differentiating among her four girls. She was unable to set disciplinary limits, either giving in to the child's regressive pull or withdrawing completely. For example, when Helen was sick the mother allowed her to stay home from school but then left her to play golf. The mother was unable to see her sick daughter's need for her. She refused to deny Helen permission to smoke, fearing she might disobey and in such an assertion establish herself as "separate." She recognized her need to control all the girls, as she put it, "to bind them up," but this she feared to do with Helen.

Father

Helen's father was a depressed, distant, detached man who under stress became circumstantial and disorganized.

Past History

He idolized his own father, a businessman who spent most of his time out of the home. He became more involved with his father as an older adolescent and young adult when he entered the family business. When he was 8 years of age his 10-year-old brother died. His parents refused to acknowledge the brother's death and left him in a temporary grave for 10 years. Helen's father recalled his childhood as being lonely, because of his parents' preoccupation with the death of this son as well as with the business of earning a living. At 17 he had a serious sinus operation. From then he felt even more isolated and alone, viewing himself as a damaged person who was doomed to rejection even by his peers. He did marry, however, and became successful in his business although it became an overwhelming preoccupation; a repetition of his own father's behavior.

Relationship with Patient

The father's view of his child was colored by his own autistic and grandiose thinking. His relationship with Helen was characterized by an angry insistence on "due respect" for him and his wife which in essence was a demand for distance. Nevertheless, his wish to win her love and affection led him to give in directly or indirectly to whatever she requested. Helen knew she could manipulate her father and both used and feared his weakness. He had difficulty in setting limits to Helen's use of money. He also had difficulty setting limits to his own gift giving; the gifts were often what he wanted to give rather than what Helen needed; for example, he brought home antique jewelry for her and men's shirts for himself because he was able to buy them all at a bargain. Although the father was at least intellectually able to see the need for limit setting, the mother proved to be better at following through.

Treatment Problems with Mother and Father

The primary problem with Helen's mother was her tangential and circumstantial manner of speaking, her poor ego boundaries, and extreme ambivalence. In any given conversation she could shift from a description of a specific interaction with Helen to talking about all the four girls with little awareness of the relationship between them; she was even unaware that she was doing it. This became an issue particularly in the family sessions where Helen found her mother's manner exasperating and frightening. Helen felt overpowered by her mother and unable to interrupt this behavior for fear of hurting the mother or of being hurt by her. Indeed the mother did feel any interruption as an attack and a criticism rather than an attempted clarification. Her need to control her children as symbiotic objects seemed to have been increased by her illness and her anxiety about her impending death.

The father's anxiety about his wife's illness and the possibility of losing her was overwhelming to him. He attempted to handle this by either withdrawing or becoming over involved in a chaotic and somewhat confused manner. During the casework he was able to control these feelings. His strengths were his intellectual abilities and his substantial financial support of the family.

PARENTS OF GEORGE

Let us now consider in more detail the history of Mr. and Mrs. Graves to illustrate the origin of their difficulties in their own childhood as well as its effect on their relationship with their son.

Mother

Past History

Mrs. Graves had many memory blanks in her early childhood and we can only surmise that such amnesia suggests that she had many difficulties. She hardly remembered her mother's looks, let alone her personality. Mrs. Graves was the second of two girls, her mother appeared always to be physically ill and was never "there" for her children, thus probably initiating the cycle of deprivation and abandonment that was to take such devastating toll over two generations. (There is a good possibility that her mother spent a lot of time in the hospital.) Mrs. Graves remembers her mother never being there to take care of her when she had childhood diseases. She remembers throwing tantrums on the neighbor's lawn to break up fights between her father and mother. Her mother and father did not sleep together. Only after months of treatment could Mrs. Graves recall how her mother, a nurse, frequently gave her painful enemas and cathartics.

Mrs. Graves' father was in the real estate business. Although he drank a lot, he appeared to take a more active part in her life than did her mother. Her memories of him are also sparse, although she does remember him yelling a lot. She appeared to have invited this yelling by provoking him into battles on purpose, for example, joining in an argument her sister was having with him and pursuing it long after the sister had left the room.

Adolescence and Adulthood

When Mrs. Graves was 13 years old, she and her sister found her mother with her head in the oven and the mother was taken to a mental hospital never to be seen again. Although the mother later died in the hospital, for all intents and purposes for her children she died when she was taken away from home. Mrs. Graves recalled that during adolescence she was always lonely and that there was no one to take care of her.

The mother's physical place was taken by a number of housekeepers while the father was probably seldom at home. Mrs. Graves and her sister were left much on their own. She began to steal, truant, and generally act out, in all probability to defend against the abandonment depression. "I wanted most to be accepted. . . . I was mad at something. . . . I was in a vacuum, nothing was going to bother me. . . . I wanted someone to say: 'So you stole; I love you anyway. . . .' I desperately wanted to be loved. My father must have tried, but the same way I do, by yelling that he loved me. You can't kiss someone goodnight just after telling them they're a jerk."

Mrs. Graves recalled how much she wanted to get caught and how amazed and disappointed she was after 52 days of truanting from school that neither her teacher nor her father knew about it; or, if they did, neither one cared enough even to scold her. She also recalled that at that time she lost control and banged a cat on the floor until it died. She finally was sent to a boarding school because of her unmanageable behavior. Here limits were set to her behavior and she appeared to function fairly well. At age 17, her father remarried and neither she nor her sister liked the stepmother. In later adolescence she began to act out again, this time sexually and at age 20 she became pregnant and had an abortion. She again felt depressed and abandoned: "What's the use . . . why bother . . . for what . . . to succeed in school didn't make me feel any better."

Soon after the abortion she met and after a short courtship married her husband, hoping to find in him and his wealthy family what she had not had, a mother, a father, and a family. Again she failed; she couldn't get what she hungered for, and she reacted with a pent up anger which she expressed in both emotional and physical withdrawal.

Motherhood

Mr. Graves, having no apparent interest in his son George, left Mrs. Graves alone with the child most of the time. After his birth George was colicky, cried all the time, and clung to his mother. She resented the father's lack of interest. George was big for his age and Mrs. Graves began to expect a lot from him very early. She seemed deeply involved with George wanting something from him, the love and acceptance that she was actually supposed to give: "Love me, please don't love daddy more" was her constant plea.

Recently, when she found a love note in a pocket of George's clothing she thought: "I've lost you before I've found you." (She was partially aware of her need for George; as she said: "a dependent encompassing, complete giving is what I must have.") As George grew older and bigger she became awesomely aware of a sexual feeling: "I've even felt attracted to him. . . . I care, I care and I felt like screaming it at him every day of his life." Her symbiotic needs compelled her to resent the treatment focus on George. "All the importance is entirely attached to George— I'm left out—what about me?"

To protect herself from the avalanche of these feelings, Mrs. Graves withdrew from her son. "If I give up anger there is nothing in its place. I tend to give the impression I can handle things—I had to at an early age. It is my defense. If I let someone else take over then what do I have? My husband wasn't going to be there when I needed him. I've been hurt, hurt, hurt—show me that you care. . . . I'm physically in better shape when my barriers are up."

We see here the extraordinary emotional difficulties Mrs. Graves had both as a child and later with her son. She invested all of her frustrated hunger for love and acceptance in her new born son. Little wonder then that it was almost impossible for her to let him go.

Father

Past History

Mr. Graves was a tall, silent man, who sat quietly in his chair reflectively puffing on his pipe, and spoke in a low keyed calm voice. He described himself as aggressive in business, accustomed to handling affairs that were quite complicated and making many very important decisions. At home, however, he admitted that he might be too quiet and possibly withdrawn from his family since he left much of the management of the children to his wife, and focused primarily on his relationship with her, and not with his children.

Childhood

Mr. Graves was born to very young and wealthy parents, who led an active social life and did a great deal of traveling. His childhood memories were vague. Mr. Graves recalls his parents as being fun-loving, superficial, materialistic people who were too busy with their own lives to be interested in him. He was left in the care of a governess until he was 8 years of age. However, on the whim of his parents, he was swept along with them on their many trips to Europe and other places where he was often left to fend for himself in a hotel. He recalled being sensitive and emotional as a child and crying a lot. To describe his loneliness, he said: "I felt in the way and wished I could grow up fast so I could go with my parents. I hated being left alone. It was terrible to have them go off and leave me." He always felt badly when they went away." I never got the time of day from my father. I've only been close to him in the last ten years. My father wasn't much of a one for children either." His father was described as a philanderer who never even showed up at family functions such as birthdays. The mother always made excuses for the father, denying any wrong doing.

Mr. Graves recalled that throughout childhood he was very emotional: "As a child when I got emotional I couldn't function." He almost drowned at age 9 and was saved by the chauffeur but could not remember where his parents were or what their reaction was to this event. He seemed to get his only stability from his paternal grandparents who had a farm in Vermont where he would go in the summer time. He had pleasant memories of the warm smell of the barn and of his grandmother working and cooking in the kitchen. His parents would stay 15 miles away and come to visit them on Sundays. He recalled once having run after his parents' departing car as far as he could until exhausted. He fell down crying, feeling a sense of helplessness, futility, and defeat.

He described his early relationship with his parents as follows: "They did everything to take care of my physical needs, but their care was all on the surface. There was no warm love and the only kind of emotion I was allowed to be involved with was good manners. All deep emotions got swept under the rug. The physical shell was there." He described two maternal aunts and the mother's grandmother all of whom showed affection but wanted more love from him than they gave. "They were too busy with their own lives." His paternal grandparents seemed to provide a much deeper love. He visited them every summer until he started camp at age 11.

Adolescence

After age 11 he was given more freedom and independence but never took advantage of it because of fear of the "consequences." At 15 he got into a fight with a boy who had picked on him until he exploded and "almost beat him to death," which scared him and impelled him to try harder to suppress his anger.

He finished high school and college, and joined the Naval Air Corp. He met and married a "beautiful model," but remained married only for a short time. He and his wife mutually agreed to part as their interests were so opposed. Shortly after the divorce he returned to college for graduate work where he began to date Mrs. Graves whom he married, again after a short courtship. At the time of the marriage he needed $3000 to purchase a house but his parents refused to give or lend it to him. It seemed to be just another instance of their customary habit of withdrawing their support whenever he needed it.

Fatherhood

When the children came along Mr. Graves left their care to the mother. He had little interest in them, and withdrew more and more into his business. "I was unable to get down to their level, I suppose because I never had a good relationship with my own father." He permitted his wife to dominate him and the household and would conduct only those tasks which she demanded of him and these he did only to keep the peace. He handled confrontations with George as he was growing up by evading any involvement and suppressing feeling.

RÉSUMÉ

The pathologic link between generations so emphatically described in these parents suggests the epidemiologic aspect of the Borderline Syndrome. The chain of disorder is passed down from generation to generation each providing its own fatal link. To borrow an analogy from infectious disease, each Borderline parent is a contagious agent carrying within himself the seeds that will spread the disorder to yet another generation. Treatment is the most effective weapon to combat this disease, since it enables the parent to work through his deprivation in therapy rather than acting it out against his own children. However, I seriously doubt that all the parents with a Borderline Syndrome can ever be treated, and for the reasons cited these parents seem unlikely to respond to efforts at education. Their problem is not lack of knowledge but lack of awareness of how destructive their behavior is to their children.

In Chapter 5 an overview of the problem has been described, which is studied in further detail in Chapter 10 through the casework treatment of George's mother and father. Chapter 6, in which the intensive psychotherapy of yet another Borderline mother is described, affords a unique opportunity to examine the inner workings of the tie that binds.

CHAPTER 6

Parents: The Tie That Binds—Clinging

By way of a report on the intensive psychotherapy of a Borderline mother of a 5-year-old child, this chapter studies the clinging defense mechanism from two perspectives: its defensive function in protecting the mother against feelings of abandonment and its destructiveness to the child's efforts to separate and individuate.

As the basic theme reported in the preceding chapter was clarified, I felt a need to pin it down further through direct observation by treating a Borderline mother in more intensive psychotherapy than once a week.

At that very moment, as sometimes happens, fate presented me with just the opportunity I was seeking. A 33-year-old Borderline woman with a 5½-year-old daughter came to me for private treatment. She had been acting out her conflict with her own Borderline mother through her husband, alternately clinging and rebelling. After 1 year of psychotherapy three times a week she decided to divorce her husband, which led to a dramatic upswing in the intensity of her clinging to her daughter to defend herself against her feelings of abandonment.

This provided a unique opportunity for intensive detailed study of the clinging mechanism. When the mother clung she "felt better"—that is, less anxious—but the child developed symptoms of separation anxiety. When I interpreted to the mother the destructiveness of her clinging to her child she would curb it and then experience and describe in the next interview her resultant feelings of abandonment. The child, on the other hand, would not only feel better but also, relieved of her own fears, would take further steps to separate and individuate. In the course of these sessions there was an uncanny one-to-one relationship in the interaction between parent and child: the patient's presenting her clinging in interviews, my interpretation of the destructiveness of the clinging, and the patient's efforts to curb the clinging followed by feelings of abandonment on her part while the child improved.

This experience dramatized and placed in such bold relief the basic psychodynamic theme of this book—that the Borderline mother with-draws emotional supplies at her child's efforts to separate and individuate —that I felt it warranted an entire chapter.

This report also makes clear that the more intense the feelings of abandonment, the greater the need to cling, the smaller the capacity for self-observation; the mother could not see that she was unable to perceive her child's needs but was reacting to the child strictly in terms of her own needs. She would curb the clinging, her self observation and her perception of her child's needs would increase, and then with the next stress and intensification of the feelings of abandonment the self awareness and perception would disappear again. Finally, at no time during the treatment did the mother feel that she was curbing the clinging in her own interest but, rather, that she was doing so to prevent her daughter from suffering the same fate that she had suffered at the hands of her mother.

MRS. BROWN

Mrs. Brown, a 33-year-old, slender, attractive brunette, was married and taught at a local college. Her chief complaint was depression, dissatisfaction with her work, and conflict with her husband whom she described as cold, insensitive, stingy, ungiving, and depriving. He objected to her working, but demanded that she pay more than her share of the family expenses. She could not respond to him sexually, though she was able to have an orgasm with her lover. (A good example of object splitting with projection of the negative image of the mother on the husband and acting out of resentment at deprivation through an affair.) Although she functioned well at her job, she derived little satisfaction from it. Her chief satisfactions were found in her relationship with her 5½-year-old daughter Margaret and in the affair she was having with another teacher.

Family History

The patient described her mother as being cold and without feeling, but said that "I bought her line." She described her father as an irresponsible Don Juan, who was hospitalized for a suicidal attempt when she was 26 at which time the mother divorced him. A younger brother, now aged 26, the mother's favorite, has been chronically ill with asthma since the age of 3. His illness always required much of the mother's attention, and finally impelled him to move away from her to the West.

Past History

Mrs. Brown was born in a large eastern city, the oldest of two children. A compliant, compulsive child she was subtly terrorized by the mother's threat of abandonment. If she did not obey the mother would withdraw. The mother, whose lifelong ambition to be a professional woman had been frustrated, coerced the patient to fulfill this goal for her. The patient complied, spent much time studying, and did well throughout her schooling. Her first abandonment experience came at age 8 when she was sent to summer camp for the first time. She became panicky and depressed, instigated the camp authorities to recall her mother to take her home. However, the mother's obvious rage at what she viewed as the patient's unruly behavior created an even greater threat, and the patient reluctantly agreed to stay, having "the most miserable summer in my life."

In high school the patient was quite aware that she had difficulty in getting involved with boys. Her boyfriends had to be approved by her mother, and since very few of them were, dating was sparse. She graduated from a local college, left home for the first time to attend graduate school, and had her second clinical episode of abandonment depression. "I completely fell apart. I was depressed and afraid, spent all my time in my room, and was unable to study." After 6 months she transferred to a college from which she could commute home on weekends and began an affair with one of her professors which lasted for 3 years until the end of her graduate studies. At this point the professor suddenly died, her father attempted suicide, and she had to leave college to take a teaching job. She left home again, this time going South to teach. Here she had her third clinical episode of abandonment depression. She described herself as "totally coming apart," depressed, lonely, and frightened—exactly as she had felt the first year at college. At this time she met and married her husband quite consciously in order to "not be alone." Thus she clung to the husband to defend herself against the feelings of abandonment. The marriage was filled with conflict from the beginning, since her husband, a replica of her mother, was demanding, obsessive, rigid, cold, ungiving, and rejecting.

Psychotherapy

In the first year of psychotherapy the relationship with the daughter, Margaret, remained at the periphery while the problems with husband and lover were worked through. During this time I made little reference to the patient's reports of her clinging and her daughter's obvious separation anxiety. However, after about a year of therapy, as the patient decided to divorce her husband her clinging to Margaret increased, and I began interpreting its destructiveness to the daughter. As we worked on this problem, I asked how it had begun—that is, what was the origin of the tie that binds.

Feelings about the Birth of Her Child

Patient: "When Margaret was born I felt like a woman, fulfilled. I loved the stage when I had to be up with her at night—even though I was tired. I resented having to leave to go to work then. I never resented efforts to take care of her. I loved her needing me, I thrived on it. I never let her cry, I always picked her up. It reached monstrous proportions. I hated to leave her . . . that is, go out at night. I hated having someone else take care of her. She ended up crying all the time and if she didn't get picked up she'd throw up. I used to rock her to sleep on the theory that you can't spoil infants. All a child needs is to have love poured in endlessly—obviously I was satisfying myself." Here the patient described her identification with and use of the child to repair her own feelings of deprivation at the hands of her own mother. "The physical experience of holding Margaret was like plasma to me. It got so bad my pediatrician raised hell with me—told me to stop picking her up. I did it but I was very upset. I couldn't bear to hear her cry and leave her there. I felt like it was murdering her. I did it though and it worked."

What happened when Margaret learned to walk? "She walked at 14 months. It occurred coincidentally with a lot of other things. Those two weeks were the worst depression I was ever in. Margaret was born in May, I returned to teaching in September. I had wanted a summer vacation but my husband said 'no,' so I had done some summer teaching. Then the next summer the in-laws invited us and we went. I was annoyed because I wanted to go away with my husband and Margaret. When we got there company was there for the night. I was in no shape to be up around the clock. I was upset the whole time, angry at my husband and myself. I remember that was the time Margaret first walked on her own. I still recall it. On the drive back she climbed out of the crib and I knew she couldn't do it on the trip up. I felt 'she had moved on.' I was not happy about her advancing out of babyhood, but I have enjoyed later stages of development to my surprise. I knew infancy would be great, but didn't expect to enjoy other stages of her growth. Before I never faced the reality of her growing up."

"I wanted the infancy state to last forever, never thought of her growing up. I saw myself surrounded by a large family—I had the fantasy of not crying anymore if I had children. I would age with them, but they wouldn't grow up—I never thought of that. Having Margaret was like heaven, greatest thing I ever dreamed. Nothing I've ever done has made me feel as good as the love and affection I poured into her. It is only clear now that she is going to move on and I have to do something about myself."

Comment

Three aspects of this report require emphasis: (1) Mrs. Brown's use of her daughter as an object to make up for her own feelings of deprivation from the past, to the exclusion of the child's needs. (2) The fantasy that the child would be her possession or object forever—strong enough to replace reality. (3) The gratification she felt during her child's infancy.

Although every mother feels special gratification during her child's infancy, the gratification of the Borderline mother has a special quality to it; that is, it is in great contrast to her feelings later when she desperately struggles to ignore the reality of her child's growth and development.

This has given rise to a clinical observation of the so called "symbiotic smile," which is almost diagnostic of a separation-individuation problem. When the mother is giving the evaluation history her facies is usually angry, depressed, guilty, and withdrawn as she describes her adolescent's various transgressions. When the therapist then changes the subject and asks the mother what kind of an infant the adolescent was, this depressed, withdrawn facies breaks into a beatific smile as the mother recalls and reports the pleasure of the symbiotic stage.

Psychotherapy of the Mother

Prior to this point in psychotherapy Margaret had had school-phobic symptoms, occasionally not going to school because of getting "sick" in the morning, occasionally requiring the mother to go to school with her. Mrs. Brown reported that "Margaret's behavior made me further aware of how I cling to her and how I treat her like my mother did me. She sounded off at me and I was so mad I could have killed her. She is the only person I have a total attachment for. When she walks out of the apartment I'm never sure she will be back. Since she was born I haven't moved without her. I can't see our relationship through her eyes. I don't know what it's like to have a mother who loves you. With Margaret I'm being good to her so she'll love me. I was so afraid of my husband taking her away from me that I gave him anything he wanted in the divorce settlement."

At this point Margaret was starting day camp and was complaining to Mrs. Brown that she did not want to go—clearly testing to see if the mother would let her go. Under some pressure from her mother Margaret went off to camp in tears. Mrs. Brown, in a quandary over sending her to camp, but unconsciously wanting to cling by keeping her at home, did not think of asking the camp officials whether Margaret's behavior indicated that she liked camp. I interpreted to the patient that she was holding on to Margaret to defend herself against her fear of being abandoned—these fears by now being an old topic in therapy. I said that "Margaret must feel that she cannot grow up without losing her mother's support." I then interpreted that she was sacrificing her daughter's welfare to the demands of her neurosis. Mrs. Brown checked with the camp officials and found that Margaret was enjoying herself immensely. Consequently, she insisted that Margaret continue.

Mrs. Brown then reported the following in the next interview: "When Margaret was to leave for camp I felt like I did when I left my mother and went to college: I was going to die, but mother insisted I had to do it. I cried my way through the whole summer." Her clinging defense interrupted, further memories of being abandoned returned. For example, she continued talking about her year at college where she felt abandoned, was unable to work, flunked her exams, was suicidal and paralyzed, and was finally rescued by her affair with one of the teachers. She also reported having fantasies of starving herself to death, as this was probably the only thing that would make the mother sorry.

In the next interview Mrs. Brown went further into her conflict with her own mother. If she expressed anger, she said, the mother would withdraw completely, would cut off her oxygen supply. The madder she got the more she was afraid of dying. Several interviews later Mrs. Brown returned to the subject of her daughter. "I am in a bind about Margaret since I have never left her. My mother never listened to me; she always made me stick things out and I never functioned when I was away at college. When Margaret gives me flack about going to camp, I can only see myself and I don't want to do to her what my mother did to me, I don't want to force her to go out." I interpreted this as a rationalization for holding on to Margaret. The patient then recalled the memories of how her husband and her mother both withdrew from her at the time of Margaret's birth and that Margaret was the object to replace them.

Two themes dominated the content of Mrs. Brown's interviews, side by side: Margaret's difficulties with day camp and Mrs. Brown's reliving in psychotherapy the period of abandonment at age 17 when she went away to college. She dreamt about it at night, felt afraid of being alone during the day, recalled that she got through those years only by compulsively working. Following this, she reviewed her next abandonment experience when the father was hospitalized and she left graduate school to go South to teach.

During this time whenever her former husband came to take Margaret out for the day, Mrs. Brown would report that she was furious at him for taking Margaret out and at Margaret for going with him. "I think I'm never going to see her again. If I let her go I will drown. When she goes away I'm in a vacuum. She's my reason for living. That whole part of me goes with Margaret almost physically."

At the end of the summer when plans had been made for Margaret to spend 2 weeks with her father, Mrs. Brown reported that Margaret was fearful about going, had nightmares of being kidnapped. This time, however, Mrs. Brown, in better control of her feelings of abandonment, instead of clinging to Margaret reassured her about her fears and encouraged her to go. Margaret went and enjoyed her holiday. I reinforced Mrs. Brown's efforts by saying that she had responded to the message implicit in Margaret's behavior in an appropriate and constructive way—which was proved by Margaret's response—that is, she reassured Margaret that she need not fear for her continued emotional supplies and should go with her father. When Margaret returned, however, Mrs. Brown said: "I was fearful that I had lost her; but our relationship was never better, we are both happy and this is the first time she has returned without being cranky."

In the fall, as it came time for Margaret to resume school, Mrs. Brown with better control of her impulses to cling said that "for the first time I can't wait for Margaret to start school." She later reported that Margaret went off to school happier than she had ever been. Several months later, in November, when Mrs. Brown was finally beginning to have a relationship with a man, Bruce, she complained for the very first time of being bugged by her daughter. "Margaret asks if I'm coming to a school meeting when I've never missed a single one since she was two, I'd tear myself inside out for her schedule. Now I need time to collect myself before teaching and I can't put up with all of her demands." I mentioned that having clung to Margaret to deal with her fear of abandonment she had had no independent existence and had probably encouraged Margaret's demandingness and because of her guilt about using Margaret was not able to assert her own independence. Mrs. Brown responded that "from the day Margaret was born I wanted to do the opposite of what my mother did with me, I'm not getting total gratification out of Margaret any more. It used to be a total plasma injection. Seriously, I couldn't have spent more time with her."

As Mrs. Brown began to get more involved with Bruce, Margaret became anxious. The worm now turned. Mrs. Brown reported that "Margaret is testing me about my going out and being on my own. Today the plans were for her to go stay with a friend after school and then come home. This morning she threw a temper tantrum about going to school. She was in tears, said she didn't feel well, didn't want to go. I said she had to go. She went into the bathroom and slammed the door, I got furious. She came out, slammed the door, threw herself on the floor, kicked her heels hysterically shouting that I was a terrible mommy if I made her go to school. For the first time I was able to look at her as something other than myself. Not a thing the matter with her, I knew I was right. I could listen to her and could hear her as myself talking to my mother. I let her get away with murder. Mother always had candy in the house for company but was furious if I had a piece. I finally realized that it was important for me to win and I forced her to go to school."

In the next interview Mrs. Brown reported Margaret's response to this seemingly drastic maneuver. "The change in Margaret is fantastic. Butter wouldn't melt in her mouth. She's cheerful, happy, a changed child." I interpreted that Margaret felt her mother had neither overindulged or used her but loved her—that is, she had recognized Margaret's need to have limits set and had had the strength and confidence to carry it out. In the next interview the patient reported that she left Margaret home with a babysitter for the first time to come to the interview.

Several weeks later Mrs. Brown reported that "Margaret threw another temper tantrum on a Friday night when I was going out and wanted her to stay with her friends; but I handled it and went along and later she was in a great mood."

"However, I'm still afraid to completely let go of Margaret. If my relationship with this man doesn't work out I'll be left alone, even though I can see it's good for Margaret. I can only do it because I have Bruce. I need more from Margaret than I do from Bruce."

During the next interview Mrs. Brown reported further separation-individuation on Margaret's part: "The change in Margaret is fantastic. I didn't see her all day and she was cheerful and relaxed. I can't get over it. She's blossoming. Her inner tranquillity astounds me. She's capable of handling things herself. I'm caught in the middle between wanting my freedom and feeling abandoned if I get it." Several interviews later Mrs. Brown said: "Sometimes I'm so pleased about Margaret I can't get over it. I was able to spend the whole weekend away from her without being lonely or depressed. Christmas will be the acid test. I couldn't have done this last August. I feel separated from Margaret's life but not left out."

After Christmas vacation when Margaret had spent time with her father, the mother reported: "Deep down I'm mad at Margaret for visiting her father. I'm upset at seeing her again. I'm mad at her because she doesn't need me anymore. I'm the world's biggest Jewish mother and can't stand it anymore. I could have killed her this morning." I interpreted that she was angry at her daughter because her daughter is more on her own. Mrs. Brown responded that "she's more mature than I am."

Two weeks later Mrs. Brown reported that she excluded Bruce from her relationship with Margaret. "I'm ambivalent about letting Bruce in on my relationship with Margaret. I would just as soon keep him outside but on the other hand it's beginning to look funny." I interpreted that she wanted Margaret exclusively to herself and questioned whether this was good for either of them.

Again 2 weeks later as Mrs. Brown began to make inroads on the exclusivity of her relationship with Margaret she reported that "I'm having difficulty with Margaret, I'm not spending 24 hours a day with her, she's no longer the exclusive center of my attention and she gets cranky and irritable before Bruce comes to visit. I have difficulty disciplining her because I wait until I get furious." Feelings of abandonment are always just under the surface—"a piece of baggage I carry." The very next day: "I'm upset at not seeing enough of Margaret, I can't handle the feelings of abandonment. Can't stand being alone. I'm so mad at myself for signing the visitation agreement with my ex-husband. Either I'm working or Margaret is off with him. I'm in a state of terror that she's going to leave me."

A few sessions later: "I'm realizing that having Margaret around is not helping anymore, maybe because I'm letting go. Before I never faced the reality of her growing up." Margaret then got a severe cold and the mother reported that "when Margaret coughs I'm afraid she will die. As Margaret grows I feel I'm losing my last support. I am digging my own grave."

A little later Mrs. Brown finally asserted herself with her ex-husband telling him that Margaret wanted to change the visiting agreement. Mrs. Brown had been unable to do this previously because of fear that if she asserted herself he would take the daughter away from her. I again reinforced her efforts saying she was acting as a mother interested in Margaret's welfare and not in using her. These efforts again brought her feelings of abandonment to the fore and the very next interview she said: "I feel like I'm at a funeral all the time, yet I deserve it. The fear is almost physical, I get sick to my stomach, totally frightened. My motivation for standing up to my ex-husband is so that Margaret won't think I'm a cream puff. I realize that it may be good for my character someday, however, when I do it I do it for her."

By this time, a year of psychotherapy had passed; it was summer again, and Mrs. Brown reported: "Unlike last summer Margaret is raring to go to camp. At her age I did nothing happily, I was miserable at camp. I was scared to go and scared to come home. I almost wish that Margaret didn't want to go."

Mrs. Brown now had conflict between her desire to be with Bruce and her feelings of guilt about leaving Margaret. "I feel guilty every time I go out. I can't put my feelings about Margaret in perspective." I interpreted that she did not want to put her feelings in perspective. The situation itself was clear: Margaret was testing her and the problem was not Margaret but her guilt about being on her own. She must set limits to Margaret's testing for Margaret's own good. Mrs. Brown said: "Margaret is my last mooring, giving it up is painful."

When Mrs. Brown set limits to Margaret's testing and discussed the situation with her, Margaret told her mother that she was afraid the mother would marry and had had a nightmare that someone would kidnap her and take her away. Mrs. Brown continued: "Margaret said finally that she didn't want me to stop seeing Bruce because of her, because it would make her feel bad and I would bitch at her about it and she didn't want that. I told her no one can take her away from me." I asked Mrs. Brown if that's all she should have said to Margaret and she replied that "Margaret just needs to be reassured that I'm not going to leave her." I interpreted that Margaret's questions aroused the patient's fears that Margaret would abandon her if she should go out on her own and because of her wish to cling to Margaret the patient failed to meet Margaret's need—that is, to point out that her relationship with Bruce could not exclude Margaret, that there was room for both, and that someday Margaret would have a relationship with a man of her own. "That's what it's all about."

Several weeks later Mrs. Brown reported and reflected on the change in herself and her daughter in the last year. "Last year on Margaret's birthday I felt like committing suicide. My ex-husband had just called me to tell me that he was going to remarry. This year I had an absolutely marvelous time, I couldn't believe it was either me or Margaret. Margaret said mommy helped me get the party ready but then I didn't need her and I went off for the afternoon with my boyfriend. Margaret knows and I know when she needs more freedom. I keep pinching myself. It can't be true."

The treatment of Mrs. Brown and Margaret clearly illustrates the extraordinary tenacity of the clinging defense mechanism. It envelops the personality like a tree whose roots have deeply burrowed their winding and tortuous way to the very core of the personality. It can only be extirpated by the kind of slow painful, tedious work that Mrs. Brown undertook in her psychotherapy with such great courage and at such great cost to herself.

The rewards of such an effort are great: the final and ultimate severing of the pathologic link between generations; the interruption of the vicious epidemiological cycle of disorder and the final and realistic fulfillment of every mother's wish—not to inflict on her child what she suffered at the hands of her own mother but to truly nurture, encourage, and enjoy the unfolding and flowering of her child's unique individuality.

This study of the psychotherapy of a Borderline mother demonstrates in microscopic detail the two essentials of the tie that binds—clinging: the defensive function of the clinging for the mother and its destructive effects on the child's separation-individuation. The clinging defends the mother against her feelings of abandonment, but at the same time it deprives the child of the emotional supplies necessary for separation-individuation.

This case, more clearly than most, illustrates the mechanism of the Borderline Syndrome—the relationship between the tie that binds and the deprivation of emotional supplies. This nuclear process, although present in every Borderline adolescent, is usually more camouflaged than in the vivid picture presented in this chapter.

PART TWO

The Therapeutic Process: Inpatient

CHAPTER 7

Theory of the Process

MILIEU THERAPY

Why an Inpatient Service?

The usual indications for hospitalization are protective in nature; a person who is severely disorganized, homicidal, or suicidal should be hospitalized. There is another more positive indication for hospitalization of the Borderline adolescent: when ambulatory therapy cannot bring enough influence to bear on his defenses to enable him to work through the abandonment depression. The structured environment of the inpatient service has the unique advantage of monitoring the patient's entire 24-hour behavior and of funneling all of the patient's thoughts, feelings, and actions toward the psychotherapeutic interview. This makes it extremely difficult for the patient to maintain his characteristic defenses of denial, avoidance, projection, and acting out.

The treatment program (at The Payne Whitney Clinic of the Cornell New York Hospital) has been designed to meet the Borderline adolescent's therapeutic needs based on his psychopathology, that is, his abandonment depression, his narcissistic orally fixated ego structure, his distorted object relations, and the implications of these for psychotherapy.

Salient Characteristics of the Borderline Adolescent

The salient characteristics of the Borderline adolescent are the following:

1. A history of severe oral deprivation and frustration.
2. Narcissistic orally fixated character structure with ego defects manifested by the following: motivation by the pleasure principle, seeking immediate satisfaction and immediate relief of tension; low frustration tolerance, poor reality testing, poor ego boundaries, and inability to tolerate the frustration of containing feelings, hence the tendency to act them out;

105

resort to fantasy rather than reality for gratification, emphasizing passivity and irrational acting out rather than rational activity in dealing with emotions and life situations.

3. The prominent use of maladaptive defenses such as denial, projection, avoidance, and acting out as defense mechanisms. The management of the latter is particularly crucial for therapy. Acting out discharges feeling, thereby preventing it from arising to consciousness and being available for therapeutic use in the interview.

4. Maladaptive object relations. Because of the introjection of his parents' attitudes the patient has very poor object relations. His relationships with others are based on projection of these inner attitudes derived from his parents and therefore represent fantasy rather than reality. He deals with people as reproductions of his parents who are going to abandon him rather than as realistic individuals who may be potential friends. He has no basic trust and tends to be at times withdrawn, isolated, provocative, manipulative, and hostile.

5. Maturational lag as seen in inadequate development of social and achievement skills. One of the principal developmental tasks of ages 6 to 12 is the acquiring of social and achievement skills—the tools for mastery of the environment. Most of our patients have been either on drugs during some of this time or so unable to be assertive that they have not learned these skills.

Design of Milieu

1. *The oral deprivation and frustration.*   An inpatient facility with a high staff-patient ratio and a carefully designed structure of discipline gratifies to some extent the patient's oral dependent wish to be cared for and on this basis alone decreases frustration and aggression and begins the process of enabling the patient to feel that we are interested and do care. For some of these patients it is the first time in their lives that they have received *any* effective assistance in dealing with the anarchy of their impulses. For others it is the first time they have experienced satisfaction from achievement and social relationships rather than from fantasy.

2, 3, and 4. *Ego defects, maladaptive defenses and object relations.* The staff sets up a standard of consistent expectations of realistic healthy behavior, and when the patient deviates from this standard in one way or another it is brought to his attention [50a–50d]. The manner in which this is done varies from a simple remark all the way to a graduated series of room restrictions from 15 minutes to 24 hours long. While restricted to his room the patient is asked to think about his behavior, which is then discussed in the next interview. The confrontation focuses the patient's attention on the meaning of his behavior as the therapist attempts to relate the behavior to his feelings. This attention to behavior reinforces the patient's feeling that we are interested and can help. By helping him control his impulses we are doing for him what his parents were unable to do for him and what he was unable to do for himself.

At the same time as the defense is interrupted the patient's depression comes to the fore. Control of the acting out shuts off this escape valve for feelings and causes them to rise to consciousness where they become available for discharge in the interview. Thus the stage for interview psychotherapy and the development of insight is set. A constructive discharge of feelings in the interview is substituted for destructive discharge by acting out.

The patient's distortions in his attitude toward the staff can be brought to his attention where they become grist for the psychotherapeutic mill. At the same time, as the patient is externalizing the old negative introjections he begins to make new more positive introjections from the attitudes of the staff and their expectations. In this way he replaces his maladaptive defenses with more constructive ones and begins to learn new ego techniques of self-mastery and adaptation to the environment.

5. *Maturational lag.* At the same time in school, in occupational therapy and recreational therapy, he begins for the first time to learn new social and achievement skills which were left by the wayside in earlier developmental periods.

Whether in school, on the floor, in O.T., or in R.T. the staff confronts the patient with his deficiencies in dealing with reality and emphasizes the necessity of dealing with reality constructively. For example, a patient may prepare for a test inadequately, but, not perceiving either his inadequate preparation or his poor performance, may think he did quite well. The teacher will point out his poor performance, and then question his preparation, stressing that one must make realistic preparations to meet a real challenge and implying that this requires effort and delay of immediate satisfaction. Emphasis is also placed on realistic achievement as opposed to fantasy for gratification. This can be done also in occupational therapy; a patient building a cabinet may plan it poorly and execute it impulsively and then try to assert that it looks better than it actually does.

The goal of these policies is to provide an environment that through consistent expectations and appropriate limits (1) demonstrates our competence to treat the adolescent and relieves his need to test our intentions, (2) helps to undo the pathology of his earlier developmental years, (3) prepares him for interview therapy, and (4) provides him with constructive learning experiences. We anticipate that he will learn to develop self-control, which is the only basis for self-respect and true autonomy. We expect that instead of being a slave to all his impulses he will gain an ego structure strong enough to enable him to decide which impulse he will express and where and in what manner he will express it.

The Setting of Limits

There are two horns to the dilemma of setting limits: too many rules will repeat the parents' rigidity and two few will be interpreted as a lack of interest. We try to steer a middle course: a reasoned, gradually escalated response to the patient's behavior with the goal of teaching control. We prefer to accept mistakes in judgment rather than the hazards inherent in the alternatives of rigidity or permissiveness. Since we are attempting to teach ego control, the limits that are set must as much as is humanly possible be based on reason and on an individual response to each situation.

Restrictions

Room restrictions are an important part of the limit setting. The duration of the restriction is directly related to the degree of lack of control that the patient demonstrates. The less control the longer the restriction. When a patient is out of control the nurse will ask him to go to his room. His doctor will come to see him as soon as possible to examine briefly, while the issue is still "hot," what the patient was feeling before he lost control. The doctor will then restrict the patient—from 15 minutes to 24 hours. The incident will then be examined in full in the next regularly scheduled session.

I call this "the velvet glove within the velvet glove" technique. The inexperienced often think of restrictions as being punitive. They are just the opposite, since they meet the patient's emotional needs. The only factor that supports the restriction is the patient's willingness to substitute our authority as a means of control for his lack of control. We do not permit use of force.

In some patients it was not until we instituted 24-hour room restrictions —which indicated to the patient how seriously we viewed his behavior and how firmly we intended to deal with it—that the therapy got "off the ground." The restrictions are not an end in themselves but a means to an end. They must be combined with efforts to focus on a therapeutic understanding of the feelings underlying the act. Restrictions are usually necessary only in the first phase of therapy before the working through has begun. Thereafter behavioral episodes can usually be handled by interpretation rather than by restriction, since we assume that the patient now has the capacity to control his behavior. It is fascinating to observe the effort and will a patient will employ in trying to control his behavior once he has become aware of its destructive import.

PSYCHOTHERAPY

The milieu therapy, described in the preceding section provides the essential framework for the psychotherapy. The psychotherapy has many of the qualities of a scientific experiment, since it is specifically designed to deal with the developmental theory of the problem outlined in Chapter 2.

For example, two steps are designed to deal with the theory that the patient's clinical picture reflects his use of acting out as a defense against the feelings involved (mourning and depression) in separating from a symbiotic relationship: (1) physical separation in a hospital and (2) control of acting out by setting limits. The effectiveness of these two steps can then be verified by whether or not the patient begins to experience the mourning and depression when he is deprived of these defenses. This is exactly what happens, as you will see in the pages that follow.

The goal of treatment is as specific as the developmental theory and the therapeutic design: the resolution of the acute symptomatic crisis (the abandonment depression) and the correction and repair of the ego defects that accompany the narcissistic oral fixation by encouraging growth through the stages of separation-individuation to autonomy.

The treatment is a process, a continuous series of changes, one laying the groundwork for and flowing into the other in a natural and logical manner—smooth transition from one phase to the next depends on the application of the appropriate therapeutic procedure. Although for purposes of exposition I divide the process into the three phases of (1) testing (resistance),* (2) working through (introject work or definitive),* and (3) separation (resolution),* the reader should keep in mind that these are major trends and there may be much overlapping and back and forth movement. Each phase has its own characteristics, which are briefly outlined below and will be developed in detail in later chapters.

Phase I: Testing

This phase extends from the onset of treatment to the control of acting out, the beginning of the depression, and the establishment of a therapeutic alliance.

---

* Rinsley's terms for these phases.

1. *The goal* is the control of acting out and the establishing in the eyes of the patient the therapist's competence and trustworthiness.

2. *The patient's clinical condition.*   The patient, motivated by the protest and wish for reunion instigated by parental abandonment has been acting out to defend himself against feeling the depression and remembering the abandonment. Thus underneath the acting out he is depressed and feels hopeless. He resists the therapist's efforts in order to prevent final separation with its associated depression. The control of acting out which brings affect to awareness and memory into consciousness enables the patient to begin the painful work of mourning involved in separation.

3. *Therapeutic relationship.*   The patient is resistant, and significant communication occurs in actions, not words. He is constantly testing the doctor's competence and trustworthiness, challenging him with a variety of defiant acts. There is no therapeutic alliance in Phase I.

4. *Therapeutic activities.*   The doctor sets limits to control the acting out defining it as self-destructive. Repeatedly he points out the relationship of affect to behavior.

Phase II: Working Through

This phase extends from the control of acting out through the period of depression until separation is achieved and the depression subsides.

1. *The goal* in this phase is to achieve separation by working through the rage and depression associated with mourning.

2. *The patient's clinical condition.*   The patient is very depressed, his acting out is progressively reduced, he has a greater awareness of the relationship of feeling to behavior, and he is better able to control behavior and to express feelings in words.

3. *Therapeutic relationships.*   The testing phase having been successfully passed, a rather shaky but definitely working therapeutic alliance develops between doctor and patient—the patient begins to trust his doctor. Problems and conflicts now tend to be verbalized in the interview rather than expressed through acting out and efforts to manipulate people, and it is possible now to use words more effectively than actions.

4. *Therapeutic activities.*   When the patient gives up the acting out, a second line of defenses ensues against the depression such as withdrawal, evasion, denial, and blocking. The doctor removes these defenses by interpretation and guides the patient back to the depression. He encourages verabalization as an alternative to acting out for relief of the depression and begins to investigate the origins of the depression in the conflict with the parents. At this point he deals with any regressive acting out by inter-

pretation rather than setting physical restrictions as he did in Phase I.

5. In the later part of this phase joint interviews with the parents are begun (see page 112).

Phase III: Separation

This phase extends from the resolution of the depression until the termination of hospitalization. Its duration may vary a great deal.

1. *The goal* is the repair of ego defects and pathologic character traits, and the reworking through of anxiety over separation from the therapist and over becoming independent and autonomous.

2. *The patient's clinical condition.* Depression has abated. The patient now functions better but he experiences great anxiety over separation from the therapist and over becoming autonomous. He defends himself against this by clinging to the therapist and also by transient episodes of regressive acting out.

3. *Therapeutic relationship.* The patient, now reexperiencing with the therapist a repetition of the original anxiety over separating from the mother, clings to the therapist in order to avoid the anxiety.

4. *Therapeutic activities.* The doctor supports the patient's autonomy and interprets his regressive defenses.

In Phase III, after the family has begun to work out new patterns of relating, the patient, in line with the need for autonomy and independence, is encouraged to visit out of the hospital with the family. He is also encouraged to deal with his conflicts with the parents by himself on these visits. After each visit conflicts that arose with the parents will be analyzed in interviews with the doctor and the social worker. It must be kept in mind that there is not sufficient time to completely work through the patient's separation anxiety, and this then becomes the focus of his later outpatient psychotherapy.

Treatment of the Parents

The parents are not permitted to see the patient during Phase I in order to minimize both the parents' and the patient's resistance to separation. Separation is as painful for the mother as it is for the patient, and she resists it accordingly, as does the father.

However, the parents are seen weekly by the social worker whose treatment goals are as follows: (1) To enable the parents to verbalize their rage at the separation and thereby to relieve their guilt and attenuate their resistance. (2) To investigate the nature of their conflicts as parents, as well as the source of these conflicts in their own development. (3) To discuss the open conflicts between the parents that impair their parental role with the patient. (4) To interpret the unconscious conflicts interfering with the parental role. (5) To give support, advice, and guidance as to what the appropriate parental role should be. (6) To investigate destructive patterns of family communication and to suggest more appropriate ones. (7) To prepare the parents to deal with the confrontation with the patient.

Joint Interviews

In the latter part of Phase II, when the patient has verbalized his homicidal rage and suicidal depression and when the parents have become aware of their conflicts in the parental role and have, to some extent, learned a more appropriate parental role, it is necessary for parents and patient to be brought together.

These joint interviews have a specific and limited purpose: not to do family therapy as such but (1) to expose the family myth; (2) to restore more appropriate patterns of emotional communication in the family, the patient doing now what he was unable to do originally, that is, express his rage verbally and work it through with the parents; and (3) to find more constructive ways of dealing with family conflicts. This initial confrontation always arouses great anxiety, which immediately leads to regression on the part of both patient and parents. However, after successful confrontation and catharsis of the underlying emotions the family is freed to seek better patterns of adjustment. This crucial operation finally brings a strong shaft of hope to the patient.

Thus the patient progresses from one phase of treatment to the next in an orderly sequence propelled by his emotional conflicts and guided by his therapist.

CHAPTER 8

Phase I: Testing

The testing phase (as outlined on pages 109–110) extends from the beginning of treatment to the control of acting out and the establishing of a therapeutic alliance. It is obviously crucial. If its ingredients are not recognized and properly handled, the remaining hours or even years of therapy may be rendered ineffective. Why is this first phase so important? Why does the adolescent attempt, often very ingeniously, to thwart the well-intentioned efforts of the therapist to help him? What are the dynamics of this encounter and, more important, what do we do about it?

The adolescent is defending himself against feeling the abandonment depression. He has been repeatedly hurt and deeply disappointed by the deprivations and abandonment by his parents. Nevertheless, he clings to and tries to keep alive the pathologic symbiotic tie to his mother. His façade of resistance, rebelliousness, lack of concern—though tenaciously clung to—actually masks a feeling of utter hopelessness, his despair and dread of abandonment. His despair stems from the impasse that has evolved in his relationships with his parents. He feels that their abandonment indicates they do not care, and in his thwarted dependent, still symbiotic state this is extremely painful, producing rage, depression, fear, guilt, helplessness, and emptiness and void.

He is fearful and anxious as he enters treatment. Although aware on some level that he needs help, he is afraid that if he allows a relationship to develop with the therapist he will risk reexperiencing the abandonment of his earlier relationships. In addition, driven by the wish for reunion with the mother, he feels a need to fight anything that smacks of separation. He wants reunion, not consolation for his loss. His first unspoken questions will be: "How do I know you [the therapist] are any different? Can you understand me? Can you do the job? Will you not also abandon me if I give you my trust? Can I rely on you?" The adolescent's testing aims to answer these questions.

The therapist must go through a "trial by fire" before a therapeutic alliance develops. Words, at this point, are not used to convey or express feeling, but to manipulate and test. Behavior is the principal means by which the patient expresses his emotions.

He employs acting out not only as a defense against feeling and remembering, but also as a vehicle for testing. Although acting out is self-destructive, it is not so painful for him as risking trust and placing his all-embracing symbiotic needs in the hands of a person that he, as yet, has no reason to trust.

The patient makes a virtue out of a necessity by extolling the benefits of his acting out and of his manipulations, all the while hoping that his doctor will have the ability and good sense to see through him. After all, what else can he do—he is grappling with overwhelming primitive conflicts, such as wishes for reunion and fears of engulfment on the one hand and abandonment on the other.

How does the therapist handle this testing? The patient's acting out behavior is conceived of as both a defense against mourning and separation and a means of testing the doctor. The goal of treatment is to pass the test by controlling the acting out, thereby enabling the patient to resume the work of mourning involved in separation.

In this first stage the essential vehicle for communication for therapist as well as for patient, is not words but actions. The patient, communicating mainly by actions, scrutinizes the therapist's actions for feedback.

Another dynamic motivating the test is to determine if the therapist "cares." The parents have usually felt too guilty to set limits, which the patient has interpreted as further evidence of their lack of caring.

The following example shows how permissiveness leads to both disappointment and contempt for father and to feelings of impotence. The patient says: "They would say I coudn't. I did it anyway and then they would say you will stay in next week. I would go out and there was absolutely no way they could have handled me." The patient described how this made him feel powerful. "I could wear down anyone. No one could have controlled me. They tried everything. They even tossed me out four times. I packed my bags. After a day or so my father would come and apologize to me."

The therapist asked: "What did you feel about that?" Patient: "He was a pussy. He let me get away with everything. He was playing my game and I always won like with those curfews. I never kept them. The weekend I stole the blankets, I called up from the store and told my parents I was there and they said, 'okay'."

The basic job of management is to set limits in order to control the patient's acting out; to convert the patient from an actor and nonfeeler to a feeler and a talker, that is, at another level to interrupt his defenses against mourning so that the separation process can proceed and repair can be accomplished; and at a third and final level to establish the psychotherapist's competence and trustworthiness.

Since the patient's emotions are not yet available for interview therapy, he is seen daily for short periods of time. Meticulous attention is paid to the meaning of his behavior—what feelings it expresses. Limits are set by use of floor restrictions.

We control for the patient what he is unable to control for himself. Our interest in his behavior and in setting limits replaces the parents' lack of control. These two factors—interest and control—go far toward answering the questions that the patient's behavior asks—yes, we do care and we do know what we are doing; we can help. In addition, suggestions are made that the patient's behavior is self-destructive; and tentative preliminary investigations are made as to why someone would want to be so self-destructive.

Setting limits has the additional goal of preparing the patient for interview therapy. Control of the patient's acting out by damming up this channel for the expression of the rage underlying the depression enables the depression to emerge more clearly into consciousness, bringing with it the painful memories, all of which then become available to the patient to reinstitute and work through the process of mourning.

At the same time it provides the prerequisites for making the patient aware of the relationship of feeling to behavior, so that conscious control of behavior can be employed, thus furthering the work of mourning.

At the same time that the suggestion is made that dealing with feelings by acting out is harmful an alternative is offered—a more constructive way of dealing with the feeling might be to check the impulse to act out and verbalize the feeling in the interview.

The environmental milieu plays a crucial role in controlling the adolescent's acting out behavior. Since the adolescent has usually been subjected to an endless series of inconsistencies, provocations, and failures to set limits on the part of his parental figures, he is subject to a riotous set of distortions in his perception of the behavior of authority figures as well as considerable defects in his capacity to control impulses.

The staff members of the adolescent unit, now the authority figures, serving as substitute parents, attempt to treat these defects in ego functioning by applying a set of constant expectations. The adolescent is expected to behave as much as possible in a mature, adult, healthy, and realistic fashion. Deviations from this standard then become the subject of therapeutic investigation.

At the same time, the adolescent is able to use these figures in his new environment and their consistent and constant expectations as a new source of introjections to enhance the functioning of his ego. He begins to learn how to control his impulses and feels that he is now a more acceptable person, which helps him to perceive authority figures in a less threatening and distorted way.

Nevertheless, as he did with his parents, the adolescent inevitably will probe the staff and their attitudes for loopholes of permissiveness or inconsistency which he will then exploit.

It has long been the adolescent's "job" to find and exploit these loopholes; it is now the staff's job through frequent conferences to identify and understand his exploitive efforts in order to maintain consistency in their attitudes toward the patient. Inconsistencies in management on the part of the staff provoke in the adolescent the same disappointment and rage that was provoked by his parents' inconsistency in their efforts to help him to manage his needs.

The adolescent expects the therapist as well as the staff to "know" what is best for him and to have no compunctions about saying so. When he suspects either that they do not know or that they will not tell him, he views it as a repetition of his own parents' behavior and his feelings of disappointment impel him to regress and act out. Therapist and staff work in tandem, jointly expecting the adolescent to behave in a realistic, healthy fashion and jointly focusing on control of his acting out.

ILLUSTRATION OF TESTING, PHASE I: ANNE

Let us now follow what happens to Anne as she enters the hospital. Her appearance on admission was striking: shoulder-length black hair, partially covering her eyes, pale white skin, her only makeup blue and white eyeliner, giving her an almost ghostlike appearance. She dressed either in bluejeans with a black turtleneck top and black boots or in very short miniskirts. She wore one blouse open on the sides to the waist without a brassiere. When visited by her parents (we had not yet learned to restrict visits), she would demand that they bring in all sorts of unnecessary items.

The content of her initial interviews was more or less as follows. She did not want to be here—there was nothing really wrong. Why should she follow the stupid rules? People do not live by rules. She denied depression, but said: "No, it is just a feeling of vagueness, numbness, emptiness—I'm not really unhappy, it is just that I don't care. All I really want is out." She wondered why she did not feel more depressed in a horrible situation like this. She hoped something would happen so that she could get out of the hospital.

Anne's initial acting out consisted of her exhibitionistic appearance wearing miniskirts, her negativistic, sarcastic, flip attitude toward the therapist, writing provocative letters to her friends about hospitalization, procrastinating in school, phoning friends to make provocative statements, and failing to keep her room clean.

We began to limit the acting out by forbidding miniskirts, monitoring her letters, limiting the telephone calls, and expecting her to be at school on time and to keep her room clean.

Dealing with an adolescent's testing is much like negotiating with the Russians—you no sooner have one issue under control when another pops up. The patient's imagination and ingenuity is diligently applied to avoiding and evading the limits in such a way as to place the therapist in a "bind." The better the bind the better the test. At this task they are real "professionals" while the doctor is still an amateur.

Anne continued to test us by ingeniously violating all our limits. For example, one of the questions she forced us to resolve was: How mini is a miniskirt? She would wear a shockingly short miniskirt, and when she refused her therapist's request to change it she would be restricted to her room.

Later the patient was told she could not wear any of her short dresses until she let down the hems. She complied with some but kept others of minilength in the closet. She was finally told that if the hems were not let down the dresses would have to be sent home. She protested the imposed limits to the nurses and other patients, but never to the doctor.

When she appeared to be responding to the limits as to school, room, and dress another issue popped up. She was found to have installed a red light in her room to burn incense. (Incidentally, the therapist's counter-transference caused her to tell the patient her red light must go, but that they could compromise on amber.) It was decided that the incense and decorations had to be removed and that the room had to conform to the hospital pattern with a white light.

At first each of the patient's infractions required the therapist to come to the floor. Within several weeks, however, once it was established that we would consistently enforce the rules, the patient responded to correction from a staff member. For example, the first time she wore a miniskirt the therapist had to come to the floor to tell her to change it. After this prohibition was finally settled a firm and unrelenting word from the staff was sufficient to bring compliance.

The anger that had previously been dissipated in this behavior now began to come out more directly. For example: "I'm not picking up this room, you can tell the doctor that if I am in O.T. and she wants an interview, I'm going to refuse to come down. If she comes near me I'll throw something at her face." She is saying, in short, that the doctor is unreasonable, does not understand her, and is "square."

At this point the patient was totally unaware of the relationship between her acting out behavior and her emotional state. For example, she did not realize that after an upsetting visit or phone call from her parents she would resume acting out by staying up late and dressing inappropriately.

The first breakthrough in her awareness of the relationship of feeling to behavior occurred about 10 weeks later, when the doctor (countertransference again) forgot to leave an order giving the patient permission for a visitor. The patient was furious but rather than verbalize it she acted it out, refusing to go to bed on time, wearing heavy eye makeup and perfume, and a shirt borrowed from one of the male patients. She remained in the next interview only 5 minutes and said: "This interview is a waste of time—you forgot what was important—you demand things of me, but forgot what was important to me," and stormed out.

In the next interview, it was pointed out to her that she expressed her anger at the doctor in the same destructive acting out manner as she had with her parents. In addition, it was suggested that verbalization might be more constructive. Still angry she denied any connection: "People are trying to change me. When I get out nothing will change. I will still have the same tastes."

This connection between affect and behavior was made many more times until the patient began to grasp it. Then the doctor could handle the issue as follows. After observing some acting out on the behavior chart, she would say: "Well, I wonder what's bothering you"? The patient would answer: "Nothing, what do you mean?" Doctor: "Well, you stayed up late, your room was a mess, you are dressing inappropriately. We both know something has happened to upset you."

In the course of the interview, the upsetting incident would come to light and gradually the patient would make the connection herself, so that finally the therapist would only have to say "What's up" and the patient would be able to reply, "Oh, you mean because I did this or that."

Two weeks later the issue was brought home in a much more telling way. One night the patient had stayed up till 2:30 in the morning, discussing her desire to take drugs with the staff. In addition, her room was once more in disarray. At the next interview the doctor said: "Something is bothering you Anne." Patient: "No, I am in a good mood." (Patient's flat denial.) Doctor: "No, you were up till 2:30 a.m. and your room is a mess again."

Patient's rationalization: "I've been going to bed for weeks on time. I wanted to wash my hair and stayed up late—that's all. I just felt like disobeying the rules." Doctor: "You haven't been breaking the rules lately. It looks as if something special must have happened."

Patient: "Well, I came down at 10:00 p.m. to call my mother and found out that she was going to sell our house, move to an apartment, and give away my cat." The patient denied any anger saying: "If I had been in any other mood, I might have really been annoyed. They don't care about me. They throw my stuff away." She continued to deny that she was expressing anger in her behavior, but finally she admitted: "Well, it is true I guess, when I am angry I break the rules."

The patient's acting out of her anger at the parents' behavior was pointed out again; its self-destructive quality was noted, and suggestions were again made that it might be more constructive to check the impulse and talk about the conflicts in the interview. Gradually, the patient, identifying with the therapist's attitude, began to internalize this perception and to check the impulse to act out.

Later she talked about her anger in the interview. For example, following one of these episodes the doctor interpreted that "Your mother's behavior made you angry and depressed and you continued to react in the only way you knew how: in the hospital by breaking rules, whereas at home you had done it by smoking pot, staying out late." Patient: "I wish that were not true, because it makes me feel awfully immature to realize that it is."

Throughout this period the patient felt angry at the doctor but she rarely expressed it directly. She alternated in interviews between denial of her feelings and refusal to talk. She would say to the nurses: "The doctor is a machine and she doesn't care about me." At one point, she tried to enlist her parents' aid to get a change of doctors.

As inroads were made on the patient's acting out, she began to experience affect in a dream: "I am not used to being like this—dreaming all the time—it is like I don't go off so much—like I realize something is boring me—I realize I am cut off and it doesn't happen."

"I don't understand why all these things have happened all of a sudden in the last few weeks. I am feeling something different that I didn't feel before. I want to divert myself. When I am with a whole bunch of people, I want to drift off. I might have felt this at home if I hadn't only done things not to feel it. At home I always had a little warning beforehand— not like I was depressed—but I did something, that is, took pot to keep something else from happening."

The patient was now more able to express her feelings verbally, but she was being blocked by the fact that her therapist could not accept her hostility.

Twelve weeks after the start of therapy she again persisted in testing limits, procrastinating in her schoolwork, coming late to breakfast, and dressing inappropriately; in interviews she became demanding: "What about my packages? Can I have my yearbook? Remember to leave the order for visitors. Can I have Christmas presents?"

The therapist responded by confronting the patient with her acting out, particularly her arriving late for breakfast. The patient answered: "Seeing as I get no passes I don't see any reason to get up in the morning. I was annoyed so I stayed in bed." Here she made the connection herself between anger and acting out. The therapist reiterated: "You are expressing your anger in your behavior." But (countertransference again) instead of pursuing the expression of feeling at this point the therapist drew the patient away from her anger to talk about her parents.

The patient talked about her mistrust of words—how they were used in her family to evade rather than communicate. (She is probably unconsciously asking the therapist to prove to her in some way that there is a reason now for trusting words.) She recalled that she was angry with her father on the telephone because he told her only what he thought she wanted to hear, and later she became aware that her anger was provoked by his lack of involvement.

For the first time the patient began to become aware that gifts and fleeting relationships were demanded by her as a substitute for the affection she felt she never received from her parents. She recalled an experience with her former therapist who once suggested to her that she might get another set of parents. In response to this she ran away from home and met a strange boy, Paul, on the train.

The patient recalling the episode said: "I met Paul on the train and got attached to him. That's what I do when things go wrong. I look for people so it makes me think you may be right. Still I don't think I have anyone." Therapist: "Yes, maybe that's the meaning of all those gifts you demanded." In this interview, anger at the therapist is connected with acting out behavior and with anger at the parents which is later acted out. Even the cause of this anger, the feeling that the parents do not care is approached for the first time, as well as its connection with acting out, such as demands for gifts.

For 5 days following this interview there was no acting out. However, the pressure of the anger returned, the patient became sarcastic, angry and resumed her constant requests to the therapist. The latter, again because of her countertransference, did not focus on the behavior, clarify its meaning, and get the patient to verbalize her anger. The acting out continued

The patient was late for school, again wore inappropriate clothes, became exhibitionistic, left her room in a mess, and talked about wanting to get away from the hospital.

Finally, unable to get through to her therapist as she had also been unable to get through to her mother, the patient took marijuana from another patient who had smuggled it into the hospital. The patient was transferred back to the restricted floor, and the therapist interpreted the patient's acting out as anger at her and suggested that she verbalize it.

Finally, the stored up rage came out. Patient: "I was angry about everything you have done to me—I hate people telling me what to do—this place is getting me down." The therapist pointed out that what was bringing her down was her conflicts that she brought into the hospital. . . . She was running away. A firm stand by the therapist enabled her to release more anger. Patient: "Well, I'll tell you, I am mad at you and it is really hitting me. I don't want to hear what you say. I don't want to believe I am crazy. There is something I want to hold on to about myself and I feel it has been taken away."

On the restricted floor, she procrastinated and became sullen, preoccupied, and weeping. She attempted to make the therapist feel guilty saying: "You don't trust me. Everybody expects me to fail." Therapist: "You got yourself into this mess." Finally the patient said: "I know I did it to myself and I can't be mad at you." Therapist: "You have been mad at me for months." Patient: "Yes, I couldn't tell you, I was too scared. You control my life, but you sit there like a machine saying, I don't know what we are going to do with you. What do you think you are, you Bitch?" The patient's anger is finally coming out in verbal form.

Therapist: "You have been playing games with me for months now." Patient: "This is what you want. You want me to be depressed and unhappy and when I wasn't you had to do this to make me suffer. I didn't know I was angry when I did all those things."

"When you told me I stayed up after my parents' phone call because I was angry, I thought that was absolutely absurd. Now I know there is no point in my telling you what I think you want to hear, because it won't get me downstairs any sooner." The patient's recognition that the therapist was more or less in control of the situation was immensely reassuring. Following this ventilation of anger the testing phase subsided and the patient entered into the working through phase.

ILLUSTRATION OF TESTING, PHASE I: GEORGE

Let us now look in on George Graves whose testing phase took a somewhat different course. I began to supervise George's treatment about 6 weeks after admission, at which time he had made token efforts to control his acting out, but beginning to feel depressed, was demanding that he be allowed to visit outside of the hospital and be moved off the restricted floor. The doctor was unaware that the patient's control of behavior was only a token one, and that his demands were a request for more external controls.

When the doctor cannot control the patient's acting out, the patient experiences it as a rejection, is disappointed and angry, and acts out more; in fact, he continues to act out until the doctor "gets the message" and really sets the necessary limits.

Before his first visit out, the patient was anxious and jokingly asked the staff for ten darvon, and on return from his visit he was unable to sleep. The next day he was irritable, angry, discussed drugs with other patients, refused to make his bed or attend the floor meeting. In the interview, despite this behavior, the patient pressed the doctor for further privileges saying that he felt normal when he was out, did not want to come back, and that he wanted to go out and stay out for good.

The patient, on the verge of experiencing his depression, did not trust the doctor's competence to help him control himself. Therefore, he continued to test his therapist and at the same time revealed this intent by reporting his disillusionment with doctors and parents to the staff.

The doctor still unaware of the test acceded to the patient's request and moved him to a less restricted floor. At this point the patient's anxiety mounted, his acting out continued, and when the doctor still failed to perceive the message the patient acted out sexually with another patient; the doctor finally "got the point" and transferred him back to the restricted floor.

Here the patient was both angry and depressed, broke down and cried, and said that he was going to "screw himself." In the interviews George was furious with the doctor for moving him, tried to provoke the therapist's guilt by saying that he thought the therapist was a friend of his, he trusted him, he never thought he would do this to him; at the same time, George denied his acting out and his depression. He continued to press persuasively upon his doctor to be moved off the restricted floor again.

After several weeks of forced confrontation with his acting out, George managed to control it, began to feel depressed, and finally started to express in the interview the feelings that underlay his behavior—that he was angry at his mother and that he did poorly in school to aggravate her; that he did not have a good relationship with either mother or father; that he hated them; that he could not stand it if they gave him everything.

He told of his self-destructive desires, his taking drugs, and that he would have killed himself if something had not been done because he had given up. The content of this interview is an excellent example of how the real story of the history of present illness, complete with its affective force, only comes out when the acting out has been controlled. This is also the cue for the therapist to change his function from Phase I, control of acting out, to Phase II, support for the working through of the depression.

At this point it is important to encourage the patient because while the therapist is cutting off the avenues of escape from the depression he must give the patient some incentive or purpose for this pain. The therapist's approach has to be affirmative, giving the patient the feeling that the therapist knows what he is doing. He might say: "Yes, you do feel worse, you feel worse because you have controlled your behavior, but this is a good sign rather than a bad one. You have been unhappy a good part of your life, at least now you are unhappy for a purpose, because at least it is now possible to get to the bottom of your conflicts whereas before when you were acting as you did, it was not possible."

The behavior chart should be checked daily because after an effective interview there will almost immediately be a worsening of depression. Usually the next interview will start with a defense against the depression. In addition, at the time the patient has controlled his acting out and is beginning to experience his depression, if the therapist distracts or keeps him from ventilating it in the interview, he is contributing to the pressure of unexpressed feelings which may cause the patient to act out again.

George's doctor, in the crucial interview described on the preceding page, was unaware of the need to shift his emphasis from control to full ventilation of feelings and he "put a lid" on the patient's expression of his depression. The patient was acutely disappointed and reacted with a feeling of hopelessness and anger, as he had with his parents, as illustrated by the following. George had just finished saying: "I guess my therapist was right. He said I was committing mental suicide, which I was. I wasn't physically dying, but I was dead mentally."

The therapist diverted him from this expression of his feelings of depression back to a discussion of his relationship with his parents. He complied and said: "If I hadn't done what I did, they would still be there, I was the scapegoat, I gave them a good excuse to get up and scream. I stayed away from my mother, I was distant from her—from everybody. She was messed up. I wonder if she was crazy?"

George illustrated the relationship between acting out and the depression saying: "I want to get out of here. I want to get laid, get high, and take drugs." His next comment illustrates a further effort at defense: "Look, I've been here five months. I haven't done anything, I'm not getting anywhere."

The therapist rather than giving the patient some support to enable him to work through the depression, continued to use the technique of Phase I, pointing out the patient's acting out as destructive. The patient responded with anger and hopelessness: "There are times when you have to do your job, be a psychiatrist, but there are times when you can come out of yourself a little bit. What you just gave me is a very good sermon."

The transference reaction continued into the next interview, as the patient attempted to seduce the therapist into a battle. Therapist: "You are sad today." Patient: "No, I'm not." Therapist: "But you are angry." Patient: "Yes, I am, but I don't know why." Then silence.

The therapist attempted to bring the patient back to talking about his mother, but the patient, feeling that the thread of the interview was lost, began to get angry.

Patient: "What have we accomplished so far? I think nothing. We have talked a lot, but haven't said anything." The therapist continued to question the patient as to why he was angry which only made him more angry, since he expected the "psychotherapist" to know.

The therapist should have interpreted to George that his anger was a reaction to disappointment. Finally, in response to the therapist's question "What are you so angry about?" The patient began to cry and said: "I want to die rather than talk about this. I feel angry and hopeless. I want to break that table. I don't know why." Therapist: "This is the way you felt outside." Patient: "Yes it is." Then taking distance: "We're not getting anywhere—talking doesn't help." However, some of his anger at his mother began to come out. Patient: "I don't give a fuck about my mother—I don't give a shit about anyone—least of all myself. That is the sick touch—that last part. I can't stand her. Someone should have killed her a long time ago. She is lousy, rotten."

At the end of the interview he recalled an incident at age 5 when his mother threw him against the wall for wetting his pants. Patient: "She is a messed up person. I always hated her for as far back as I can remember." These latter comments of anger followed a supportive comment to the patient saying how difficult it was to express these feelings, which allowed the patient to go on with the business at hand, talking about his mother. And thus George, like Anne, progressed from Phase I of the treatment to Phase II, the working through.

CHAPTER 9

Phase II: Working Through

Passage of the patient from Phase I: Testing, to Phase II: Working Through, is signaled clinically by control of the acting out, a consequent deepening of the depression, and spontaneous recall with appropriate affect and detailed memory of the history of the environmental separation experience which precipitated the abandonment depression.

The patient has now fulfilled the conditions necessary for the working through of the mourning process and his other emotional conflicts in the interview, that is: (1) the patient is now aware of the relationship between feeling and behavior; (2) he has begun to check the impulses to act out, which allows feeling to rise into consciousness and also impels him to remember his past; (3) words are now used to express feeling rather than to manipulate; and (4) finally, with the conclusion of the testing process, the patient, assured of the therapist's competence and trustworthiness, allows a therapeutic alliance to develop that makes the first dent in the patient's feeling of despair and hopelessness.

The patient enters into a "symbiotic transference" which later has to be resolved. But nevertheless, because this is not a true symbiosis, but rather the patient's transference distortion of his relationship with the therapist, it breeds confidence and allows the patient to work through the rage and depression associated with separation from the mother.

This change in the patient's clinical condition warrants a parallel change in both the therapeutic focus and the therapeutic approach. The interview schedule is now changed to 45 minutes three times a week. The focus shifts from the environmental milieu and behavior to expression of the patient's feelings in the interview with consequent recognition and working through of the conflicts. The goal of therapy in Phase II is to work through the rage and depression at the abandonment and complete the separation process, which lays the groundwork for the repair of ego defects through new introjections.

To accomplish this the therapeutic techniques shift from those involved in controlling acting out to those dealing with the "working through" in the interview, that is, from limit setting to interpretation. With the control of acting out, there immediately ensues a deepening of the depression. Thereupon, the patient institutes a secondary line of defenses against the depression, such as withdrawal, evasion, and denial of his feeling state; this must be interpreted by the therapist to bring the patient back to accepting and working through his depression. At the same time, the therapist supports and encourages verbalization as a superior alternative to acting out to relieve the depression and eventually resolve the conflict.

The intensity of affect and the recall of memory are further enhanced by the control of acting out. Inevitably the patient begins to reexperience the abandonment, which the therapist must patiently interpret and reinterpret until it is finally worked through, and fully recognized and understood by the patient.

Each successful interview, in the sense that it brings the depression to the fore, makes the patient feel worse and initiates a reinstituting of defense. Therefore, the therapist must also reassure the patient as to the true significance of the depression, that is, it is a good sign, not a bad one. A companion goal of this phase, to be explored in detail later (see Chapter 11), pertains to the family and involves exposure of the family myth, and both restoration and reconstruction of verbal patterns of interaction.

ILLUSTRATION OF WORKING THROUGH, PHASE II: ANNE

Let us return again to Anne as she passes into this phase of therapy. The reader may note in this section a certain amount of repetition which is, after all, the essence of working through. One of Anne's primary means of relating to the world was to view it as a scene in which characters live only by manipulation of one another. She expressed surprise when informed by the therapist that this was not how all people behaved.

She reviewed her past history of manipulation of authority figures in school, her parents' manipulation of her by means of gifts, her mother's manipulation of her through illness, and her own various manipulations of the staff in her immediate world of the hospital.

The therapist then interpreted to her that it is this very manipulation of her by her parents that upsets her because she felt it meant that they did not care about her. "Nobody has ever spanked me—maybe they do care but they're afraid of me." The therapist explained that when the patient can successfully manipulate others by making them feel guilty, it makes her angry and depressed. Manipulation brings sterile success because at the moment of a minor victory she wins no love.

Following this enlightening discussion, Anne then elaborated on her parents' use of gifts: "My parents always gave me things—they had to after awhile—so I thought you would, too. If I was in the hospital long enough naturally you would have to let me move downstairs."

She then talked further about her habit of manipulating people by making them feel guilty; how she told the therapist what she wanted to hear to get passes and privileges; about her desire for a male therapist who would not be as astute in seeing through her maneuvers. Just as her mother was able to make a fool out of her father, she was certain she could do so with a male therapist. She said: "It brings a person down in my eyes if I can manipulate him." (Good examples of how the battle between therapist and patient mirrors Anne's battles with her parents.)

The therapist again interpreted that the patient was a master manipulator and that this was her chief way of relating to people. Following this interview, the patient, forced to become aware of her manipulating way of life, became tearful and more depressed. She talked about the difficulty she had in caring for people and how she was always hurt. She began to make more constructive efforts to express her feelings—but she also continued some acting out. Patient: "I didn't get any pleasure out of doing all those things. It is kind of a relief not to feel I have to fight so many of your crazy rules."

At this point when the patient had not completely given up her acting out, she expressed her contempt for the failure of the staff to perceive and control it. "I was mad when that nurse came in. I was annoyed and felt like screaming and telling her how dumb she was for letting me ask her about the short dress—or else for being dumb enough to ask you."

With the gradual realization that she was getting "no pleasure" from continued acting out, the patient's grooming became better, socialization with other patients easier, and her manner was more outgoing. Once the patient began to gain some insight into her defensive maneuvers the therapist began to insist upon verbalization and finally to stress the necessity to deal with the depression in each interview.

Under this pressure and encouragement from her therapist the patient did begin to deal more directly with her depression. Almost simultaneously with this step forward, Anne received a letter from her mother which gave fresh evidence of rejection by the mother through thinly veiled efforts at bribes.

Anne was depressed anew and angry. Prior to this she would have denied the relationship of this feeling to her mother's behavior. Now Anne said: "It is as if my mother is saying I miss you, but the message is that there is no one really to take care of me, that she can't even take care of herself." The patient then denied her need for her parents and substituted her desire for material things for her need for parental care.

This prompted her spontaneously to recall the history of her abandonment: "In a strange way my parents did seem to care. I think underneath they cared but they are cluttered up by other things going on for a really long time. I was just thinking today that if I were put in this hospital when I was 12 or 13, things might have been so different! My troubles really started with my desperately needing people, and then drugs—I needed people, boys and Jan, and then I wanted things. I can remember being in the apartment alone and it felt terribly alone—mother had a headache— things were different—she was different."

Therapist: "What kind of an influence do you think Louise (the maid) had?"

Patient: "It is kind of hard to remember her—I can't quite remember that there was a different atmosphere when she was with us. I remember first moving to the apartment and having dinner and things were a lot happier, everyone was freer." The patient then reported the onset of her feelings of abandonment. "After Louise left I started meeting people, getting really lonely."

The therapist asked: "What did you think about her leaving?"

Patient: "I don't know but I felt more acute loneliness. She used to stay with me. I didn't realize she was good for me until long after she had gone. Mother told me she didn't know where she was. I had the feeling that maybe some thing happened. I felt nostalgic, something that was part of me was taken away." Here Anne literally reported her feeling that the separation involved a loss of part of herself.

Therapist: "Was that about the time you began to have trouble in school?"

Patient: "Yes, I started getting called down. I didn't do well in the first part of the seventh grade. In the summer I really got close to Jan and Bill —we used to stay over at each other's house. Jan and I were always freer, we had less of a front with each other than I had with other people. I really was terribly lonesome. Mother started getting sicker then. I'd come home to a different friend's house each night, and father stayed in New York City."

Anne then reported her acting out as a defense against the depression. "I think I would have talked to anyone—I didn't know what I felt. I mainly acted. I did whatever I wanted to. I don't think I have ever talked to anyone really deeply. I wasn't aware of feeling lonely, but I thought I really needed somebody. I wasn't aware of feeling lonely until one or two years ago."

Therapist: "That was when you started smoking pot and taking drugs?"

Patient: "Yes, that's right. It was with Denny. I was scared at first and then it made me feel groovy. Then I felt I had something on other girls my age. I was only 14 years old then."

The parents' permissiveness deepened Anne's plight. Therapist: "You told me your parents were aware?"

Patient: "My parents told me I could smoke in my room. They would compromise and say, 'Okay, smoke pot but nothing else.' When I was home, after I quit school, I wished I had gone back. I never knew what I wanted to do. I tried to think of things I might want to do. I really wanted to see somebody. I knew I wanted somebody to come and stay, and say, 'I'll get you out of this for good.' I would have married Denny just to get away. I had messed him up a couple of times, but he stuck it out with me."

The therapist pointed out the relationship of her nostalgic loneliness to taking drugs and seeking boyfriends. This prompted Anne to give illustrations of her parents' inability to set limits for her acting out in that she continued to take drugs and stay out late at night.

During these discussions the patient's behavior continued to improve and several days later she expressed for the first time a feeling of hope replacing her feeling of despair by saying "things may actually get better." In an interview a few days later the patient said: "I don't know why, but I feel more comfortable now, calmer, waiting for something to happen. Up to now I have had no hope. I have thought things would go on just like before. But now things do seem to be getting better. In fact, I am coming back to when I was comfortable, and I kinda expect things to keep getting better."

Rage at Mother

When her doctor discovered she was spending too much time with a male aide and suggested that she stop this, the patient expressed anger at the hospital rules and at the therapist; this then led her past the depression at the loss of the mother-surrogate to the more basic Separation-Individuation problem with her mother, and her homicidal feelings emerged.

She began expressing her rage at her mother as well as her guilt over this rage: "Mother would try to ruin things between me and Jan if she could—like Jan would come to visit and mother would say: 'when is she going to leave.' Mother would say she couldn't go out and get things for me to eat because it was too much trouble. Jan and I would be talking at night and mother would pound on the floor and say 'be quiet.' She was jealous. All of a sudden, when Jan would come to see me, mother would want to do things with me. She would suggest that we go out to eat, and that Jan should visit somebody else.

"I never remember a mother-daughter relationship, maybe just a bit when I was young. I ended up hating her. I wish I didn't. Talking to her makes me pissed off at the world. Sometimes I could pound her into the ground. Then she'd get sick and I'd feel bad and I'd take her to the hospital. A couple of times she would come up to slap me and I'd push her away. I felt I could kill her a couple of times. I wound up feeling sorry for her.

"Everytime I would hit her she would call me a tramp. She found out about Bill, but she told me that before it even happened. She always expected me to be rotten, no matter what happened. If she had been a good little girl herself, then I don't think she would have been so worried about me. Besides, she expected me to turn out like my real mother.

"She lacked sensitivity. Maybe somebody messed her up a long time ago and that's why she was unable to understand. She was married once and she was bad, but I don't think she ever knew what it would be like to love without convenience."

Anne then again recognized the relationship between her behavior and her anger. "It is funny, I thought I was doing all those things because I wanted to do them. I spent a lot of time with Bill—I'd be upset and he would come over to my house, and then when he left I would be upset again. We would watch TV or go to a movie. I'd also go over to Jan's house. But, when I was 13 or so, Bill and I broke up and Jan moved away. Things were still groovy in a way, but we were more separated.

"Then I started to smoke pot and go out with Denny. When Jan and I got together we used to look back to when everything was okay—2 years before when I wasn't smoking pot. My parents didn't hassle me as much about Bill and I stayed away from them as much as I could, and I had stuff to look forward to, such as being with Bill or going to Jan's.

"I think that there is a kind of loss that goes with smoking pot. I was kind of happy but I knew that it couldn't go on, but I didn't want things to change so radically. I had to have someone to hang on to. I figured I could focus all my attention on Bill and Jan. I was out of school, nothing to do, just waiting and waiting. My mother expected me to be rotten no matter what happened."

Anne then began to wonder why mother expected the worse to happen and attributed it to her adoption. She then sought further causes for the mother's behavior and expressed her disillusionment and anger at this behavior.

After 6 more weeks, the patient acknowledged how depressed she felt and that talking about her past made her feel worse, but that she couldn't get away from it in the hospital as she could on the outside where she would use drugs to relieve the depression. She expressed disappointment with her parents that they did not stop her—that they remained insensitive to her need for their real interest and love.

She also expressed disappointment with previous doctors because they had not stopped her—that the mother and psychiatrist tried to get her to use birth control pills, thus encouraging the acting out.

At this point the patient began to fight the deepening abandonment depression: "I am upset, I want my freedom, I want to get out of here." She expressed anger at the hospital for bringing on her depression and not taking care of other patients well enough. The therapist interpreted the depression to her as related to abandonment and pointed out that she used to react to it on the outside by taking drugs and clinging to people, and how here she must find another way.

Concurrently, the patient's periods of participation and activity were getting longer, and her periods of depression and withdrawal were getting shorter.

She talked about her use of friends to avoid loneliness and depression and that at age 12 and 13 her peer group broke up—this group had meant much to her from age 8 or 9. She then began to cling to Bill—recognizing that she clung to him as a substitute for the relationship with her mother and also realizing that her relationship with the maid, Louise, had meant a great deal more than she had thought.

In the next interview she talked about her willingness to go home to live with her parents, but expressed her fear of returning to the same situation: her father disinterested or not at home and mother sick all the time. This discussion led to some awareness of the symbiotic relationship with the mother, that is, their mutual dependence. "Instead of me following her example, she follows mine." The mother always needed someone to take care of her.

Patient: "Mother treated me like a friend. She clung to me, she wanted me, but she didn't want any of the responsibility of caring for me." When Louise left, mother asked Linda to come and stay, and then she wanted her to go home very suddenly. She used to do this. She'd get the idea of having someone stay, and then she'd get bored and perhaps a little jealous and say it was too much trouble, so she made her go home in a very rotten way.

"My mother would say: 'We don't need her around, you and I can do things.' When she was around Mama treated her more like a servant and when she was gone, Mama just got sick, went to bed, and I had to take care of her."

The therapist pointed out that the mother repeated this behavior with Jan also, and the patient responded with: "When I was with Jan she would say to me 'let's go on vacation' a kind of bribe to get me away from Jan, and when I would keep pulling away and making excuses not to go with her, she would ask Jan to go with us. She would be nice to Jan when she could tell her she was having a hard time with me, but if Jan stood up for me she would make her go home—like she doesn't know how to act like a mother with me."

After Anne had reviewed her search for relief from loneliness with her friends and with Bill, the therapist asked her to try to recall what she had felt when Louise left?

Patient: "When Louise left, mother became depressed and tried to fill her life with me but it was too much for her. Mother then imported a playmate about my age to help take care of me and was either jealous of this girl when we were together, or used her to take care of me completely." Anne continued: "It may seem strange to import a playmate, but in my house it became a matter of course."

The therapist empathized with the patient's loss of the maid, Louise, who gave her some real security and with her need for a mother at this time. The therapist again interpreted the lack of mothering, the depression, and the use of drugs and friends to ease the pain of her abandonment.

Anne replied: "Louise was the closest thing I ever had to a mother—she never talked to me as a kid. It never dawned on me till I was older how wonderful she had been. When I was sick, I would want her to come in, but she would only come in for 10 minutes and turn on the TV and I would want her to stay longer. When I was older I expected less."

This then led to the feeling of what life was like after Louise left: "Mother in the hospital, me at home alone watching TV and father away or preoccupied and paying no attention to me as if I wasn't there. I felt I wasn't living. I didn't care about living. I didn't know how to get out of it. I went to see a doctor who was afraid of me—afraid to stop the shots he had given me. He asked me if I thought they were doing me any good! I said, 'I think we should go on.' Imagine that! Pretty stupid wasn't it that I should be in control."

She began to perceive that her parents had their difficulties also: "They hassle over me like an object—and use me like a pawn." She previously had only been able to see them in terms of the misery they caused her, but now, she perceived that her father was cut off almost completely from his family and had little to do with his wife. He was more frequently away than at home so her mother was lonely too.

Gradually as she expressed her depression and rage she was able to recall positive aspects of her mother. "I guess I miss her in a funny way. When I think about her I'm not always angry. I think about good things—that she was nice when she came to visit me in school. I want her to be all like that part of her that is nice and that I miss. It's funny I said I missed her—I never thought I would."

Since Anne had been able freely to express not only negative but also some positive conclusions about her parents, she was considered ready for a visit from her mother. As we feared and half expected, Anne's dread of the mother's withdrawal aroused by the anticipation of this visit promoted her retreat into her old defenses: she appeared in dungarees and a sloppy shirt and her hair half covered her face. The visit, however, was not the disappointment she had fortified herself for. Her mother was more direct than prior to admission and actually gave Anne some support and encouragement. Seven months had elapsed since the mother had seen Anne. During these months the mother had seen a social worker once a week to review her problems in relating to her daughter. As a consequence, the encounter between mother and daughter seemed to give the patient real hope of the possibility of change for the better, and further alleviated her depression.

Now the therapist left for a 2-week vacation: despite which the patient continued to work on her parental conflicts with her substitute therapist. She also continued to relive her feeling of abandonment, because the separation from her regular therapist sparked memories of Louise's leaving and revived the abandonment depression. Now she was able to review these feelings with appropriate expression of mourning for the loss, accompanied this time by her recognizing her guilt about her mother's many hospitalizations.

The father visited 2 weeks after the mother, and Anne noted that he dealt with her evasively rather than directly. This was followed by a joint visit that made it clear that her parents, threatened by Anne's new-found self-assurance, combined to defeat and render useless the patient's attempts to be direct in her verbal communication with them. Therefore they again visited separately for the next few weeks while plans were made to begin the joint interviews to attack this problem. Anne at this point may be considered as on the threshold of Phase III.

ILLUSTRATION OF WORKING THROUGH, PHASE II: GEORGE

Let us now turn to George as he moved into Phase II. He continued to test the doctor. For example, he demanded that his parents send him additional records. The therapist refused and pointed out to George that his demand for records was only testing to see how much he could "get away with." The therapist then related this maneuver to how easily he could push his father around to get what he wanted. George responded that he really did not need the records and agreed that he was in fact only testing the doctor.

He then talked about his mother. "She never gave anybody a break. She was a domineering bitch who overemphasized details and had no understanding of anything. I hated her for it. I was aware I hated her. I don't feel hatred like that towards my father. I always tried to please him, but not her. When I did something bad I felt rotten thinking of what it was doing to my father, but I have always felt good about what ever worry and distress it gave to my mother. But, I was upset at the same time too because I have to admit down deep I loved her, and she was not all bad. She could be nice and want to do things for me. She took us out for lunch sometimes and that was fun, but she was a bitch too."

Exploring further, George reached his homicidal rage: "Sometimes I had thoughts about killing her. They bubbled up inside, and I would feel like I was going to explode. I thought about stabbing her in the back with a knife or hitting her. One time I had a knife in my hand just fooling around and I had these evil thoughts and I laughed, a wicked laugh, and she was really scared to death. I swiped at her and that let the pressure off a bit. Boy, that brings back memories.

"One reason I hated her had to do with my father—he never disciplined us. It was always her, she was always punishing one of us and she was very hard on us. I'd go wrong in school, want some help and understanding and I'd get screaming and yelling. I'd be home studying till 9 and get straight A's. I rebelled—no bullshit like that for me. Once in the 8th grade, she said, I had to get all C's or better, so I made 2 B's, 3 C's and a D in Physical Ed. I was supposed to stay home every day after school for 6 weeks because of that D. That's crap, I wouldn't take it. I was so angry I disobeyed and in 3 or 4 weeks the rules went off."

At this point the patient looked very depressed and the doctor said: "You look hopeless and depressed."

Patient: "Yes, I am, but I am sure they are trying, I hope they are anyway." At this point the patient switched saying: "I'm not going back to the same old thing at home. If I ever go home, I will be on my own anyway. I will do what I want, and if things don't work out the way I have planned I will only be home for a little while."

He then adopted a second line of defense by arguing with the doctor about why he had been transferred back to the restricted floor. The doctor interpreted the change in subject as an effort to get away from the depression.

Patient: "No, I can talk about my mother—I flash back a lot to her. My angry feelings toward my mother were probably the most important; more important than my feelings toward my father. She was the trunk and everything else was just branches. It all went back to the third grade and her pushing me in school. It really hurt me when she yelled at me. I really wanted to please her very much in the beginning. Then I went the opposite way because I never could please her—nobody can please her, I know that now. She was a perpetually unsatisfied woman. She was looking for something and couldn't find it—she'll never find it. I am looking for something too and so far I can't find it."

Following this interview, anger at his mother having been aroused, George resumed his acting out by "exploding" at a nurse on the floor. In the next interview, the doctor interpreted the anger at the nurse as an acting out of his anger at his mother, which George denied vehemently. He turned the conversation sharply to challenge the doctor about how long he would be on the restricted floor, when he could go home, and so on. The doctor responded in a consistent, patient, but firm manner, and pointed out that the patient was again challenging him and was trying to get away from the main subject—anger at his mother.

The patient then expressed his anxiety over his anger: "When I get angry I am not me anymore, I am really a different person. I am disoriented and I feel like I am going to burst so I have to do something and it doesn't matter what it is, but it is always self-destructive. I like to do self-destructive things, but then when I get back to myself again I really get scared. While I am doing the things I'm not scared at all, I really enjoy it." (The tension created by the anger is so great that he must have the release that he obtains by acting out. To experience this release without conflict, he must suspend the perception that it is self-destructive.)

"Then when I come out of it I think about how hopeless things are and see that if I keep up like that I'll end up in the garbage heap—that's what really frightens me. I really don't want to act the way I do, but I can't help it I'm all fouled up. I say to myself, who am I going to become acting this way when I am out of it, and then I feel the other way."

Several interviews later, the patient again began the interview with denial, challenging and testing the doctor. When, however, the doctor again responded firmly, he returned to the theme of his mother, this time mentioning his reaction when he first noticed that his mother was having an affair. He felt furious and bitterly disappointed with his father for doing nothing about it and sorely felt the loss of his mother's attention. (This occurred when George was about age 12.)

However, after reviewing the material, he again became defensive to fight off the depression which ensued, saying: "I am sick of being miserable. I want to get out of here. Can't I go on vacation for a week? I would like to get away from all this."

The therapist interpreted these last remarks as a defense and also encouraged George to come to grips with his depression.

At this point the therapist's impending vacation exacerbated the patient's rage at abandonment as follows. George started the interview saying: "I really feel like acting out. The same feeling I had on the outside when I was getting into trouble. I can taste my anger just like when I was outside. I don't want to think, I want to act. It gives me a feeling of power."

The doctor interpreted first that this may be a reaction to his going away.

Patient: "I can't know if I am really angry with you. I have no right to be angry. It's not valid at all, but I feel terrible. You have a right to go on vacation." George then revealed the extent of his dependency: "I guess the trouble is I am too dependent on you and when you go away I fall to pieces. I would like to scream, explode, I don't know what to say."

The doctor then explained that George was reacting to his leaving as a repetition of his abandonment by his mother.

Patient: "I feel now as I did then [meaning age 10] I feel I am losing something, but I don't know what I am trying to accomplish by acting out. Maybe I am trying to hide something. I think I am sane. I don't care about anything. I say to myself 'you are trying to hurt me, so I'll try and get back at you.' I know you're not trying to hurt me, but I feel left alone and that hurts. It is the same feeling I felt with my family. Instead of sitting down and saying what was good I acted out and tried to kill myself. I am not giving you a sob story, this is the truth. I feel like a child talking this way. I really can't face up to it, I can't take it like a man. It makes me feel angry that I am not as powerful as I thought I was. I am really just a cry baby."

The expressions above of genuine feeling on the part of the patient, and his willingness to admit these unacceptable feelings are the most significant evidence of the strength of the transference and the success of the therapy to date.

The patient continued to review the origin of his conflict with his mother and finally in the last interview before his regular therapist returned and in the first interview after his return, he reviewed in detail the experience of his abandonment by his mother and his reaction to it.

"Before the 9th grade, I was hanging around with a group of friends and we were getting into a little trouble now and then. My mother used to ask what we did and I used to trust her at that time. One day I told her a few things we had done and asked her not to say anything, but she got on the phone and called up all the parents of my friends and told them. The next day I had no friends. They were all mad at me and this lasted for 6 or 7 months.

"I would stay home with nothing to do and that was when I really began to get sick. I don't think about it much anymore, but it used to make me feel terrible. It was terrible staying home every day. I used to get teased by these friends constantly and I never got angry with them. I'd get angry with them now. I should have smashed their heads in. I wanted to tell my mother what she had done, but I never could tell her. I hated her. She used to ask me what was wrong. It really was a very bad time for me, it hurt me very much.

"About now I really started doing lousy in school, getting poor grades. When I went into the 10th grade, I flunked twice. Then I began to lose respect for my mother, and to do things to spite her, but it carried over to my father and I would do things to spite him too."

This painful recognition came out in fits and starts. When the patient stopped the therapist immediately said: "You make a good start, but then you stop, and why is that?"

Patient: "I know I have anger, hate and love for them, but I can only take it to a certain extent. I know they didn't care about me, but I don't like to talk about it because it hurts me."

The therapist responded: "Do you stop because it hurts to talk about it?"

Patient: "I think I have said my feelings till I'm blue in the face. It is hard enough saying it once let alone saying it over again. I thought I wasn't getting enough attention from my mother, my brothers were taking it away."

Now the therapist brought George back to the 9th grade experience.

Patient: "I felt lonely and isolated and had no friends—just because I told my mother something and she went and screwed me up. I had a fairly good attitude in the 9th grade, but in the 10th grade I didn't care about anything. I lost trust in people, really started hating my mother. I should have told her but I couldn't.

"I started to get back at her in my own little ways. I was riding in the car with my father one day and he asked me what I was trying to do to my mother. I screamed at him: 'what is she doing to me.' She got the message, she used to say: 'You hate me don't you,' and I would say: 'Oh no, mother.' Sometimes my mind shuts off and I can't think of anything to say. What was I saying just now?"

Then George brought himself back: "I liked to see my mother get upset, I felt so much hatred for her. At times she seemed so sad I used to go to the park but then I would fantasy all day long about what I could do instead of staying at home. I had spurts of anger and would yell at her, I'd feel very lonely that nobody cared about me, not even my parents. That is why I feel so lonely today."

The therapist pointed out that the patient seemed somewhat detached from what he was saying.

Patient: "I've had so many feelings, so many times, that I have run out of emotions." After a pause he went on: "These feelings of sadness and loneliness go back to that, but I don't feel like that at the moment. It does go back to my mother's telling the confidence I gave her. If I felt that angry all the time, I would be a wreck. I think I am ready to talk about all the things that happened with my parents. I have some explaining to do to them—why I acted the way I did. I don't know if I can, but I would like to try.

"I reacted to people here the same as I did at home, but I think I have done a good job in controlling it. I have been having a battle with myself. The other day I was lying on my bed and started screaming at myself: 'stop, stop it, don't react to these people this way! You are just ruining yourself.' I tried to stop in the past but couldn't, now I think I can.

"I used to have constant conflicts with myself and my self-destructive side would always win out, and I'd go out and screw myself. I thought I was just completely gone. Now when I get into these moods where I feel nobody cares, I can think it through and do the constructive thing. I used to get a sadistic kick out of doing the bad thing. Now I really care about what happens and don't have to do self-destructive things, and for the most part I can talk about the way I am feeling."

George here described the effects of control of his acting out which permitted him to seek alternate ways of dealing with his feelings. He went on to describe his symbiotic needs: "It goes back to the same old feeling, jealousy. I have to be the center of everything. I know I say I don't need attention, but when attention is directed to others I get this feeling nobody cares about me. I know it is all wrong, and that I have no right to think that way. I get so upset I can't even enter in when I know I want to."

When the patient's regular therapist returned for the next interview he continued right where he had left off.

Patient: "I get this feeling of loneliness and emptiness and sadness. I found out it was all caused by my mother. I never thought she cared. I never got any attention or love from her and it carried over from the past into the present, and it is the reason I have reacted the way I have to this other patient [female patient]. I have really been very jealous lately."

Patient then recapitulated the conflict with the mother in terms of his relationship with the female patient, Bess: "When I got no attention from her I got very angry. I stopped working in school and would be angry all day and would overreact, and only when I talked to the doctor about my mother did I stop. Mother didn't care so I let myself go." The patient then reviewed again his acting out in the 9th grade, and redescribed the traumatic incident of his mother's betrayal of his confidence, when she phoned the mothers of all his friends and told them "all about a bunch of things I did with my friends."

After reviewing what he had presented in the previous interview, he went on to say: "When mother attempted to direct her attention to someone else I felt she didn't care about me—so I'd do stupid things and it ruined my whole day. I would really do lousy in school unless I had a good day with her—it depended on whether or not I had a good day. She did give me more attention than anyone else, but her looking at someone else made me angry. At home I felt my brothers were getting all the attention and I wasn't getting any. I wanted her but couldn't get her, so I went out and screwed myself. I was really stupid too."

The doctor offered the interpretation that when he was not the exclusive focus of this girl's or mother's attention he got angry. He needed exclusive attention, a need which was by its nature insatiable.

Patient: "I guess my overreaction to Bess goes back to my mother and my home. The problem now is, now that I know about it, what do I do about it? I overreact to the slightest thing she does with someone else, but still I know she likes me. I'm too sensitive. That time with my mother, too, when I was in the 9th grade, the emptiness and sadness was unbearable so I blocked it all out by not caring and became self-destructive. When you block something out, you think it doesn't affect you but it really does.

"I need someone to love. I need to have everything revolve around me —it's unrealistic I know. I want to be everything in some person's life. I had it when I was younger, but I haven't had it in a long, long time with my mother!"

When the therapist again questioned why George needed this, George said: "Well, I don't know. Sometimes I think I can do things on my own. Sometimes I'm not sure I need someone to love." Facing this possibility, the patient shrank back saying: "No, I don't really mean that. I guess I do want to be dependent on somebody. But I'm *not* going to let myself get so dependent on somebody that I can get myself screwed up."

Following this, George talked about his difficulty in talking to the mother, how she would withdraw making him feel worse; he said: "Since she didn't care, and wouldn't understand. I felt sad and lonely because she wouldn't talk to me."

Then under increasing apprehension about the impending confrontation with his parents—that is, now he must attempt to discuss with them matters that he has been unable to touch upon since age 13, thus running the risk of further abandonment—his anxiety rose to such a pitch that to handle it he regressed into serious acting out by tricking one of the hospital aides to obtain some "pot." This he smoked on the sly and wrote a letter asking to sign out of the hospital.

He was thereby expressing his dual desire to strike back at his parents as well as at the hospital for "permitting" him to have pot. Throughout this period until the pot was discovered he was truculent and challenging in every interview, remained adamant about his intention to sign out and responded to all confrontation by the therapist about his real feelings with denial. When the pot was discovered, and he was confronted with it, George finally revealed his unbearable anxiety as the reason for his desire to take pot to get relief. He was given convincing support by his therapist and agreed to joint interviews with the parents.

CHAPTER 10

Casework Treatment of the Parents

At the same time George was going through Phases I and II of the treatment in the hospital his parents were being seen in casework treatment by the social worker. This treatment also consisted of three phases: the preparatory phase before the joint interviews, the joint interview phase (the parents being seen individually as well as in joint interviews), and the phase following the joint interviews.

I decided to devote a separate chapter to the joint interviews because they are of special importance. I have indicated in Chapter 10 at what point in the casework treatment of the parents the joint interviews began. Therefore, if he wishes, the reader can skip to Chapter 11 and then return.

The Borderline Syndromes of Mr. and Mrs. Graves have been vividly presented in their individual histories. The following detailed accounts of their casework treatment illustrates all the cases of mothers clinging to their children to defend themselves against their own feelings of abandonment; of fathers crippled by their own developmental difficulties and unable to respond to the mature demands of fatherhood. The reader is urged to re-read pp. 85–89 at this point. In the following pages, one will appreciate the stubborn resistance to change of both parents and patient—the tenacious strength of the tie that binds.

GEORGE'S MOTHER

Mrs. Graves was transferred to the adolescent program social worker after several months with another worker. Her former social worker had encouraged her to dwell on her past, which resulted in a deepening of her depression and created a frightening dependency on the social worker, to the point that Mrs. Graves was having frequent and severe anxiety attacks. Our aims were to give Mrs. Graves enough awareness of her difficulties in parenting, together with their historical origin in her own childhood, to enable her with our guidance to allow her adolescent to separate and individuate, that is, to induce her to give up clinging to him as a defense against her abandonment feelings and to become a more effective parent. We pinned our hopes on change in parental behavior rather than change in character structure.

First the social worker asked Mrs. Graves to give her a blow by blow description of a typical day's activity, along with the feelings she had doing these things. This very quickly led into Mrs. Graves' feelings about the children and her husband and her inability to wait out their delays and procrastinations when she wanted something done.

Discussion of some of her past accomplishments, for example, education and jobs, allowed the social worker to support her shaky sense of self. This led to a description of her pregnancy with George and her feelings about both the pregnancy and giving up her work. She did not like giving up work and continued till she was 7 months pregnant. After the birth of her baby she had a terrific desire to return to work, but could not do that and take care of George because she had no help. George was a very demanding baby. She could not take her frustrations out on her husband —so she took them out on her child: "At least he'd cry." She then spoke about the hardships she encountered with her husband's business uncertainties and the subsequent moves to different cities that the latter entailed.

Mrs. Graves began the second interview by describing the interdependence between herself and her husband. She described how intensely she needed a definite reaction from him and that she would often try to provoke him to react by getting angry. He responded by wanting peace at any price which only aggravated her more. She described how difficult George was as a baby and how her husband failed to take part in his care or to give her support. "I tend to give the impression that I can handle it . . . like whistling when scared . . . if I let someone take over then what do I have?" This described Mrs. Graves' dilemma perfectly. Her husband unable to satisfy her and her dependency needs unmet, she took over control of her family herself, remaining frustrated, angry, and frightened. She was unable to give up this control because she had learned that her husband would only let her down further.

The third interview raised some concrete issues about how to handle the acting out of her two sons who were still at home. The social worker stressed the reasons she and her husband should pull together, which led into a discussion of her handling of George's acting out, including her feelings of guilt and ambivalence about him. She related how her ambivalence was intensified when her husband left handling George completely up to her, right or wrong.

Mrs. Graves' first inkling that George and she might have similar feelings as well as background (i.e., rejection, withdrawal, and acting out) came in the fourth interview, when the social worker was aware that enough of a relationship had developed to allow her to explore some of Mrs. Graves' history to tie it in with present feelings and problems. This is when Mrs. Graves confessed her inability to remember even what her mother looked like and told about the arguments between her parents; even then she felt in some kind of control—because she could break up the arguments by throwing temper tantrums on the neighbor's lawn.

She appeared to have both positive and negative memories about her father. She described herself as "never a happy child." Mrs. Graves then spoke about her own acting out and the feelings behind it—rejection, a need for attention, and a plea for love. The social worker proceeded to compare these feelings to George's as the likely basis of his acting out.

In the fifth interview, Mrs. Graves, continuing the thought trend from the previous interview, described the "volcano" in her before George came into the hospital. She discussed her resentment of her husband for not helping to handle George, but, on the other hand, her fears in thinking that her husband might help her cope with the boys at home. With this clue the social worker broached the idea of Mrs. Graves giving up some of her controls while at the same time she worked with the husband to take over these same controls and more responsibility.

Mrs. Graves also described her dependency on her husband and her complete retributive withdrawal after he had left her for a weekend to go duck hunting. "I'll show him I don't need him—if he doesn't need me I'll get even." She described much the same feelings about the patient and his acting out. "If he hurts me, I'll hurt him."

In the sixth interview, Mrs. Graves continued to describe her dependency needs and her conflicts with her husband. "I want him to be punished . . . if only he learns more about himself, I could love him more." Mrs. Graves began to see the reversal of roles in her family, how she was "the big bad wolf" and her husband was "sweetness and love." At the same time, she discussed her unreadiness to take a "back seat," how she still was unsure of her husband. The husband was at this point supporting Mrs. Graves' efforts at discipline of the children, but he had yet to take the initiative in these matters himself.

"My husband hurts me by saying and doing nothing," said Mrs. Graves to illustrate her feeling of rejection.

The social worker was again able to draw a parallel between this feeling of rejection by her husband and George's feelings of being neglected and withdrawn from by her.

Mrs. Graves once spontaneously and with great effort told of a love affair she had not mentioned before. She related how she had given her husband broad hints about this relationship with the husband of a friend.

She recalled her great embarrassment when her husband wished them to continue to see the other couple socially. She mentioned that she retreats to this affair in fantasy whenever she is disappointed in and withdrawing from her husband. Recognizing her anger at Mr. Graves' lack of response to her hints, she finally told him directly about the affair and was quite upset at his lack of immediate reaction. He still wanted to continue seeing the man socially. Mrs. Graves finally made her husband choose between her and his friend: "Whom do you like better?" At the same time, Mrs. Graves spoke about her difficulty in letting go of the controls in the management of her family and how empty she felt without them: "I don't know where I belong."

At the same time, Mrs. Graves was able to talk about the positive way she and Mr. Graves were handling the boys at home and how pleased they were with the results. She, however, noted that somehow George was always more difficult. "I was madder at George."

In the seventh interview Mrs. Graves related how she transferred some of her unmet dependency needs from her husband to George. "I am a clinging mother . . . I say, love me please—don't love daddy more."

In the next interview Mrs. Graves reviewed in more detail her feelings of being let down by her husband. She discussed the difficulties in their sexual relationship, how she always complied with him, because she was afraid to hurt him, and how the odd part was that a great deal of their relationship was based on sex. She then spoke about her further disappointment in her husband's family and how somehow she had hoped they would have taken the place of her own inadequate family. These discussions raised her anxiety to such a pitch that she had an anxiety attack.

In the ninth interview the social worker reassured Mrs. Graves that that attack was not a serious matter and assuaged her fear that she was "crazy." What actually brought on the attack was that her husband in discussing his neglect with her expressed how dependent he was on her. This raised Mrs. Graves' fear of abandonment, if he needed so much caring himself. "When emotions are brought up my defenses go down . . . what did my mother mean by dying and leaving me . . . I might be left again . . . I get this overwhelming feeling of loneliness . . . I'm afraid my husband can't control outside forces."

By the tenth interview Mrs. Graves and her husband discussed their feelings in more detail. Mrs. Graves was now less angry and her husband was able to tolerate more of her anger without withdrawing into his customary passivity. Mrs. Graves emphasized how hard this was for her as she was used to being mad. "My anger is my defense, when I'm not angry, I'm scared." She recalled that when her mother and father let her down, she'd be angry rather than hurt.

In the eleventh interview Mrs. Graves elaborated on her abandonment depression and her own defensive acting out both as an adolescent and young adult and how disappointed she was that she did not get caught. She herself now drew the parallel between her feelings and the patient's. "Show me that you care—I've been hurt, hurt, hurt . . . nobody else gets hurt but me, couldn't they see that? I'm no idiot, I know what I'm doing, why don't you ask me how I feel? I wanted George to owe me. As he rejected me I felt hurt. I hurt him, he'd hurt me back—then I'd reject him more . . . I told him: 'you'll shape up over my dead body or yours. . . .' I had to find the punch that would get to him. I'm physically in better shape when my barriers are up [one of her favorite and recurrent phrases]."

Following this emotional breakthrough and violent revelation of her abandonment feelings, Mrs. Graves became more resistant, withdrawn, and had little to say in the next two interviews. The social worker interpreted her withdrawal as another defense against her recently revealed intense feelings of abandonment and tried to make Mrs. Graves perceive the effects of her withdrawal in the treatment and on the people around her, that is, her husband and the patient. Interestingly enough Mrs. Graves further revealed her intense dependency at this time through a dream of being admitted to the hospital.

It was at this point that joint interviews were started. We were encouraged that Mrs. Graves and Mr. Graves had gained enough understanding of themselves and of George's acting out to warrant our bringing patient and parents together to attempt to work out a better pattern of family communication. Here our interviews began to focus more on Mrs. Graves' relationship with George as well as her husband.

With this shift in focus, Mrs. Graves again felt abandoned by the social worker and showed her resentment by withdrawal. When the social worker canceled an appointment, Mrs. Graves sent her a spiteful letter terminating their relationship. It was only after much firmness that she was persuaded to come in for the fifteenth interview. She said she was not going to be hurt again, that she had felt badly at the previous change of social workers, and that she would not allow her defenses to be let down again.

She recognized that this attitude might be self-destructive but "hurting myself is an old friend." She declared that she had lost faith in the social worker; that she was "on again, off again"; that none of us knew what we were doing. She was really conveying her fear of again being abandoned. She said: "I will cooperate up to a point. I will cease to interrupt or talk . . . but I don't intend to put myself in a dependent position again . . . it's all or nothing . . . the love affair is over . . . I will not tell you my feelings, what goes on inside me is my own business." The social worker pointed out to Mrs. Graves the difficulties inherent in sustaining such an attitude of aloofness and interpreted it as a reaction to the change in their relationship, that Mrs. Graves felt the change as an abandonment, became angry, and withdrew.

In the fifteenth interview, Mrs. Graves returned to talking about her relationship to her husband. She told of her pleasure in shocking her husband with the news of the affair she had with their mutual friend. However, she had quickly tired of his anger and bewilderment as she had with her own. Whenever her husband got angry, he sent her flowers, which enraged her even more. "He rewards me for something I did wrong . . . he makes me full of guilt and anxiety." She deliberately undercut him by canceling a date with the friends with whose husband she was involved rather than allowing him the dignity of doing so.

Mrs. Graves then admitted that she had taken two tranquilizers to control her talk in the interview and that she did not intend to reveal more of her feelings. She wanted to remain separate, to block the social worker, to pay her back for letting her down by calling off an interview. In addition, Mrs. Graves related her feelings of being left out now that the focus of treatment had shifted to her son. With these feelings of abandonment coming to the surface, she asked questions such as: "Who am I? If I can't be considered important, then what am I?" She talked about her dependency and how frightened she was that she would lose those around her—yet damned them when they are there. She was able to recall and see the similarity of her feelings of abandonment by her mother and her desperate loneliness and anger at her mother's final desertion, her death.

By the sixteenth interview Mrs. Graves' defenses were again intact. She came in talking glibly about the patient and her desire to have him independent soon. "When does he fly from the nest? . . . you don't want a stone around your neck . . . only for a part of your life." The social worker began to investigate if the patient's reentry into the family situation was not shifting the balance of Mr. and Mrs. Graves' relationship and interfering with their dependent ties. Mrs. Graves admitted that her husband appeared to be more assertive and she was floundering in her efforts to find a proper way to behave and respond: "If I don't get angry I don't know who I am. I'm not myself any more."

In the seventeenth interview Mrs. Graves related the details of an anxiety attack in which she felt she just had to hold on to her husband with a "don't leave me feeling" (again a plausible reaction to the shift in their previous relationship).

In the eighteenth interview she talked about feeling left out of the treatment scene now that the focus of treatment was more on the patient. She tried to retrieve attention for herself by talking about her own feelings of being abandoned and never feeling loved. She repeated that one of the few memories she has of her mother was of being hurt, of enemas and cathartics. She spoke about some of the maids she felt close to and how one by one they dropped out of her life. But the memory of one maid she still cherished and maintained that she still loved her.

Following this interview the Graves' went away for a long-planned 1-week vacation. George was upset by this and later told them so. Mrs. Graves came in for the nineteenth interview resenting any responsibility for the patient's feelings. "I feel like I'm walking on eggs. I can't do anything to please myself without hurting George."

The social worker tried to link up her own feelings of being abandoned with those of her son. Mrs. Graves was gradually able to see a relationship between her own behavior and feelings and those of her son's, but she was not sure how much she was willing to go back into her own experiences to understand George. However, she had already explored somewhat the sea of her past, the tide had already begun to turn, and Mrs. Graves began to investigate how painful her feelings were for her, hence her defenses of anger, counter questioning, and constant surface involvement to keep people away from her and then the feeling of total loneliness that followed: "I can't keep it up all the time—I have nothing to give. Hurt as I am I can't give anyone any love at the moment. It's so much harder to give love when its demanded. I get that leave me alone feeling. Don't ask me. Don't make me feel responsible for every feeling I have, and that George has . . . it's like dragging something from me when already I am empty—I tell you again, I have nothing to give—I want to get. Can't you see that I am the one who needs attention?"

By the twentieth interview Mrs. Graves seemed stronger and able to tolerate the shift in the family balance better. She allowed her husband to handle the patient's threat to sign out and allowed her youngest son to criticize her. In the twenty-first interview Mrs. Graves "acted out" by reading a letter on the social worker's desk, thus discovering that the social worker was pregnant. Mrs. Graves felt quite guilty about finding out about the social worker's condition in such a stealthy way and finally admitted it, yet could not discuss her feelings about it further.

In the twenty-second interview Mrs. Graves, beset with fresh guilt toward the social worker was again trying to withdraw, but the social worker, conscious of the part of her countertransference, skillfully drew parallel lines between Mrs. Graves' past experiences and her feelings about the social worker's pregnancy. She was awakened to her need to try things on her own; this was heartily supported. However, as soon as this was discussed, she reverted to her resentment at having had all the responsibilities for her children. She reviewed George's birth and childhood, and recalled her feeling of total helplessness: she hadn't known what to do when George cried, or when he walked and followed her around—wanting to be with her all the time: "I'd panic . . . I'd hide from him . . . I'd put him in the bedroom and I wouldn't let him see me . . . once he'd catch sight of me . . . I was caught. I never knew what to do with him." In this same interview Mrs. Graves related how she felt reprimanded by the social worker when she no longer permitted her to be in the office alone. However, at the same time Mrs. Graves betrayed her disappointment that she had not disciplined her to stay out of the social worker's office sooner.

Now the treatment had definitely shifted. Mrs. Graves was no longer treated so much as an individual, but more as the mother in a family unit. We were in the separation stage of treatment. First the therapy had dealt with her as an individual, then as a wife and mother as well as an individual in these roles.

In the twenty-fourth interview Mrs. Graves spoke about how she and her husband had bandied back and forth the discipline of the children as a weapon to get back at each other, that is, whenever her husband set some rule, she would not go along with it, and vice versa. She admitted this, recalling that: "I almost drowned the children in the bathtub and he lay calmly on the couch, with me saying to myself, you stupid ass, how can you let anybody do this."

In the twenty-fifth, twenty-sixth, and twenty-seventh interviews Mrs. Graves talked about practical matters of taking care of her home, her children, and her husband; and about her fear of responsibility and, on the other hand, her fear of losing control. She spoke about feeling unneeded if she didn't have controls at home. "I fear losing the known . . . giving up controls . . . it's part of my life. If I give them up I'm going into the unknown. I've been living off my children and husband for my own fulfillment. I'd love to let go, but it's the only way I know." She spoke about her past relationship with her husband and her transfer of feelings from her mother and father to him. Awareness of this inappropriate transfer of emotion enabled her to see her husband more realistically.

In the twenty-eighth interview her husband had gone out of town on business and many of her old abandonment feelings returned even with so short a separation from him. She said she tried to keep these feelings "under wraps" until she could see the social worker and discharge them and get some support. She pled: "Please somebody say I'm right to feel so lost!"

The remainder of the treatment interviews were concerned with working with Mr. and Mrs. Graves as a husband and wife rather than mother and father or sister and brother to each other. We constantly confronted them with their dependency on each other and encouraged them in mutual respect and independence. Their sexual relations were discussed from the same point of view. For both of them sex had been an expression of dependency, effectively blocking the development of an adult relationship.

Mrs. Graves' treatment is far from finished. However, she has been brought to awareness of her needs, taught ways to control her acting out and to behave appropriately as a mother. Mrs. Graves has expressed a willingness to continue work on these aspects of herself—yet the danger of disappointment or failure still looms in the future. She must continue to be seen until she is better able to handle her problems on her own, with an adult realization of what her responsibilities should be as a wife and as a mother of three children.

GEORGE'S FATHER

The goal of therapy with Mr. Graves was to help him deal with his dependency on his wife and his passivity in such a way that he could assert himself and better fulfill the roles of a father and husband. In the beginning he was superficially pleasant, emotionally quite removed and distant, and only aware of "his love" for his wife. He denied both his anger and his frustration in regard to his son. Although obviously annoyed at being asked to repeat his son's history, he grudgingly complied. Encouragement from the social worker enabled him to express the annoyance and frustration he felt at having to repeat this history to the courts, to other social workers and doctors.

In the second interview he admitted that there were "some minor" difficulties with his wife that he would usually ignore. He said: "Getting mad goes against my grain, I have a high boiling point." The social worker pointed out that he expressed much of his anger in passivity and withdrawal and that he might be better off by verbalizing it.

By the next interview Mr. Graves had taken this suggestion seriously and made tentative attempts to let off steam. As he got positive results at home he became enthusiastic about the idea. He started to set limits for the children but was blocked in doing the same with his wife by his fear of her anger and withdrawal. He related that his wife when angry withdrew from him sexually and he did not let emotion show because of his fear of disrupting his relationship with her.

By the fourth interview Mr. Graves was talking more about his dependency on his wife and his willingness to accept almost anything at home to have her approval and "peace at any price." This admission puzzled him since he knew that in his business life he was so much more aggressive. Concurrently, he would discuss his poor relationship with his parents, how little attention he would receive from them. He was unable at this time to relate this need for affection to his relationship with his wife.

Mr. Graves' initial resistance was manifested by his beginning every interview with a concrete issue such as some difficulty with insurance or the court. This behavior was interpreted as a resistance. The source was not explored at this time, and instead he was reflected back to the business of the interview. In the fifth interview, he discussed his feelings of hurt, anger, and disappointment at the failure of his attempts to handle George. These feelings were hidden by his emotional withdrawal. "I felt completely defeated. He did the same thing again. It was very frustrating. I smacked him a couple of times saying: 'For God's sakes cry so your mother knows I am doing something.' I found it difficult to punish him when his mother demanded it, especially if I wasn't angry."

In the sixth interview Mr. Graves described how he was trying to be more active in the management of the remaining two boys at home. He began to discuss some of his feelings with his wife and was surprised to find out how his withdrawal from his children had affected her. She told me that she felt it did not matter to me. This led to an awareness that he had been missing an "awful lot" that was going on in his family and he became genuinely eager to learn how he might change to rectify some of the past.

In the seventh interview, Mr. Graves dramatically illustrated his extraordinary dependency on his wife by spending the entire interview talking about his own anxiety at his wife's anxiety attack. He voiced his fear of her having a nervous breakdown, saying: "My god what if I have to send her off." The social worker attempted to reassure him about his wife's emotional strength.

In the eighth interview, Mr. Graves returned to the previous theme this time stressing the importance of physical affection from his wife relating it to his inability to get any reassurance from any other kind of emotional expression from his family. The ninth interview crystallized Mr. Graves' dilemma at home. He was beginning to assert himself but was made extremely anxious by his wife's withdrawal. He emphasized his own inability to function when his wife denied him her approval and affection. The social worker questioned whether it was his wife's withdrawal or his great need for her that troubled him and suggested that he not accept his wife's withdrawal so passively but attempt to talk things out. He responded with resentment at the anxiety it caused him to discuss his wife with the social worker but nevertheless said: "This might save my family. I didn't realize it was heading to 'nowheresville'." This interview was evidently too much for Mr. Graves because in the next interview he was extremely resistant, claiming that he was tired, unable to discuss very much and was quite worried as to whether his self-assertion might cause his wife to continue to withdraw from him.

In the tenth interview Mr. Graves' resistance subsided and he was able to sketch out in more detail the greatest dependency on his wife. "I need to know that she is happy and doesn't need anything else. I need to know she loves me physically." He also spoke of how frightened he was to show too much emotion himself as this meant getting involved and that he would not then be able to function. "I can't operate, if I let all these things hurt me." This awareness caused his anxiety to reach a peak and he became resistant, wondering whether George and his wife should not learn to accept him just as he was and why he had to change. The social worker stepped in to suggest that he might be angry with her for forcing him to face these uncomfortable things. He responded: "I don't like to be probed and it's difficult to reveal these things to someone I don't know. It would be easier with a gray haired old doctor." His resistance continued throughout the eleventh interview.

By the twelfth interview Mr. Graves' resistance was broken through and he burst forth with his continued dilemma, that of asserting himself and then having his wife withdraw, and his anxiety about whether he would be able to handle her coolness and win back the warmth of her affection. The social worker pointed out that Mr. Graves was caught in between his son's needs, his wife's needs, and his own needs. If he asserted himself for his own needs and for his son he might lose what he desperately needed from his wife—her approval: "She's punished me in the past; she'd be cool toward me for 2 or 3 days and she'd know she could hurt me, that's why I take a back seat. I'm weighing her against George and that's what I'm saying. He's got to go on his own and we can still live our life together as best we can." The intrusion of the patient and its part in upsetting Mr. Graves' dependency on his wife was then discussed. Mr. Graves was finally able to express his desperate fears of his wife committing suicide and his losing her for good.

In the thirteenth interview Mr. Graves appeared very depressed and sadly related that his wife had told him about the affair with a mutual friend. He was angry but quite obviously frightened to even discuss it. He related again how the physical show of love was so important to him and how he could tolerate almost anything but this kind of desertion. "I'm trying to be rational, but I feel terrible inside. I'm very much in love with her. I wish I weren't. It hurts me so much. I'm not showing anger over this affair, I'm doing everything to show her I love her." The social worker pointed out that if he felt angry no matter how he tried to hide it, his anger would probably show in his controlled behavior and this in turn would be seen as withdrawal by his wife.

He responded: "I'm so upset that I could take that little runt and wipe the street with him." To reassure Mr. Graves about his anger the social worker discussed how intense feelings of anger were quite common but that there was, however, a world of difference between feeling them and carrying them out and also that he seemed unable even to tolerate the thought of anger. He agreed, saying: "Anger just makes me sick because of what I would like to do, pack my bags and get out. I feel terrible, I know how much I would miss her. I want to get her to love me again. I'm afraid to do something rash." Finally, revealing the extent of his dependency and the pain of his dilemma, he said: "I want to hurt her but I'm afraid to disturb the situation. I want things the way they were [before George's treatment was begun]." He then lamented the loss of the status quo with his wife that ensued following the onset of the treatment and George's hospitalization.

This interview again raised Mr. Graves' anxiety so that he began the next interview with his usual defense of citing concrete issues to avoid talking about his painful feelings. The social worker at this point interpreted this behavior as a way of avoiding discussion of the issue raised in the previous interview—his feelings about his wife's affair. After a good deal of pressure on the social worker's part, he admitted that he had wanted to stop the interviews and that thinking about his anger frightened him. As he returned to wishing he could restore the status quo of their marriage, the social worker suggested that perhaps this feeling had been revealed to his son who probably would interpret it as a rejection. He admitted that this might be true, saying: "I'm not sure I can handle all of George's monkey wrenches."

In the next interview (the fifteenth) held in conjunction with the joint interviews much of the time was devoted to discussing Mr. Graves' resistance to discussing his feelings. "It's a question of emotional investment in a future obligation. How far is he going to go? What is the end result? I want some guarantees about the consequences of treatment in terms of reality and finances."

In the sixteenth interview with the onset of joint interviews his resistance began to take more subtle forms. In the joint interview he suddenly pronounced that the patient would have to do all the changing, he would not. "We've learned a lot and we've changed some but certainly there are things that won't change." His vacillation back and forth between awareness and resistance was indicated in the next two interviews. In the former he discussed his fear of losing his dependent relationship with his wife if he took more responsibility for the family, admitting that he was actually affected by his wife's mood. Then in the next interview he again said that the patient should do all the changing and not he or his wife. In the nineteenth interview he was again complaining about his inability to continue treatment because of finances. The social worker now being fully apprised of his financial condition was aware that this was a flimsy defense and interpreted it to him.

In the next interview Mr. Graves talked about his own struggle for independence from his family of origin. Just when he was beginning to feel financially independent from his parents, the hospital bills forced him to get money from his parents. He spoke about not wanting to cowtow or be beholden to his parents. "Whenever they gave anything it always was on their terms." He recounted that one of the most important days of his life was the day he was able to take his parents out to dinner.

The social worker interpreted to Mr. Graves how his son must feel about being dependent on him to relate this to his feelings toward his own father—the grandfather had let down the father and the father had let down the son. Mr. Graves resented these comparisons, saying: "Nobody got my parents off the same hook." He then again went back to lamenting "the good old days."

When he came to the twenty-first interview Mr. Graves was very upset over a disagreement he and his wife had had. He asked for advice as to how to make amends. His wife, he said, was able to talk circles around him. "She's a good talker, she makes me feel foolish, but I desperately fear she may leave me or be taken from me." However, in the twenty-second interview he showed that he had been able to take over more responsibility for his own son's future as well as for his other two sons. But when the social worker tried to get him to elaborate on his fear of loss, in an abrupt about face, Mr. Graves denied such feelings. In the twenty-third interview he voluntarily mentioned that he could not afford to revolve all his emotions around his wife's. He knew she was hurt because she was no longer the center of attention, but that was reality. He never had listened to his wife so he never had to handle her. The results of these discussions were beginning to show in the joint interviews as Mr. Graves began to take much more responsibility.

In the twenty-fourth interview, he seemed better able to grasp what his role of father should be and seemed to understand what was expected from both his wife and George. The difficult part for him was that he seemed to miss the regular attention he used to get from his wife. However, in the twenty-fifth interview he even discussed the fact that since he had taken some assertive steps to assume his natural role as a father, his sexual life with his wife had improved.

In the twenty-sixth interview he had had to be away the previous week on a business trip and upon his return, he found his wife distant toward him and he again had to cope with her withdrawal. However, he no longer was devastated and tried somewhat successfully to discuss her feelings with her. "I like myself much better, I am beginning to see what was missing in our marriage." In the twenty-seventh interview he continued to talk about his taking on his new responsibilities as well as the anxiety that this entailed for him.

Mr. Graves continued to take more responsibility, especially with George when he began coming home for visits. He even asserted himself with the social worker and the doctor when he felt that they should be handling certain responsibilities such as getting a bill from his son's tutor. He became angry and defensive when George brought up a couple of things he did not like about his father, but he was able to express these feelings after an initial refusal to discuss them. He began to discuss his fear of the patient's coming home and how this would affect the family, particularly his relations with his wife. He made plans to continue the treatment after George left the hospital.

This series of twenty-seven interviews outlines clearly Mr. Graves' clinging to his wife and his passivity as defenses against the fear of abandonment that was aroused by his efforts to become assertive and take his natural position as the father of the family. He was aided not only by his work with the social worker but also by the recognition in the joint interviews of the destructive effects of his passivity in relation to his son. Although he has become aware of the problem and has begun to make efforts to deal with it, he still has recurrent anxiety about his own capacity to cope and will require a good deal of supportive treatment in the future if he is to be successful. He continues to harbor underneath his awareness of conflict, the wish to restore his dependency with his wife through the exclusion of the patient, a conflict requiring more work.

Slowly, painfully with great reluctance and resistance Mrs. Graves was brought to an awareness of the tie that binds, that is, her clinging to George to defend herself against her feelings of abandonment. The destructiveness of this behavior on his efforts to separate and individuate were pointed out. She continued to struggle but was much more able to control her clinging behavior. Similarly, Mr. Graves was brought to an awareness that his passivity and dependence on his wife were defenses against his feelings of abandonment which were destructive to his son's efforts to develop a masculine identity.

CHAPTER 11

Phase II: Joint Interviews

The purpose of joint interviews is to alleviate the communication block between patient and parents that facilitated the acting out, to establish new verbal channels of communication, to enable verbalization of anger about the abandonment previously impossible for the patient, and to foster insight into the pathologic family dynamics so that the latter can be worked on both individually and collectively.

Preparation and timing are important to the success of the joint interviews. Minimum preparation of the patient includes control of the acting out and working through of the homicidal rage and suicidal depression associated with the separation.

Preparation of the parents in weekly visits with the social worker requires working through of the mother's resistance to separation, that is, her clinging, and the recognition and relief of both parents' anger and guilt as well as an awareness on their part of how their own childhood conflicts impair their functioning as parents, that is, how their need to defend themselves against feelings of abandonment by clinging to their adolescent is destructive to his growth and development.

As the joint interviews begin, the patient, in the setting of a transference relationship with his doctor, must face again the pain of abandonment by his mother to find a better relationship. If the interviews are begun too soon they will only create greater conflict and feelings of abandonment, which will produce further acting out by the patient.

As the patient faces the start of joint interviews, his anxiety rises and he regresses to avoid the pain. Therefore, he needs added support from the therapist. His regression must be interpreted as a way of avoiding the pain of confrontation with the parents which he feels promises a repetition of the feelings of abandonment. He fears that if he asserts himself with his mother, she will withdraw her approval. As the patient tries to express his rage in the interview, he does run head on into the family's defenses, and therefore he does reexperience, in the setting of the interview, the feelings of abandonment that began his clinical illness.

The patient's effort to assert himself and express his rage come up against the mother's and father's defenses against these feelings. The mother has maintained her control by demanding compliance and withdrawing her approval at any sign of self-assertion. The father is usually quite dependent, withdrawn and passive—at least in the home. The patient's verbalization of his anger not only violates the mother's unconscious code of conduct but also threatens the neurotic bind between aggressive mother and passive father. They defend themselves by creating a common barrier against the patient. When the patient comes up against this barrier he sees it only as excluding him from the family, and his loneliness wells up, his anger increases, and he becomes further depressed, hopeless, and hostile.

How the parents handle the patient's behavior strongly affects the outcome of these interviews. Can they accept the patient's hostility? Can they in turn verbalize? Can they change? Can they let go and permit the patient to grow to autonomy without withdrawing supplies? The work with the father tends to go faster than with the mother, since the mother is more intimately involved in the symbiotic bind with the adolescent. She becomes more and more defensive and resistant as the patient becomes more verbal.

The crucial resistances again are the mother's defenses against separation. In some instances this might be severe enough for her to remove the patient from treatment rather than permit therapy to separate her from her adolescent. As the mother feels more abandoned, she becomes more resistant. The therapist must continue to encourage the patient's verbalization and interpret the parents' defenses against the patient's anger. The conflict must then be worked through in the interview. With the beginning of the joint interviews, the content of the patient's individual interviews consists more of the current family dynamics and less of past events.

JOINT INTERVIEWS: ANNE

Let us now return to the case of Anne and see the effect of the joint interviews. Patients and parents have been prepared. The therapist was clearly aware of the family dynamics; that is, there was a symbiotic relation between the patient and the mother, and the mother was dependent on and clinging to the patient, using the patient to fulfill her dependency needs and excluding the father from the relationship. The father was withdrawn from and avoided both the wife and daughter, but tended to support the wife against the daughter—the patient was caught like a pawn in between. The first therapeutic problem in the joint sessions was that the patient's anxiety at the necessity of facing once again her parents with her anger and taking a chance at reexperiencing the feelings of abandonment had caused her to shrink from direct communication, that is, to fall back into her old pattern of acting rather than verbalizing.

This was interpreted to the patient and it was explained that the parents were not conscious of their own behavior, and that the patient really had no alternative other than to attempt communication directly with them.

In the next several interviews the patient did this quite freely, and articulately expressed her anger; this led to what she had feared and became the major therapeutic problem of the joint interviews, that is, the mother's resistance to separation.

The mother's fear of losing the patient caused her to try to frustrate the therapeutic process in every way possible, with almost as much ingenuity as the patient had shown in the initial testing period with the doctor. She would physically cling to the patient at the end of each hour, profusely hugging and kissing her and protesting how good the interview had gone (although it was obvious to both patient and parents that it had not gone well).

Whenever Anne would get close to the father, the mother would withdraw and remain silent. She attempted to divide the patient from her therapist, the therapist from the social worker, and the father from the social worker. She attempted to bribe the patient with gifts.

In response to this Anne reacted to the mother's pressure by becoming more depressed and withdrawn. Patient: "Sometimes I get real lonely when I think about my parents. I guess they care, but they will never give me what I really want. There should be somebody who cares—not just you in the hospital."

In these interviews, the patient began to wonder if the father would recognize the mother's behavior. In this context she mentioned her adoption: "They wanted someone to give things to—they didn't have much with each other."

The patient, realizing the mother was quite upset, was afraid to confront her and was torn between whether to deal with her directly—expressing the anger at the risk of losing what little support she did have—or to maintain the old symbiotic pattern and give up her efforts to individuate. Patient: "This was the only form of relationship I had with them and I am afraid to destroy it because there may be nothing to replace it."

At this point we became concerned that the mother's need to maintain the symbiotic hold on the patient might cause her to take the patient out of the hospital in a final effort to frustrate the therapy. Nevertheless, we decided it was necessary to take this risk. As the pressure mounted, the mother began to complain of physical symptoms and the patient wondered if her mother could really endure the pressure, saying: "Mother had frequently complained that my behavior would kill her, and both mother and father made me feel responsible for mother's symptoms."

Finally, with the therapist's support and pressure, in a dramatic joint interview, Anne confronted the mother and told her that she felt her own mother did not want her to get well, and that she would not as long as the mother keeps playing these games.

The mother took this as an attack and attempted to make the patient feel guilty saying: "Are you happy now—you picked me apart in front of Daddy and all these other people."

As the mother got more upset, the father made it clear to the patient that he did not want the mother to be upset—thus repeating the pattern that had existed for many years before hospitalization.

With interpretation of this pattern, the mother finally expressed what she had been protecting herself against—her anger and disappointment with the patient.

Patient said: "I was messed up when I came to the hospital."

Mother: "I think you were messed up since you were born."

Patient: "I think mother thinks I was born crazy—she hated me almost. When I was 8 years old and mother was in the hospital, I was staying with friends and acting out—father came home and said she would be all right, and then said: 'Are you satisfied, you'll kill her if you don't stop it, you already have her in the hospital'—all she has to do is look upset and I think she is going back to all those horrible ways of getting sick."

The patient was encouraged to express directly what she felt and take the risk of the repercussions as far as her mother's illness was concerned. In the next joint interview the patient was able to deal directly with both mother and father, and her anger at the father's lack of assertiveness, his lack of involvement, and his deferring to the mother all came out with gradual awareness on his part of the role he played in the patient's illness. The father also expressed at this time some feelings of hopelessness about the patient and her illness.

Following this joint interview, the mother, claiming to have an exacerbation of her porphyria, placed herself in the hospital and reported that she would not be available for interviews for awhile. A check with her doctor revealed that the flare-up was minor but he had hospitalized the mother at her request. Nevertheless, the next interview between the patient and her father led to a substantial clarification of the father's role.

The father had been unaware of what he had been doing to his daughter while attempting to preserve the precarious relationship with his wife. As a result, the father visited the mother in the hospital to confront her with her distorted behavior towards the patient, thus removing his support. Afraid that her parents might try to smooth things over again Anne said:

"Mother can't change—I'll have to go it alone. I wonder if it is not a stronger pull to stay sick. There is no way to contend with father's weakness and mother's sickness. He has to let me know that he cares about me—I can't play these kinds of games. This is the only place that cares about me—I can't stay here the rest of my life—there isn't any other place that can care about me without destroying me. I have been dependent on them and haven't done anything alone except mess myself up."

At this point the mother visited home from the hospital, and for the first time the patient also visited. The father was now playing a much more appropriate paternal role and supporting his daughter. The mother was now able to allow the patient free time with the father and did not make a scene at leave taking. Anne's depression now cleared up completely—there was no acting out—her behavior was quite constructive—family communication had been restored and the patient was about to move into the last phase of therapy.

The joint interviews had brought about the following: (1) a verbal channel of communication had been opened up between the patient and her parents, (2) the father had gained a good deal of insight, changed his role, become more of a father figure, and was more involved with his daughter and more assertive with his wife. Now as he gratified some of his wife's dependency needs, the latter was more able to relinquish her clinging hold on her child.

JOINT INTERVIEWS: GRACE

The management of the mother's resistance is so crucial to the success of the family sessions that another brief example is given—the turning point in Grace's interviews with her family.

In joint interviews Grace's mother was withdrawn, depressed, and resistant. In an early session she attempted to project her daughter's difficulties on events outside the family circle; for example, rejections by peers and intrinsic "bad" or "selfish" qualities in the patient herself. Grace persisted in explaining her former depression, her unhappiness in the family, her frustration at the compliance the parents demanded; and she proclaimed her intention to continue to express herself in the future. Both parents became noticeably more threatened and defensive. They viewed family sessions as a battleground in which Grace was "attacking" them and they had no alternative but to use every method at their disposal for defense.

The first major turning point was reached during the third session when both parents continued to project. They insinuated that Grace was either parroting the words of her doctor and the Clinic or that she was under the influence of drugs; in either event they effectively negated the validity of all she had said. An extra session was held the following day to point out that the parents were going to the extreme of attacking Grace's therapist in an attempt to avoid what she was telling them.

Thereafter the father appeared more insightful and accepting of Grace and was much less defensive and more direct in family sessions. However, the mother continued to be withdrawn, showed little affect, and expressed herself only with sarcasm.

Grace's mother often stated that she was either not feeling anything or was so emotionally drained that she could not speak. She walked out near the end of the fourth session. In the fifth session the mother revealed her hurt at Grace's separation from her, her persistent wish to keep Grace a little girl, and her fear of further closeness with Grace because of the risk of once again being hurt by separation. Grace responded that she desired closeness with her mother but would never return to the old role of compliance; if the mother expected that, Grace could not guarantee that she would not again hurt her mother.

In the following session (the sixth) Grace's mother was again withdrawn while Grace spoke of her desire to have a relationship in which she could freely express herself. Grace's mother did not respond but sat stoically with her mouth closed. The father explosively erupted in anger at his wife, telling her that she was pretending not to have any feelings for Grace because she did not want to risk any further closeness. Thereafter, the mother was more verbal and acknowledged her "terror" of being hurt by Grace again. She said that all she felt was "confusion," that she did not want anything but a superficial relationship with Grace in the future, and that since not all children need to grow up with a mother, in the future Grace could do without her.

The mother now escalated the intensity of her withdrawal by not coming to the next session. In addition, she also withdrew from her husband. The father appeared alone for the seventh session informing us that his wife could not be present because she could not start her car. He then revealed that his wife had been very distant toward him during the intervening week and had refused to discuss Grace. We made a suggestion to reschedule the session for later in the week but the father said that he and his wife were leaving on a business trip the next day. It was then arranged over his reluctance for him and his wife to stop at the Clinic on their way out of town.

The mother in the eighth session was emotionally flat and withdrawn. Again Grace addressed herself to her mother, telling her how she desired that they resume their relationship on mutual terms and expressing the feeling that her mother's withdrawal implied that things had to be on mother's terms or not at all. Grace then indicated that she would never comply with her mother's terms as it had been one of the factors that brought about her illness. As the mother still would not reply, the therapist pointed out that her withdrawal from Grace and from her husband during the previous week had alienated them both. The therapist stressed that important relationships were at stake, and asked the mother if she really wanted to alienate and anger the people who were most important to her.

The mother finally responded saying that she could not really accept what her daughter had said to her and had decided to comply verbally with anything and everything so that she would not have to hear anymore. It was again pointed out that she had made a verbal not an emotional commitment and that the net effect of it would be to increase the distance between herself and her husband and daughter. Grace then pointed out that her mother was handling the conflict by compliance and withdrawal, similar to the way Grace herself had handled conflict in the past. Frequent hammering on these points throughout the session finally elicited some change. For the first time the mother expressed a desire to understand; that she did love Grace and desired a relationship with her and wanted time to work on understanding.

JOINT INTERVIEWS: GEORGE GRAVES

The first joint interview began with a discussion of the possibility of the George Graves' signing out and his parents' refusal to have him come home. Then the mother began to talk a great deal about herself, her own problems and anger. The patient responded minimally saying that he got nothing from her, and then the mother explained and apologized. The patient did express some of his anger, but the mother overdid her solicitude. The father was equally solicitous thereby making it difficult for the patient to be free about his anger.

The patient began the second joint interview by giving a note to his father asking for a pair of pants (he already had more than enough); this was obviously a test. However, the parents ignored the emotional context of the request and discussed the concrete issue. The parents proceeded to take over the interview—the mother by asking the patient to express his anger, but actually dominating the interview, causing him to withdraw and not communicate.

The handling of the "pants" issue (a bid for acceptance), which the parents overlooked, recapitulated for the patient his abandonment which threw him into a depression. This was further aggravated by the mother's domineering behavior—sarcastic statements about the patient's anger which made it harder for him to talk; the interview went further and further downhill.

After this interview the patient was furious and depressed. Two hours later he walked out of school and had to be seen by his doctor; he expressed his anger at the mother, at her aggressively taking the note from the father; he stated he felt sorry for his father because his mother dominated him.

The therapist had to (1) put a stop to the mother manipulating the interview, (2) encourage the father to talk more, and (3) interpret to them the patient's withdrawal. After these procedures were instituted, the next interview went better. George talked about his anger at the father, the father's lack of interest in him, and his fury at the father for not standing up for him. He then went back to talk about his anger at the mother from the third grade—how he loved her but felt she had broken his faith.

However, the mother and the father kept interfering as the patient tried to express this anger. They ignored his attempts to talk by taking over the interview and talking about what the patient's future would be. As the doctor brought them back to the patient's anger, however, the mother continued to interrupt George's expression of his feelings. A good dialogue developed between the father and the patient; father said he was hurt by the patient's behavior. The patient under the doctor's guidance then expressed a lot of his feelings of anger at the mother. The interview concluded with the patient saying how much he wanted the father to wear the pants. At this point the mother still needed to be restrained to allow the patient to work through his feelings.

Through the doctor's appropriate therapeutic maneuvers in the next interview, the parents were finally brought to a real emotional confrontation. The doctor interpreted first to them that they were denying emotions by their chatter. He then blocked the mother's constant efforts to interrupt and cut off the patient and blocked the patient's efforts to withdraw; he constantly brought them all back to the emotional issues, supported the patient in his expression of anger at the parents, and when the parents retaliated with a counter attack, again supported the patient.

The patient did verbalize his feelings of futility, anger, and hopelessness to the parents, particularly to the mother, but also to the father—a repetition of what he had done with the therapist in individual sessions before.

The parents responded with a counter attack; they did express some of their own anger, but they joined forces in saying they would not change. The patient had to change—he was the one who was sick (an expression of their hostility toward the patient for revealing his feelings).

The patient, feeling hopeless, got angry, and walked out. The interview ended by stripping all three of their façade—the bare bones of the emotional situation at home were revealed and recapitulated in the interview with the patient giving the characteristic *clinical* responses of hopelessness, depression, and acting out.

At the beginning of the next interview the mother presented a gift of oranges and got no thanks. The patient tested the parents by telling them of his move to a better floor and said that he was depressed. The mother, instead of reacting realistically, came back with false oversolicitous sympathy and the patient remained silent. The doctor confronted both the parents and the patient with their avoidance of their feelings; then he confronted the mother with her oversolicitous behavior, asking her if she was angry. She denied it at first, and her anger then was overlooked in a colloquy about an incident on the patient's record.

The doctor confronted the mother again; this led to a definition of the mutual hostility between mother and son. Confrontation first of the mother and then of the patient brought forth the mother's feeling about the patient's behavior before hospitalization. To the mother the doctor said: "How do you feel about what was happening in the past?"

Mother: "Well, we realized that it was hard for him."

Patient: "He asked you how you were feeling—tell me that."

Mother explained: "I could have broken your neck. I was confused, desperate and dying inside without any understanding."

Patient: "What did you do to correct things?"

Mother: "I yelled and screamed and told you: 'Don't leave this house,' and you would go out anyway. I remember once I called the police on you. They asked what did you do, and said it is not what he did but what he might do and they wouldn't get you. You had me right by the balls."

George: "You have them?"

Mother: "No, I don't."

George: "I don't think you really were angry."

Mother: "Oh God, we did so much."

George: "What did you ever do to help? You sent me off to a psychiatrist."

Mother: "We were angry with him and he didn't help. He kept saying let him do as he wants."

Therapist intervened by asking George: "Why don't you tell your parents how you felt about them?"

The patient finally opened up with an enormous amount of feeling, shouting: "I wished I were dead. I would have been dead in a few months. I had no feelings. I was mentally dead. I couldn't laugh or cry. I had so many defenses. I didn't know the difference between . . . [the mother interjected a question here and the doctor pointed out that she always interrupted the patient and asked her to let the patient go on].

Patient: "I hated both my parents. I didn't really think they were trying. I was getting angrier at my mother day by day. She cuts everybody off. She cuts my father off a million times right in the middle of a sentence. He never did anything to deserve being that pushed around."

Father: "You hate me too?"

Patient: "No, but it hurt me to see this happen to you. I wanted to act for you, but I couldn't. I'd come to your defense and you'd turn on me."

Patient to mother: "I really had blood curdling anger toward you."

Mother: "What would you like me to be?"

Patient: "Just a regular mother who knows her place and is not domineering. Take some advice about yourself and stop being either angry or withdrawn when you are told something and listen."

The mother admitted some of these deficiencies, but said that she needed these defenses—everybody needs them.

Patient replied to the mother: "You slash at everybody else, but you don't like it yourself."

Then the father actually toned down the patient's criticism of the mother and then said that he was not going to change: "We made our mistakes, but we are not going to change our ways. I am getting mad now, no one will change me. I have been James Graves for years and I am going to stay the same man. You don't have to understand that George but you have to take it."

Patient: "You don't have to change, but I am not going home to the same situation."

After the patient ventilated his enormous depression and hopelessness to the father, the father responded: "We can only change so much. Maybe if we had been in a hospital for a few years we could do better, but otherwise not." (This is a good example of the father's lack of perception of the patient's verbal attacks on him with a subtle counter hostile attack.)

Now the mother also joined in. Both the mother and the father responded to the patient's hostility by a subtle counter attack of their own: "We are not going to change."

Father: "We all have some problems, George. My understanding of this is you couldn't live in the environment so you became emotionally disturbed."

George: "Yah, I was sick."

Father: "My understanding of this is that a person who can't cope should just be told to cope with the situation."

The patient tried to support the father, saying: "When he made an effort, at least it was appropriate, but mother's efforts never were appropriate. I was really hopeless."

Father: "I never got anything back from you so I lost hope too."

Patient: "Yah, I know you did."

Patient: "Mother gave up on me a long time ago, but you gave up just before I came here. Then I went to pieces. I was very dependent on you."

Father: "You felt we didn't care."

Mother: "Can I ask a question?" (The father and son were trying to get close to each other which made the mother anxious and she interrupted to cut it off, completely ignoring the depth of the feeling that they are expressing to each other.)

The mother talked about what she did for the patient, how she felt scared and helpless, and had finally given up. The patient pushed her further to see what she was really feeling and she said: "Furious, for god's sake—I was hoping you would leave me alone."

The patient expressed the intensity of his anger at the mother and re-called the time he pushed her in the kitchen and implied homicidal fantasies about her when he was playing with the knife. Then he spoke again of the ninth grade, when the mother "told on him" to his friends.

The mother withdrew and looked in her purse; George said: "she doesn't know what it is all about, she can't remember it"; he became sarcastic.

Patient talked about his anger and his father said: "The one thing we have learned here is the tremendous effect Dr. X and R. L. had on you."

Patient, feeling extremely hopeless, said: "I just want to live my own life."

The father, missing the total emotional import of what the patient is saying, said: "What's the matter?"

Patient: "I am mad at myself and you people don't understand me." The patient then got up and walked out.

In ensuing joint interviews, the father's passivity and withdrawal, the mother's domination and hostility, and the patient's withdrawal and counter hostility continued to be worked through with a great deal of interpretation on the part of the therapist—particularly of the mother's behavior.

The dialogue with the father was always better than with the mother—about the father's lack of assertiveness and the patient's disappointment in him and a review of many examples of this at home. However, the mother and the father continually and repetitively interrupted the patient. The patient's direct expression of his anger at the mother interfered with the neurotic bind between mother and father, in which father was dependent on mother and handled his hostility toward her by passivity and withdrawal.

Following this interview the parents, despite our objections, took a week off for a vacation coincident with the father's business trip to Florida. George became angry and depressed, denied that it was related to the parents' trip, and threatened to sign out saying that he had improved and was ready to leave.

On the first interview after their return, however, he verbalized his anger at their being away on vacation, to which they made absolutely no response. There was a long silence following which the father laughed and said: "Is this a contest of who should talk first?" The therapist brought them back to the issue.

The patient related that he felt they walked out on a combined effort and that he could not understand how they could do this. There still was no response, except that the parents were plainly annoyed. When the therapist confronted them with the lack of response to the patient's anger at being abandoned they began to talk about the issue in terms of feelings that they themselves had as children when they were left by their parents.

At the end of this interview in the elevator George said to his doctor incredulously: "They did not understand what I was saying." George's disappointment in this interview culminated in a feeling of helplessness and again he insisted upon signing out. By this maneuver George clearly turned the tables on his parents. He was now in command. He was not admitting to feeling abandoned or helpless but was acting powerfully and was in charge with his efforts to sign out.

He sat rather impassively putting the parents on the spot. They were now pleading with him to stay. However, there were several important changes that took place in this joint interview for the first time.

Father, usually passive and withdrawn, was quite assertive with George, expressing a very definite interest in him and setting realistic limits to the patient's fantasies as to how life would be at home if he left. The mother did the exact same thing. For example, the father emphasized that although they want the patient home, he was sick and could not leave the hospital except on advice.

The mother questioned George: "Does all this have to do with our going on vacation? That we took off without discussing it with you?"

George: "That's true in a way. Your going away gave me my incentive for signing out."

Father: "You're paying us back." The father continued: "You have invested a great deal here, so why take a chance on wasting it?"

Mother: "George you are still self-destructive. You continue to harm yourself to get back at us. We goofed and now you are goofing yourself because of your anger, your hurt and your loss."

The mother continued: "You are angry, and hurt and you're acting out like me. Throwing up your hands like I used to do. You can't be that way. I understand that we went away and left you. We want to try. Don't act like me. Work it out, without acting it out." The mother said this in tears.

She continued: "In the Fall I felt an anxiety attack when Daddy went away. I felt deserted, depressed and angry and couldn't cope and wanted to quit. That's the way you feel. I know it but you have to fight as you're trapped. The doors are closed." After this impassioned and quite genuine appeal by the mother, the patient indicated that he might be willing to retract the request.

The father continued: "George we really do care. I do and your brothers do. Tell me when I desert you and we'll work it out." Both the mother and father continued to protest in a most appropriate and passionate way that they did care about the patient and that they were interested in him and wanted him to be helped with the result that the patient finally relented and retracted his letter to sign out. This was the first break through toward a change of the parents' attitude toward the patient.

In the next interview, the parents continued in a much more active interested fashion but the patient responded in a passive aggressive manner. After several more interviews devoted to working through the patient's anxiety about facing the parents and his handling of this anxiety in a passive aggressive manner, the patient finally did speak out at the mother and the father, leading both parents to a further awareness of the family conflict.

With the change in the parents' behavior and an increased verbal communication of feelings in the joint interviews, the patient's conflicts shifted from anxiety about parental rejection to anxiety over the extent of his dependency needs and a fear that although the parents really had changed he still would be completely dependent on them and would not behave any differently. Again the patient, rather than verbalize his anxiety about his first visit out, handled it by acting out, refusing to make his bed and go to school to provoke the doctor to cancel the visit. But the doctor shrewdly saw the truth of this ruse, interpreted it to the patient, and encouraged him to go out on his visit. The patient visited his family and then in joint interviews, although initially withdrawn and depressed, he began to talk about how the parents had changed but that he was afraid of his dependency and wanted to run his own life.

Throughout the course of this latter interview, the mother and the father both played an astonishing therapeutic role, constantly confronting the patient with his denial of reality—that is, interpreting to the patient that he would talk about his fear of dependency to them and then shift to talk about his anger at the doctor to avoid facing his dependency.

At this point we felt that the parents had changed sufficiently to dispense with the joint interviews from their point of view but that George's defensiveness continued to be so strong that it would be necessary to continue these interviews past the usual point when the patient starts to visit his family. The home visits then became the content of the joint interviews—

George's efforts to avoid his anxiety about being independent by provoking his parents to restrict him, thus putting himself back in a dependent position.

In these interviews verbal communication supplanted acting out, and the parents curbed both their clinging behavior and their fantasy projections toward George so that they could better perceive and respond to his adolescent emotional needs.

CHAPTER 12

Phase III: Separation

When the patient has worked through most of his depression, the communication block in the family has been relieved, more verbal patterns of exchange instituted, the basic pathology of the parents—such as the mother's holding on and the father's withdrawal—at least recognized and rectified to some extent, the joint interviews are usually terminated; the patient then passes gradually from the working through phase to the last or separation phase. On occasion, as with George, it may be necessary to continue the joint interviews into this latter phase.

Although the prospect of leaving the hospital impels another working through of the patient's separation anxiety there is not sufficient time to settle the matter once and for all and it therefore continues to be a focus of later outpatient therapy (see Chapters 14, 15, and 16).

It is important to keep in mind that the degree to which the depression has been fully worked through in Phase II will determine the amount of clinical change seen in Phase III. The joint interviews are terminated as soon as possible to encourage the patient to handle his conflicts on his own; in other words, to enable the patient to put into practice on his own what he has learned through his therapy and in the joint interviews.

The focus of the therapeutic effort shifts again from the working through of the depression and the conflicts with the parents, to concentrate on the working through of the anxiety engendered by the patient's fear of separation from the relationship with his therapist. The patient has accomplished the work of the first two phases of therapy through the establishment of a transference relationship with the therapist, which has been the chief tool enabling the patient to control acting out and work through his problems with the parents.

Now, however, we enter the final act of the drama to which the others have been preludes but toward which they have pointed, that is, working through of the separation anxiety attendant upon leaving the hospital.

As the patient enters the separation phase he develops great anxiety—

since the impending separation from his therapist revives all the old feelings of being abandoned which then come to dominate the issue of separation. The patient responds to this anxiety as of old by regressing and acting out to impel the therapist to keep him in the comfortable, dependent position and not require him to deal with the frightening reality of becoming autonomous.

A corollary of this anxiety is the patient's feeling that alone he will be unable to cope either with his feelings or with his parents who will draw him back into the old bind of dependency and anger.

It is very important to recognize the point at which the patient enters the separation phase so that the therapeutic approach may again be changed. The therapist should now stress the patient's autonomy and independence as much as possible, avoiding the use of restrictions (which were appropriate to Phase I) as a means of controlling acting out, since they tend to reinforce the dependency. He should rely strictly on clarification and interpretation as interview techniques to encourage the patient to voice rather than act out his anger and manage his conflicts by himself. Therapeutic activities now consist of interpreting the anxiety about dependency needs, clarifying the difference between separation and abandonment, allowing the patient to work through the residual feelings about abandonment, supporting the patient's new capacities to cope, and reassuring him of the realistic changes made which will lead to even greater capacity to cope. A relatively new issue comes to share the center stage —the intrapsychic conflict between the patient's wish for individuation and his guilt at separation. Let us now return to Anne.

ILLUSTRATION OF SEPARATION, PHASE III: ANNE

Prior to her first visit home, Anne became anxious as to whether she could handle herself in her home or whether she might fall back into her old ways. She signaled this by telling the nurses rather than her therapist that she was planning to invite a male patient to her home—an action that was not permitted.

After the visit home she reported that she had been anxious, that the mother had tried to infantilize her, but that the father had acted appropriately; she did not, however, mention the visit from the male patient. We later found out about the visit from the male patient himself, and when we confronted Anne she expressed her anger at the doctor for not having discovered it and at her parents for not prohibiting her relationship with this patient.

We interpreted to her that she was trying to deal with her anxiety about her dependence on and separation from the therapist by regressing into acting out behavior to force the doctor to hold her back. She was transferred to a more restricted floor and not permitted to visit out of the hospital until this was worked through. The patient had at the very first tested the parents' control mechanisms and found them wanting. Therefore her parents were told that they must inform the hospital of any irregular activities of the patient when on visit.

In the next interview the patient expressed anger at her therapist for pushing her too fast and putting too much responsibility on her too soon, and she confessed her anxiety that she could not handle her own behavior or confront her parents alone. She talked about experiencing the impending separation from the therapist as abandonment, and at last perceived that she was handling this fear by acting out in an effort to get the therapist to hold her back as her mother always had.

The therapist reinterpreted her fears with a discussion of the difference between separation and abandonment and reassured the patient that she would not have to move away from the security of her relationship with her therapist any faster than she was able. The patient then tested her mother again by calling her and threatening to elope, but the mother responded appropriately by calling and informing us, which relieved the patient. Anne then began to work through her fears of being abandoned, in the setting of the impending separation from the therapist.

She recalled the day (age 10) that Louise left and her feeling that people could only get so close—much as she loved and needed Louise, she could not hold on to her. She then remembered her loneliness and anger at her mother for not fulfilling her needs when Louise left. Patient: "When Louise left, mother was pretty cold to me. She would be sick and sleep a lot. I would get home from school and go to my room. There was nothing to come home to. My mother wasn't even around to say 'Hello.' She really wasn't a mother at all. As far as I was concerned she was a grown-up living in a world apart from me."

She then went back further and recalled some of the positive memories of her mother before Louise left. Patient: "Before Louise left, mother seemed younger—more natural. She would get up early in the morning and go for walks—then, after Louise left, she wouldn't get up in the morning—she got old—she would tell Daddy not to make any noise—she was almost a different person. I could go tell her when I did wrong, but not for warmth. Before she had real, long blond hair. Daddy would come home from work and wouldn't let things slide. Mother would get all excited about buying me a new dress for Daddy to take me to a baseball game. When Louise left my parents really started being different with each other—before, at least we all ate together, but later she wouldn't care even if he didn't come home. She would end up making jokes about his plane crashing."

As the patient returned to her fear of doing things on her own, the therapist reassured her about her capacity to handle things herself and of the therapist's support until she was on her own—pointing out that her life had been characterized either by overindulgence or abandonment and that there was a middle course until she was able to be independent. The therapist reviewed with the patient her new found assets to plan and to cope with her difficulties and suggested that if she wanted to be independent, she would have to act that way.

Anne then reviewed her past from the point of view that her passivity was not very helpful. Patient: "Actually what comes to my mind is that I wasn't living, I didn't know what life was, I did nothing for myself at all. Every step of life had to be planned by someone else. I was pretty used to it that way."

Following these interviews the patient began to take a much more active attitude toward her hobbies and came to realize that she had exaggerated her fears of separation and dependency. She took a more active role in making plans to go to school, to get a summer job; she got a part-time job for the summer while still in the hospital.

She summarized her treatment: "I have gone through three stages here: First, it was really bad and everything was a drag. Second, then I went back to being a little kid—running to you and mama. Third, now it is okay, I am growing up at last. I hope it will be more like a happy medium between the dependency I hated and the freedom I feared, like you have talked about for a long time now." After this interview, the patient gave no evidence of any regressive tugs, nor any acting out, nor any depression.

She reported how much better her parents were: "They both seem 10 years younger than when I came in—so enthusiastic about things—so happy about my getting a job." She began to dress in a more feminine and attractive manner and decided to throw away her black boots, saying: "I could not have done so awhile ago." From then on, the patient's interviews consisted mostly of current activities and planning her future at the boarding school to which she was discharged. In retrospect it seemed that the necessity for the patient to leave the hospital and the impending separation from the therapist, prompted the arousal and working through of her fear of abandonment in the transference.

ILLUSTRATION OF SEPARATION, PHASE III: GEORGE

As improvement was shown in joint interviews and both parents and patient dealt with each other more appropriately, George began to do better in school and his behavior on the floor was reported as improved—all of which impelled us to plan visiting for the first time, first in the hospital and then outside in the home. We hoped that the patient's fear that the parents had not changed could be relieved, or if not, more of the roots of conflict could be uncovered by the joint interviews; and also that the patient's fears of the dependency needs on his parents could be brought more into the open.

In this setting before the first visit the patient did not get up in time for breakfast and did not prepare his homework and put in a written request for a pass to go out. His therapist visited him and interpreted this behavior as an acting out to defend himself from his anxiety about the visit he was about to make to his parents. The patient responded with vigorous denial. The visit was then canceled and the regressive episode was made the issue of the interview before the next joint interview.

In these individual sessions the patient returned to the theme that he was too dependent on his parents and that although they may have changed some, he would continue to be so dependent that he would not be able to behave any differently. It was strongly suggested to the patient that he deal with his fear about his dependency on his parents through his interviews rather than by acting out; that actually the acting out to avoid his fear is a backward step maintaining his dependency and it would be better for him to face fear in the interviews.

The next step was his first visit out of the hospital. He talked about his anxiety; that he felt that it was too much of a "drag" to be allowed out on pass, that he did not want to leave the hospital. He needed a half-way station. The doctor interpreted, and discussed these feelings in terms of his anxiety about separation and his clinging to the hospital as a defense. Following his visit home for a full day, he excitedly reported having a good time despite some lurking anxiety. He was able to join in the activities the parents had planned with him whereas previously he had never wanted to participate in their plans. He then talked about how changes had always been difficult for him. At this point regular home visiting every weekend began.

As the parents' attitude changed and the patient's visiting out continued, George verbalized his fear of his dependency on his parents: "I am afraid to depend on them, I hate to be dependent on them. They are bastards. I expect love back from my parents, no matter what I do. I want them to care. Maybe I am too dependent; maybe I am more like a happy 11 year old. I deny the fact that I am dependent to get away from it. It makes me feel weak. They can destroy me. Before the joint interviews I was terribly afraid. I was in pain. I was afraid. It was a lot easier to tell you than to tell them."

Expressing his fear that his parents are not changed, he said: "The only thing that has happened is that we can talk better now but we still feel the same."

He was encouraged to attempt to deal directly with conflicts with his parents rather than to withdraw and to talk freely about the anxiety engendered by being on his own in his therapeutic sessions following each visit. He talked about his being frightened that he might not be able to control his feelings and that he was afraid when he left the hospital and went home that he would resume smoking marijuana: "I really feel edgy now all the time. I don't know what it could be. It's because I'm leaving. I feel ready to leave for good right now. I handle that edgy feeling by trying to forget about it. That's the way I handle most things that bother me. I don't know how I am going to stay at home. I might leave and try to get a job somewhere but I know that would be stupid. I don't enjoy being out of here at all this time. All the people I know at home are on drugs, amphetamines and even heroin. I don't know what I am going to do when I leave here with friends like that. They steal for drug money and beat people up. I don't want any part of that when I leave here. I know I won't take drugs here in the hospital but I think I will when I leave. I don't want to but it is so hard not to when all the kids are on the stuff."

This sad confession prompted the doctor to emphasize the extraordinary destructiveness of drugs for the patient. In a later interview about a month before discharge the patient rationalized his desire to cling to the hospital as a defense against his separation anxiety. He said: "I don't think I need this place anymore. I have certainly learned about myself and I am as healthy as anyone else now. I would like to stay close to the hospital because I have spent so much time here. I mean it doesn't seem right just to walk away. I'm sure I will get used to the outside fast. Do you remember when I changed floor for the second time? I was really nervous then, and it lasted about a month. I never really told you how bad off I was, I thought you would send me back to the restricted floor. I couldn't sit down for 5 minutes, and I was really nervous inside. I am feeling a little that way about leaving here but I know I can make it outside if I want to."

In another interview, he said: "The last couple of weeks I feel very angry. Before I wanted to stay but in the last couple of weeks I want to get out of here. I feel this place is bugging the insides out of me and I can't stand it and I can't stand the damn rules. I haven't been involved in anything or with anybody. I think I am trying to detach myself from this place for some reason."

George seemed to be expressing his anger at the interpretation that he was feeling his leaving as an abandonment on the part of his doctor and that his attitude of detachment was a poor way of handling it: "But I feel I have no control over this discharge decision. You just say 'leave now' and I have to go. I am used to this place and I'm scared to go outside. It's very hard to leave after being here a year. I do not know if you know it but I am a very sensitive person. I have a feeling that I do not want to leave but when I think of it I really want to go. For the most part I hate a lot of people here but there are a few people I have become very attached to like you and a couple of nurses. That's why it's hard leaving. I never did like changes ever since I can remember. When I changed from Cedar Grove to Montclair in the third grade I was about 8, and everything went bad. My mother's mother died then, too, so maybe that had something to do with the way she acted. She really changed. She used to be loving, but she got really bad when her mother died. She took it out on me. My grades fell off. She started yelling at me and things just kept getting worse. I felt very lonely then. Maybe I think every change will work out bad just like that one did. I don't know why but ever since then I've hated changes of any kind. I like to stay with what I have. Leaving here will be the biggest change in my life. I'm like a new person going out there now. There are lots of responsibilities out there for me, and after a year here I should be able to do a lot better. However, it all makes me nervous."

The therapist pointed out to the patient his improved capacity to cope with his parents, as well as with school, the changes the parents had themselves made, and his being able to continue treatment as an outpatient as long as would be necessary. George was discharged to live at home, attend a private school, and continue in treatment.

The story of George and Anne's treatment provides a narrative of what happened. Chapter 13 takes a more methodical and exact look at the results of hospital treatment of the Borderline Adolescent.

CHAPTER 13

Results: Continuity and Change

The patient, his hardest battle over, emerges from the jungle of the abandonment depression not into a cool, green, peaceful and sunlit place but into yet another wilderness of coping demands. What has been accomplished?

Although hospital treatment does not provide a cure for all their problems, it helps them to make a decisive turn in their lives. They have recovered from their abandonment depression and have begun to learn a mechanism for dealing constructively with future trauma.

It is as if the gods, wearying of the repetition of catastrophe, deemed it fitting finally to reward these unfortunate souls. For the first time in their entire life experience they have not been compelled blindly to submit to the accidents of fate.

Anne and George from birth until hospitalization met little but difficulty, failure, and defeat. By the time they had reached their adolescent years, the last way station of development, they had embarked on a pathway that would have led inexorably to ultimate chaos. They had grown older and larger in size, but had not matured emotionally. The discrepancy between their infantile needs and adult responsibilities loomed large and ominous.

Hospital treatment changed this gloomy scene and introduced hope for a better future. Though not subject to measure on the clinical scale this is by far the most fundamental achievement of the treatment. The word "hope" is deliberately used because the changes achieved by hospital treatment have to be reinforced and consolidated by follow-up outpatient treatment.

CLINICAL CHANGE

Let us turn from the philosophical to the practical to review what has been accomplished. There has been great change within the framework of characterological continuity. The patient obviously feels better; his clinical state is improved. The depression associated with experiencing separation from the mother as an abandonment is for the most part gone. Abandonment depression has yielded the center stage to separation anxiety. However, from time to time, depression again arises on an intrapsychic basis. The patient's introjection of the mother's attitudes causes him to equate autonomy with abandonment and his newly learned move toward autonomy revives the abandonment depression. Conflicts with the parents are handled more constructively and family communication is improved. The parents have gained some insight and are better able to perceive the patient's real emotional needs.

The therapeutic relationship has led to a fundamental decrease in the patient's mistrust; the patient has begun to use his increasing trust to build ego structure and to experiment in establishing better relationships with his peers. He has developed a greater acceptance of the self and a willingness to confront and to cope with his unconscious in a constructive manner. He has become more optimistic, sees his efforts as being worthwhile, and is able to look to the future with hope of more improvement.

A reinforcement of repression and other defense mechanisms, an increase in the capacity to cope, and some move toward autonomy has occurred. At the same time as the patient's capacity to master his own conflicts and to adapt to the environment has improved, he enjoys realistic success and realistic achievement for the first time, thus learning to seek reality rather than fantasy for satisfaction.

These improvements have taken place within the continuity of the basic character structure which does not and will not change until the patient has developed to the stage of autonomy. The various defense mechanisms —denial, projection, avoidance, reaction-formation—persist but create less havoc in the functioning of the overall personality than before, even at times of acute stress-separation experiences—when these defenses again assume some of their old dominance.

A subtle but important change has been the learning of a technique for the management of stress and conflicts—handling them through awareness, understanding, and verbalization of the feelings rather than "turning them off" by acting out. This alone, in my view, justifies the extraordinary investment of time and effort on the part of the patient and therapist, and the undeniable expense to the family of time, effort, emotional trauma, and money.

BEHAVIORAL CHANGE

Behavior is a key signal flag throughout treatment. In the first phase it takes the center stage; thereafter, whenever deviant behavior comes to the

fore it usually indicates a temporary regression. It is so vital for the resident to be aware of the patient's behavior that I insist that he bring the
behavior chart to every supervisory session so that I can review it while
listening to his report of his interviews.

This view of behavior led to a psychiatric version of Parkinson's law:

The therapeutic progress of the patient is inversely proportional not
only to the content but to the length of the nurse's note.

If the patient's conflicts are not seen in his behavior on the floor, they
are worked through in interviews. An example below of Anne's nurse's
notes shows the difference in both content and length of the note in Phase
I and Phase II.

Phase I

One Day

A.M. Resistive to changing into slacks this morning. "The doctor told
me that she cared about how I was feeling and would come to see me.
If she wants me to change she'll have to dress me." Seen by therapist
quite angry afterwards. Roommate strongly urged her not to cooperate
and when she became verbally abusive to staff, Anne seemed quite upset
saying: "I don't want you to get all the anger." She was reassured about
this—changed her clothes (slacks) and went to activities. Cooperative remainder of day.

P.M. Immediately after change of shift patient appeared wearing miniskirt and black textured stockings. Very resistive when asked to put on
slacks. Changed to skirt which was short but not as much so as the miniskirt. Writer questioned length of this skirt and Anne became very angry,
stating: "She told me they could be 1 inch or 1½ inches above my knee
and that's what this is. What does everyone want from me? Can't I have
anything of my own? My mail is read, I can't have visitors except my
father, I can't go out on pass with the group, now you're changing the
way I dress. Next you'll try to change the way I think but you won't be
able to. What do I have left? What's so bad about these skirts, anyway?"
At this point writer explained to patient that the short skirts were dis-
tracting and somewhat upsetting to some of the sicker patients especially
male patients. Anne responded: "Well what about me? I didn't want to
come here anyway. It's because I'm only 16 and I have to do what everyone says. Well, this skirt is 1½ inches above my knee and she said I could
wear them that length and that's as long as I'll wear them! I feel like a fool
with the skirt this long." During conversation, her roommate continued to

make sarcastic and destructive remarks encouraging Anne to rebel. For the most part Anne seemed to ignore these remarks. Anne attended evening activities wearing skirt (1½ inches above knee). Asked staff members how they would feel in miniskirts and when they reply "uncomfortable," she said: "That's just how I feel in this." Watching television with patient group.

Phase II

Day I

A.M. Withdrawn, depressed, spending time in and out of her room, frequently resting on bed and socializing with roommate. At lunch told another patient that marijuana was different and not habit forming at all.

P.M. In spite of keeping self busy and attending activities appears quite depressed and preoccupied. Changed clothes several times this p.m. "I just can't get comfortable." Restless and tense.

Day II

A.M. Appears cheerful and outgoing, socializes with patients. Procrastinated before going to school. Set hair but shakes off compliments. Seems in genuinely good spirits.

P.M. Pleasant, cooperative. Attended adolescent group alone. More than usual in room.

The data on the changes in each patient's behavior are provided daily, almost hourly, by many sources. The therapist has his notes, which are subject to the weekly review of the supervisor who brings to bear his greater experience and knowledge. Valuable supplementary comments are provided by a staff of perceptive nurses and nurses' aides who are in constant contact and report on the minutiae of the patient's day—several notes every 24 hours. The school record reflects not simply cognitive efficiency but behavior as well. The Occupational Therapist's reports similarly reflect the patient's capacity to sustain goal directed activity, and often through the sensitive observations of the therapist, throw light on the patient's general patterns of work and interaction with peers and authority. The description of each patient's performance in Recreational Therapy is also enlightening in this respect and may as well yield information on his stage of socialization or withdrawal, his capacity to handle his aggression, and his competitive drives. The Group Therapy sessions afford a spectacular ongoing demonstration of peer interaction—a group setting in which issues raised in individual therapy may be discussed, or subtly reflected by the patients involved.

The material presented below has been derived from all these sources and condensed and edited. It is presented in three sections roughly paralleling the therapeutic Phases I: The Testing Phase; II: Working Through; III: Separation. The appendix contains the follow-up reports of psychological tests* of two of these patients that were administered shortly before discharge.

ILLUSTRATIONS OF BEHAVIORAL CHANGES: NANCY

Phase I: Testing (Acting Out)

In this phase the daily nurse's notes comprised several pages. They were condensed as follows.

Floor. Has been angry, sarcastic, and rude most of the week. She continues to make fun of an elderly confused patient on her unit. Her procrastination about study hour and general testing of staff (profanity, short skirts, etc.) continues. There is much giggling and inappropriate attitude and her manner is frequently sullen and seductive. She told her doctor she was smoking in the bathroom both Wednesday and Thursday and was restricted.

School. Work complete. Vacillating behavior. Depressed, elated, argumentative, at times. Flirtatious, used profanity. Testing by attempting to read nonschool material during school hours.

O.T. Behavior fluctuates within a matter of minutes from pensive to giddy. Angry outbursts continue to occur when she is approached by staff. Resents having to show her work to staff and often deliberately puts it away before showing it to anyone. Seems removed from group.

Group Therapy. Little participation. Very resistant to bringing feelings about parents into discussion of anger at teacher. "That's a lot of bullshit." On Friday quiet and depressed during session focused on inability of others to communicate with and trust their parents.

R.T. Very involved in activities. Became argumentative when told she had to wear gym clothes for calisthenics but quickly quieted down and was cooperative. Very pleasant and conversing with peers and staff. Appears to be enjoying exercises.

Phase II: Working Through (Depression)

The patient in only 6 weeks has managed to gain control of her behavior and is beginning to express her conflicts in interviews in which the violent rage toward her mother emerges. The length of her daily nurse's notes has shrunk to one page.

Floor.   The doctor was away most of the week and Nancy was anxious and tense, but handled herself very well. She has been depressed about Christmas, but has not acted out at all and has kept herself well occupied. Some giddiness and irritability noted. States that she finds it difficult at times to control her behavior.

O.T.   Sarcastic early in week but able to function. Worked well towards end of week. More communicative with staff. Supportive of Helen.

Group Therapy.   Angry and defiant especially toward the therapist. Although sitting in the corner, Nancy participated in the group marginally. Spoke angrily concerning her father never being at home.

R.T.   Quite active in games, well occupied throughout the period. On Thursday a little argumentative, angry, and profane but quickly calmed down. Relates to peers very well. Seems to be reaching out to get Helen into the group.

Phase III: Separation

As the patient enters the separation phase, although in good control, she begins to show both her separation anxiety and her defenses against it, that is, lack of communication and irritability. The nurse's notes continue to be 1 page in length except for occasional behavioral regressions.

Floor.   Out to dinner with her parents Friday evening and has been out alone on several short passes. Has been handling these well, although in Clinic there has been an increase in irritability and sarcasm, a lack of communication with staff and generalized argumentativeness. Tends to be dramatic and condescending regarding weekend pass.

School.   Work complete. In good control of herself, cool and calm on the surface. Engaged in school work but seems to have moments when she lets it slide and then rushes "helter skelter" to catch up. Frequently confronted about the "rushed" and consequently careless appearance of some of her work.

O.T.   Anxious and hyperactive early in week—almost giddy. She had an angry outburst on Thursday and was confronted by staff about her "complaining" attitude. Denied she has been increasingly short-tempered but did seem to make an effort to gain control of herself. Started new sewing project and commented she was glad the cost of material was charged to her parents' account and would not have to come out of her allowance.

Group Therapy.   Tuesday confronted by Bill and Donald about her using angry quick comebacks as a defense. On Friday was most involved so far this year. Mad at her father for his frequent absences. Disappointed over parents' lack of involvement with her pass home. Looks on the verge of tears and states she feels very sad, when her mother tells her she cares about her. Can not believe her words because of actions of the past and present. Wondered how mother could survive when she was away.

Group trip. Acted as platoon sergeant and led group into shops in the Village. Sought out Fred and was with him throughout. Was obviously the one who had initiated going to the Village. Kept group waiting on several occasions while trying on clothes and acted as if she was unaware of this.

R.T. Behavior similar to last week. Sociable, pleasant, open with peers and staff. Good interactions with group. Seems to enjoy volleyball games and forcefully asserts herself. Generally very pleasant and cooperative.

Thus Nancy's behavioral change was dramatic.

All the sources of information—that is, therapist, supervisor, staff reports, psychological testing—concur that there has been change. The change is now about to be tested as these patients leave the protected environment of the hospital to face the conflicts of daily life on their own. The wilderness awaits! Has there been enough change to improve their capacity to meet the coping demands in this wilderness and to deal with the future traumas that are bound to come their way? Do they have the capacity to continue through the surges of emotional, intellectual, and physiological change that are a part of maturation from adolescent to adult?

The next three chapters tackle this problem by presenting the outpatient treatment of five patients following discharge: one in detail and four in summary form.

PART THREE

The Therapeutic Process: Outpatient

Hospital treatment marks only the end of the beginning since it provides neither enough time nor enough treatment for these patients to develop to the stage of autonomy. It has turned them away from the pathologic defenses and set them on their way toward growth; but a long journey lies ahead. Moreover, prolonged hospitalization when they are ready for and need to take on a further step toward autonomy could itself have a regressive effect.

These adolescents continue to suffer from separation anxiety and the effects of narcissistic oral fixation, that is, their need for an exclusive symbiotic tie, accompanied, as always, by the twin fears of engulfment and abandonment. The latter interferes with the establishing of mature and meaningful close relationships. Ego defects frustrate the patient's general adaptation, and guilt continues to impair his every move toward autonomy.

There are two basic themes in the outpatient treatment: (1) the patient's conflict with his own individuality—the anxiety, guilt, and depression that the patient feels about his unfolding individuality as well as his defenses against these feelings; (2) the conflict the patient's individuation poses for both parents—particularly the mother. The patient's individuation poses such a threat to the equilibrium between the parents that they use all their efforts to "hamstring" it. The therapist becomes the silent guardian of the patient's unfolding individuality by: (1) supporting the patient's moves toward individuation, (2) interpreting the defenses against the anxiety, depression, and guilt involved, and (3) working with the parents to minimize their "hamstringing."

The treatment relieves the anxiety, guilt, and depression associated with individuation. The patient's unfolding individuality becomes manifest in entirely new wishes, thoughts, fantasies, and feelings. The patient experiments with these new feelings both in fantasy and in action which again leads to further anxiety, guilt, and depression which must be again worked through in the interviews. As these painful affects are attenuated their effect on the individuation process is diluted and the pace of individuation increases. Through trial and error the patient, aided by "communicative matching" from his therapist, comes to discard those of his experiments that do not fit while the remainder become consolidated in his newly formed sense of identity.

DISCHARGE

Discharge from the protective environment of the hospital poses enormous problems for these patients who have such difficulty in separating and managing on their own. Discharge is felt by the patient as yet another abandonment. In addition, removal of the care taking apparatus exposes the patient to severe oral deprivation with consequent rage and depression due to the continued emotional need for supplies to build ego structure. Thus discharge seems to replicate his infantile experiences—deprivation of his dependency needs and abandonment depression.

The discharge has an equally profound effect on the family. The renewed proximity to the mother reinforces her wishes for reunion which she actively implements to pressure the patient to regress and return to the old symbiotic union. The patient, on his part, suffering depression and guilt, is sorely tempted to regress and rejoin the mother to gain relief. Once the patient leaves the hospital the therapeutic leverage is drastically lowered. No one knows this better than the patient who begins to institute his own characteristic defenses long before the planned discharge takes place. The fact that he must now manage more or less on his own is so overriding an influence that it diminishes his reliance on the relationship with the therapist who is no longer the overall caretaker.

The center stage continues to be occupied by the issue that has dominated all others since infancy—the patient's need for emotional supplies to grow and the mother's withdrawal of these supplies if he does grow.

When we recognized that hospital treatment was only a beginning, that the patients had a continued need for emotional supplies in order to develop to autonomy, and that their separation anxiety was enormous, we changed the treatment accordingly. For example, we had not properly evaluated the extraordinary extent to which the patient used the defense mechanisms of denial to deal with his separation anxiety. Failure to work adequately through Nancy's denial of this anxiety caused her use of drastic defenses to deal with her abandonment depression on discharge and almost led to a suicidal attempt. The denial prevented her from working through the depression in the interviews and thereby increased the potential for acting out.

With Bill, Grace, and Helen we placed much greater emphasis on working through the denial of separation anxiety to the point of keeping them in the hospital several months longer than the others.

In addition, to minimize further the trauma of the separation from the hospital, the patient was encouraged to continue in outpatient treatment three times a week with the same therapist, that is, the patient would leave the hospital but not the therapist. A frequency of three times a week was advised to assure that the patient's enormous need for continued supplies could be dealt with by the therapist rather than by some other means, in other words, to maintain therapeutic leverage.

It was our hope that the therapist would be able to treat the patient until the patient had graduated from high school and was ready for college. College would then provide a stable environment for a final working through of the separation-individuation problem. To minimize the parents' "hamstringing" efforts we arranged, where possible, for the patient to live away from his home; either at a boarding school (Grace) or with relatives (Bill). We advised the parents to continue their work with the social worker but, with their adolescent out of the home, they rarely followed through for more than a short period. Finally, we insisted that the patient have a well-planned daily routine prior to leaving the hospital. The effectiveness of these measures is illustrated by the later clinical course of Bill and Grace.

The next three chapters present the follow-up treatment from two points of view: Chapters 14 and 15 describe in detail the process of Nancy's first year of outpatient therapy. Chapter 16 summarizes the outpatient course of the other three patients.

CHAPTER 14

Nancy: Clinical History, Hospital Treatment, and First Outpatient Crisis

A description of Nancy's clinical history and hospital treatment, quite similar to George's and Anne's, provides a background for understanding her outpatient treatment.

HISTORY OF PRESENT ILLNESS

Nancy's clinical episode began at the age of 10 in the setting of (1) the family moving from Indiana to Oregon, (2) father spending even more time away from home, (3) Nancy being rejected by two girl friends to whom she had been clinging, and (4) her dog dying. She lost interest in school, slept poorly, and ate very little. Although previously an avid and excellent swimmer, she gave up swimming although there was a pool in her own yard. Conflict arose with her mother when the mother attempted to teach Nancy how to sew and cook.

At age 11 she began to get into fights with her girl friends and was frequently sent home for being assaultive. Her mood improved for a short period during her twelfth year when she established one good relationship with a friend. When this girl rejected her, her previous behavior returned and she described herself as feeling lonely and apart from her family and peers.

By age 13 her behavior problem had escalated and the mother found out Nancy had been changing into hippie clothes and smoking in school. The mother became enraged and accused Nancy of being an untrustworthy sneak. The parents took on the role of policemen and a constant battle ensued. The father secured the combination to Nancy's school locker and searched for cigarettes and "unlady-like" clothing. The mother embarrassed and surprised Nancy in the playground with her friends and had Nancy empty her purse to check for cigarettes.

Nancy refused to see a psychiatrist at this time, but her mother went weekly for about 6 months for advice as to how to manage her daughter. During this period Nancy was frequently disciplined by being kept home for 6 to 8 weeks at a time. Communication between mother and Nancy was practically nonexistent. Mother spoke to her only to enforce rules. Nancy felt her parents were unreasonable and interested only in making her into what they wanted.

Nancy now began to smoke marijuana and to have sexual relations, often with black boys. By the age of 14, she had begun to experiment with LSD and DMT. At this time the family again moved, this time to New Jersey, where the parents found that Nancy was associating "with the grubbiest kids in town." During her first semester at the local high school, she began to smoke marijuana openly. Her parents took her to a psychiatrist who advised them to put her in a private school which she attended for a number of months before being asked to leave because she not only used drugs and smoked marijuana but also encouraged the other students to rebel. By this time Nancy was now frightened at what was happening to her. She could not resist her urge to take DMT during recesses and was anxious about being caught. When expelled from the school, she remained home for 4 months before arrangements were made for admission to the hospital.

PAST HISTORY

Nancy was the oldest of two children, with a sister 4 years younger. She was born 6 years after the parents' marriage following one miscarriage. Pregnancy was planned and uncomplicated, and labor was uneventful. Nancy was a feeding problem for the first 6 months. The mother became more anxious and upset with each change of formula. The pediatrician's reassurance calmed the mother and Nancy finally responded by eating as she should.

Toilet training was begun at 9 months, bowel training was not completed until age 4, and Nancy had nocturnal enuresis until the age of 10. During her second year Nancy became hyperactive and irritable. She whined and demanded a great deal of attention.

By age 3 she was having temper tantrums and breath holding spells, and she began to oppose all her mother's wishes. For example, she wanted to wear bathing suits in the winter, snow suits in the summer. Her mother would teach her how to play a game one way and Nancy insisted on doing it the opposite way.

She had no trouble in starting nursery school at age 4, kindergarten at

5, and first grade at 6. Her behavior was always better at school than at home. At age 5 her sister was born, developed a urinary infection, and had to be hospitalized for 2 weeks. At the same time her father was again transferred and he had to leave home for several months. Nancy stayed with a maid and became even more rebellious and uncooperative. The family then moved to Indiana. Nancy cried a great deal, quarreled with her mother, was restless and unable to sit still. However, her behavior in school remained acceptable. At this point at home she began to "lie," which disgusted her mother. The mother took Nancy to see a psychiatrist who reported that Nancy was an anxious, lonely child who was copying her mother in an effort to get more attention from her all too absent father. He did not suggest treatment but suggested that the father spend more time with the family.

Nancy always found it difficult to make friends. She had one close friend during her seventh year whom she kept as a friend to the present. She never seemed able to play children's games. This reflected the parents' social difficulties. They had found it very difficult to integrate themselves into the local community since their arrival the year before.

HOSPITAL TREATMENT

Phase I: Testing

Nancy's initial acting out behavior in the hospital consisted of not going to bed on time, smoking cigarettes, being seductive with male patients, and wearing inappropriate clothing. As she recreated the dynamics of her family relationships with her therapist and the nursing staff, attempts were made: (1) to show her that it was she who was doing the provoking; (2) to relate what she did to what she was feeling at the time and to inquire when in the past she had felt like this and what did she do to handle that feeling; and (3) to weave a continuity between her transactions on the floor with the content of interviews.

The clothes issue proved to be the major one in the hospital as it had been at home. She would wear a short skirt and be sent to her room by the nurse at whom she would be furious. Her intense anger and rage toward her mother were displaced onto the nurses. As her customary avenues of expression were eliminated she became first irritable and anxious and then panicky. She cried, paced the floor, reexperienced LSD-like symptoms, and once in a panic, began to clutch the walls out of fear. She blamed the hospital for all her troubles. She denied that she had any problems but when asked could recall feeling just as badly prior to hospitalization. In this manner she was confronted with the reality of her illness.

The projection on the hospital as the source of her problems soon gave way to rage at her mother. The anger her mother provoked in her was enormous and uncontrollable. After expressing her anger in interviews she now acted out by scratching her wrists. Nancy: "Mother doesn't care how tense I am; she doesn't care what my arms look like, I am afraid of what I am doing to myself to get back at her. I don't know if I'll ever be able to do enough to her." The more she talked about this anger, the more she wanted to act out, and the less she could, the worse she felt.

In the third week of hospitalization, she said: "You remind me of myself—by making me talk about it, making me bring back everything that I carefully tucked away with my grass—now all I have left is sleep." She had not yet discovered verbalization. She now became more overtly depressed. She felt apart and alone and a "black sheep." Nancy: "Mother criticized me, laughed at me for wetting the bed, for being fat, or even for cooking New Year's breakfast without fresh apricots."

Phase II: Working Through—Depression

By the seventh week of hospitalization, however, Nancy's behavior was no longer a primary issue and the sessions began to move into the content of her abandonment depression. She was now tearful, frightened, and complained that her therapist made her feel worse. She began to have feelings that heretofore she had had only short bitter tastes of and had then quickly avoided by withdrawing or using drugs. She complained: "You're making me feel worse; I feel there's a piece of glass between me and other people. I can't pay attention in school, everything seems different, nothing looks real, when I felt like this at home my parents didn't know and when I did something they would ask me how could I ruin my little sister's life."

Nancy first expressed anger at her father when her therapist arrived late for an interview. She accused him of being like her father: "He's disgusting, he never called us when he was going to be late. My poor mother would sit around worried and I wouldn't know what to do . . . when he left I always feared he wouldn't come back and I guess I thought something was wrong with me—something bad that kept him away." Moving further into her depression she recalled her dog, dramatically reliving the scene at age 10, when she came home from school and was told by her mother that the dog was put to sleep and that she should not cry. Although she did not then, she now wept pathetically.

The tie to her mother was clearly expressed in a dream of running away from someone for fear of being smothered. Her first associations were trying to escape from her problems in the hospital but then she said: "My mother haunts me, I can't get her out of my mind. Yes, just like in the dream—Oh my God I think it was my mother who was chasing me in that dream."

She then became resistant and stopped talking, saying that she could not take this any longer. It was much too painful, and coincidentally her behavior worsened. When her therapist restricted her for piercing her ear and had her remove the ear ring, her resistance broke down and the underlying homicidal rage burst forth: "You're just like her, I hate her. When she had the operation last summer I hoped she'd die and one day when she was 3 hours late because of the snow I prayed that she had run into a tree. My God how I really hate that bitch!" After expressing these murderous fantasies she began to talk more in interviews and once again the acting out dropped off.

During the fourteenth week of therapy she began to verbalize her feelings of abandonment—that her parents did not care for her. Nancy: "When I talk about them I don't get as angry as I used to get, I get sad and upset. It's an awful feeling."

Her therapist's departure for Christmas vacation caused her to reexperience the feelings of abandonment when her father left, that is, her own worthlessness or sense of evil. The move to an intermediate floor after fifteen weeks, like any other change, revived her feelings of abandonment. She regressed and again began to act out. She had suicidal thoughts at this time and dreamed that her parents had come to sign her out of the clinic. Her fear of loss of control was vividly expressed in two dreams. In one she was walking through the flames of a fire she had set in the center lounge; in another she was driving at breakneck speed on a thruway when her therapist stopped her and told her to go and sit in a school bus. These fears were allayed and her behavior improved when her fear of abandonment was interpreted. This was further reinforced by her therapist helping her to control her behavior and reestablishing verbalization in the sessions to deal with these emotions.

Within a week her behavior was under control and at the bottom of her depression she confronted her feelings of utter hopelessness and despair. "I never felt that they really cared for me, if they did they wouldn't have treated me the way they had . . . but I don't know if I'm worth caring about. . . . If they don't love me, I don't care about myself and then I do things to make them care for me even less." Important memories crystallized around her tenth year. During that year her father travelled more and the family moved to Oregon. She felt depressed, alone, apart, and different. Two successive new girl friends rejected her abruptly and this doubly reinforced her belief that something was missing in her. She believed that her demands on others were inordinate; nothing could make her feel close. "I'll never make it sex-wise with anyone because I'll always feel they don't care enough for me . . . I think I'll be lonely all my life."

By the end of the seventeenth week she was feeling better and asked for and received more privileges, for example, more passes, phone calls, and outside visits.

Before her therapist left for a 2-week vacation in the twenty-fifth week she again withdrew. His departure again reenacted her father's leaving home and quickened her fears of not being able to exist alone. Though she could not express much anger about this to her therapist directly; after his departure she was able to do so with the substitute therapist.

Joint Interviews

By the twenty-seventh week she had worked through much of her depression and was ready for family sessions. She feared her parents' rejection and at first handled this anxiety by deciding to demand various things of them. In the first session she yelled at them, in the second they at her, and from the third session on, the discussions were more mutual and typical of the family dynamics. As her parents confronted her with all she had done she grew more depressed and hopeless. She talked of other patients who failed and planned to live in an apartment with an ex-patient who was on drugs. The anger toward her parents for their rejection was once again channeled to her therapist and the staff in the form of complaints about the rules and withdrawal. After this was interpreted in the fourth family session, both Nancy and her mother became furious with one another. Nancy's mother wanted to leave the room; Nancy wanted to continue to provoke her. Through the therapist's intervention they both handled this anger within the session.

After this session both parents made greater efforts to understand Nancy; they told her that they cared for her, recognized how they may have been unaware of her feelings, and acknowledged the possibility that they too had a part in all that had happened. Nancy made anxious by their response rejected them and grew more depressed as she talked. Thus she was confronting her separation anxiety. She realized that by accepting them she had to commit herself to move independently and work out her problems with them, that is, she had to give up dependency. By rejecting them or setting up a situation wherein they could reject her, she would prove her fears true and provide license for herself to continue in the dependent state. In the eighth conference Nancy and her mother discussed how each had made the other feel, expressed their wish for more understanding, and earnestly asked each other what could be done.

Phase III: Separation

As the weekly family conferences continued and Nancy spent longer and longer times at home, two themes emerged: (1) Nancy's regressive acting out as a defense against her fear of being on her own and (2) the fear of being on her own. Nancy made very unrealistic demands on her mother, and the mother assumed the role of trying to fulfill her every need. The lack of success filled them both with anger and frustration.

When the therapist interpreted Nancy's demandingness as a defense against her separation anxiety Nancy would stop demanding and then her anxiety would come to the fore. With each move forward she experienced this separation anxiety and then regressed either by acting out or withdrawing to displace her angry frightened feelings.

She and her mother then began to get along better. They did things to please each other and went to great lengths to avoid anger-provoking incidents. On weekends at home Nancy prepared most of the meals and volunteered to serve as the babysitter. The more receptive the mother was, the more anxious Nancy became about separating and being on her own. One month before discharge the therapist had to leave because he was changing his residency and she responded to this at first with denial but then was able to ventilate her feelings of anger to the substitute therapist.

As her discharge approached she became irritable, depressed, and anxious, verbalizing her fear of not making it on her own and needing rehospitalization. Also she verbalized her ambivalence about her mother —her seeking of her mother's protectiveness but her fear of it. Her separation anxiety was further reflected in somatic complaints of menstrual cramps, anorexia, headaches, and a head cold. She began seriously to doubt her own capacity to cope, her doctor's competence, and her parents' willingness to help. When the time came to leave she made no attempt to avoid the staff and her peers but was able to face them and make appropriate goodbyes. Nancy was discharged to live at home, attend a tutoring school, and see her therapist twice a week. For several weeks prior to discharge she was handling her separation anxiety with characteristic defenses of splitting and denial.

Nancy was then seen twice a week by the same therapist who treated her in the hospital. Supervisory sessions were now held every other week and tape recorded, and the recordings were typed and later reviewed. The parents were also seen by a social worker but it was not possible for the author to see the social worker regularly enough for supervision to include that work in this report.

THE FIRST CRISIS: THE ABANDONMENT DEPRESSION AND THE PATIENT'S DEFENSES AGAINST IT— THE FIRST THREE MONTHS AFTER DISCHARGE

The first therapeutic crisis was the patient's response to discharge as an abandonment. This depression had to be worked through before any further move could be made toward individuation.

She was 15 minutes late for her first interview and appeared in hippie dress. She explained she had lost the slip of paper that contained the address and had trouble remembering it. She looked angry, depressed, anxious, and defensive. She spent much time emphasizing how well things were going and denied any difficulties. She then entered into a lengthy recitation of her mother's rejection and hostility. Unintentionally she described during this recital numerous examples of her own provocative behavior.

The therapist made the following interpretation. "You are provoking your mother; your mother is not your problem. You're trying to avoid your own anxieties by this behavior. These anxieties probably have to do with leaving the hospital and resuming treatment with me."

Nancy admitted this by saying that her mother had actually been better at home but that she was not able to handle her feelings. She did not know what was wrong but she was afraid she was not able to make it on her own.

The interpretation above set limits to Nancy's acting out. After the interview she talked to her mother about her own tendency to provoke and then said ruefully that she wished to share things with her mother but was never sure whether what she said was meant to share or to provoke.

In the next few interviews Nancy appeared less irritable and tense but she still seemed to be defending herself against the abandonment depression. Investigation of these defenses was met by denial. None the less, Nancy was quite aware of the underlying tensions: "Another thing that I feel is that something is going to happen. I feel like I'm a powder keg and I'm going to blow up any minute and I don't know why. A strange feeling, I don't know what is going on and I'm out of control. I can't call the shots. Then when I went to bed I got frightened. I couldn't sleep, I started to cry, I guess it was the pent up tension, but when I went to bed I felt I just couldn't go on any longer. I felt I wouldn't be able to make it."

The therapist then suggested that her mother's letting her be more on her own seemed to make her more apprehensive.

Nancy continued: "I feel dead inside. I used to be able to go to a play, and imagine myself in the players' places, and get very excited; but last night I went to a play and I'd just as soon have been sitting in my own living room. It really didn't mean anything to me. I have no interests. I have nothing I want to do."

The crisis came to a head 2 weeks later as she reported in the interview: "Remember I told you about that feeling about exploding? Well, it happened last night." She seemed quite confused and her thinking was as scattered as it had been when she was first hospitalized. She said: "I was reading this book, *The Electric Kool-Aid Acid Test,* about the girl named Stark Naked that everyone tried to get to take LSD. She takes LSD, has a horrible experience and winds up jumping off a bus naked, grabbing a little child. She is then committed to a hospital and they move on to try to get someone else to take LSD. After finishing the book I wrote a composition about Stark Naked being deluded thinking that acid opened doors. I felt very depressed when I read the book and also when I wrote the composition. I then had a dream that night where Father told me that James, a friend, was in a mental hospital.

"The next morning on the way to the train my father actually did tell me that there were 2 years of James' life that were unaccounted for, and this really scared me. It was too eery a coincidence. I got very panicky and felt like jumping off the train, but by the time I got to the door the train had started. I started crying and went to the ladies room. I thought, 'Jesus! do I want to kill myself?' Then, I realized: 'No! I don't want to kill myself. I just have to get off the train. I have to figure out what's going on.' I got very frightened by all of these feelings coming to me on the train. At first I thought I really wanted to kill myself but then that went away really quickly. I don't really know what's up."

Nancy then gave the following association: "The passage about her running around on acid, jumping out of the bus and grabbing a little boy, going crazy and being carted off where no one cares about her. That whole scene really hurt me. It took place in the neighborhood that I lived in, and I really miss Oregon. That was a time in my life when things really weren't too bad. It seems that all of my trouble started once we got to New York City. All of this started getting to me on the train. When father said that about James in the car it didn't hit me at all but it was afterwards in the train all these things came back at once and I got upset. I realized that James also had ended up in a mess. He's straight but he's straight with his scotch and I felt there was no place for me to go whether with acid or with scotch." Nancy further related that when she felt this way she did not want to go to school, wanted to drop out and take drugs.

The therapist had set limits to Nancy's regressive defense of acting out and had pointed up the need for her to be on her own which brought to the fore her abandonment depression. Again she was impelled to handle it in the old way by renewed acting out. The therapist reinterpreted this and also again set limits to the acting out by pointing out its defensive function and its destructiveness to Nancy; that she had had these same feelings of depression at each successive move in the hospital and that she must learn to deal with the feelings in the interview rather than by acting out.

Nancy replied: "It's going to be much harder than it was in the hospital. I was in the hospital just to work out my feelings and nothing else and now there is a lot more to do. I feel like I'm getting to a part of me that's more than just being angry with my parents—a deeper part. I don't know what it is. It has nothing to do with my parents. The part that is hard for me to get at. It keeps slipping away from me. I guess I'm afraid to find out what it is. There's a part of me that I don't know about that is making me feel bad and strange and I'm going through it and I never have gone through it before."

A joint interview with the parents was scheduled for the next day to discuss the outpatient therapy. Nancy arrived in tight pants and bare feet, claiming that something was wrong with her shoes. The therapist ignored her rationalization and pointed out the provocative acting out. Therapist: "You know what your mother is going to say when she comes in here and sees you looking like this. You are really provoking her and it's like all those other times. Why are you doing it?"

Nancy: "If mother notices me I have to notice her and that means I have to try something and I'm not up to it. I don't want to have anything to do with her. I feel like leaving the house. I want to be left alone."

Therapist: "Does that have something to do with your coming in here without shoes so that you could provoke your mother? It's a way of conducting the relationship in the old patterns so you don't have to commit yourself to something more. Just like you did in the hospital."

Nancy: "I know that my mother is trying and that she seems to love me but I can't take it. I'd rather have her bitch at me and tell me I can't do things. Cause I can't stand to be close to her."

The therapist linked the provocative acting out to the previous interview by suggesting that it is a way of protecting herself against feelings of abandonment if she is on her own.

Nancy: "I'm very frightened. I saw what I was like before I went into the Clinic. Now my doors are open and I'm afraid I won't be able to keep them open. Things are closing in on me and I'm afraid I'll be back to the way I was. I wouldn't mind that because it doesn't require so much effort. I could just withdraw and not move."

Nancy then confirmed her seemingly paradoxical reaction to the mother's affirmative efforts in the following anecdote: "I felt depressed, I suggested to mother that I might go for a walk."

Mother: "OK I can see how you're having a rough time and it must be hard for you to be here and I guess there's nothing we can do but listen."

Nancy: "I wanted to hear it but I didn't want to hear it. I'd have much preferred mother giving me a lot of orders or giving me hell. I don't know how to handle mother this way."

Therapist: "You don't want to be on your own with your mother."

Nancy responded by revealing her wish to regress as a defense. "I'm both angry and disappointed at the way my mother is acting. I like her to come around in the morning and get me up and tell me what to wear and then laugh so I could have a fight with her about what to wear. I like her to bring me to the train."

Therapist: "You want her to take care of you like a child."

Patient: "Yes, of course."

Therapist: "But you're not a child anymore."

The therapist's interpretive efforts again set limits to the acting out and relations with the mother improved temporarily.

Nancy: "After our talk I realized that I wasn't trying and I tried harder to approach my mother in a different way, not to provoke her and we didn't have any arguments. We had a good time."

As the regressive acting out was controlled the next defenses against the anxiety and depression associated with individuation appeared in the interview—denial and detachment. Nancy's life at home quieted down but she became silent and withdrawn in the interviews.

Therapist: "What are you thinking about?"

Nancy: "Some songs are running through my head."

Therapist, confronting Nancy: "Here we are talking about important things and you're allowing songs to run through your head."

Nancy: "I can't help it."

Therapist: "I think you have more control. What do you come here for? What is it all about?"

Nancy: "I couldn't care less about coming here, it brings me down. It's a question of enduring. I'm going to endure this year and at 18 I'm going to take off."

Therapist: "Oh, is 18 going to make things all that different?" Nancy laughs. Therapist: "You know it's not going to be all that different. You might move out geographically but you're going to feel just as bad as you feel now."

Nancy finally said: "I just don't want to get involved and you want to get me involved. Every time I get involved I get hurt."

Therapist: "Well perhaps that has been the case in the past but you have to take the chance if you want it to be different in the future."

Nancy: "I'm too afraid. I tried to talk to my parents but I'm afraid.

If it doesn't work out all sorts of bad feelings would happen and I'll have no place to go. I get along much better with my father but my mother is a monster. She's ugly. I know that's a crazy feeling. I see her as a dragon. I think it has something to do with not having the hospital to protect me from her."

Therapist: "Perhaps it does."

The hospital had protected Nancy against her feelings of engulfment on the part of mother and therefore on returning home she had to fight that much harder to defend against her wish to be engulfed. Thus it is one thing to protect the patient against the tie that binds and quite another to deal with the patient's wish to be so bound.

Therapist: "It must be confusing to you because you see her as a dragon and she's really trying to understand you."

Nancy: "I guess she is trying to let me grow up. What I would really like to do is just bop around the street."

Therapist: "You've been through that and you know it doesn't work."

Nancy: "If they let me do it I'd be furious."

Therapist: "You know they wouldn't let you do it because they care about you."

Nancy: "It upsets me when you say that. I don't know if they do or not and I don't want to think of it."

At the next interview Nancy appeared well-groomed and was in better spirits. She said that she had again approached her mother in a different way and then reported her anxiety at the mother letting go! "Mother said I could go to Woodstock. I got surprised and anxious and afraid and angry at her and I couldn't figure out why I was angry and then I realized, here she is letting me go. She's letting me have some freedom and that makes me nervous because that's not what I want. It's really all mixed up in my head."

The first crisis—defending against the abandonment depression by regressive acting out—was resolved by the therapist's interpretations, and the patient again turned around to resume moving toward individuation and to dealing with the resultant fears of being abandoned in the interview.

Nancy now discussed an old relationship with an emotionally ill boyfriend, realizing her use of a heterosexual relationship to defend against feelings of abandonment: "I don't know that anybody can replace him in my love. It's beyond understanding."

Therapist scoffingly: "Oh, come on, this sounds like Romeo and Juliet. If your parents wouldn't have forbidden you to see this guy you wouldn't have wanted to have anything to do with him."

Nancy laughed: "I think he needs help."

Therapist: "Yeah, but it's not your job to help, what about yourself? Why do you pick someone like this?"

Nancy: "I'm frightened and I'm scared. I'm not going to have to go back to the hospital and it helps to hold on to him." She then reported the expression of her wish for reunion with the hospital in a dream: "My mother, my father and you took me back to the hospital."

The mother now received word that her own father had cancer and she became saddened and depressed. Characteristically Nancy felt guilty, and thought she caused the mother's depression: "I was feeling guilty but mother must have sensed it because she said: "don't worry it has nothing to do with you." Nancy then elaborated on her feeling of guilt about individuation. "Mother doesn't have any friends and rarely goes out. I feel guilty about going out. I feel funny about leaving her. I know it's silly because it's good for me to go out. When I come home and tell her I had a good time I think it makes her more depressed so I keep it brief and we talk about other things. I suppose I sort of feel I have to take care of my mother."

Nancy raised the question of college mainly as a spring board to deal with her anxiety about the inevitable separation from the therapist; she first asked him how long he was going to be around. Nancy: "Do you know why I'm asking you all this?"

Therapist: "No."

Nancy: "I'm afraid to go to college and I also want to know how long you're going to be around."

The therapist told her he would be here for a year and a half.

THE FOURTH MONTH

The next series of interviews dealt mainly with the conflict with the mother and with her relationship with a boy. She mentioned a boyfriend she liked but who had not dated her. She knew he had taken out another girl in the class: "When that girl comes around I feel empty, inferior like jumping in front of a subway. There's a little voice inside that says: 'Jump, jump.' It's not on my side but I know I wouldn't do it."

Comment. Here the patient responds to the imagined rejection as an abandonment and wishes to do away with herself. These feelings spring from a projection on the boy of her introjection of her mother's negative attitude and failure to give her the emotional support she craved. (See Chapter 2.)

Nancy's fear of engulfment by the mother was revealed in battles over concrete arrangements such as the time she took the train home and whether the mother would get a "babysitter" for Nancy when the mother took a vacation trip to Canada.

Nancy's anxiety mounted as her mother asked her to stay home while the mother was in Canada, not because the mother did not trust Nancy's friends but because the mother had to know where Nancy was every moment of the day. Nancy: "I think my mother wants to be in Canada and at the same time know what room I'm in and what I am wearing." Since Nancy would not agree to stay home while the mother was away, the mother got a "babysitter" and lectured Nancy on her selfishness in not agreeing to stay home alone. Also, at this time, the boy whom she had been seeing after school said that he would have to stop seeing her because she was "too straight, too much into feelings and not on the drug scene."

The patient reacted to this also as an abandonment: "I felt like doing the 200 aspirin trick when he told me that. I wish I knew a sure way to get away from this feeling. It's just like the feeling I have when my mother goes away. I can't stand to have these feelings any longer. I feel worthless and like somebody who will always be abandoned. Why do I pick people like that?"

Therapist: "That's a very good question. I think it may be a reflection of your low opinion of yourself."

Nancy: "The only people I'm comfortable with are people I feel are in more trouble than I'm in. I can feel superior, and take care of them."

Nancy: "I don't know what to do."

Therapist: "You have to understand these feelings. What you're doing right now is the best thing, talking about them. In the past these feelings would make you want to do all sorts of crazy things."

Nancy: "All I feel like doing now is crying and going to sleep. I feel I'll never have anybody again."

Therapist: "This is a boyfriend, it happens to everybody and you're going to get over it and it's not what you feel it is."

Nancy: "He was much sicker than I and it made me more comfortable to be with somebody like that. These are the kind I pick out. People I can help, people I can lord it over with my own health. I don't stand a chance with other people because they realize I'm nothing, an empty person, a phony."

Therapist: "Feeling so bad yourself, what are you doing with somebody worse off than you? How good is this for you? What you need is someone who is healthy and who can have a relationship with you. This guy was so much sicker than you, he did you a favor."

Comment. The therapist set realistic limits to the abandonment feelings by providing the patient with his perception of reality. Boyfriends come and boyfriends go; people have ways of dealing with boyfriends that make these events not so totally devastating.

Borderline patients, like Nancy, choose relationships for "comfort" rather than involvement. Since sexual attraction and emotional involvement produce fears of engulfment or abandonment they pick boys with whom they are "comfortable," that is, not anxious. They feel safer relating to someone who needs them rather than to risk a relationship based on attraction or love where they have no leverage or purchase on the partner. The partner, having the option to stay or leave, reinforces their fears of abandonment. These patients always use the word "comfortable" rather than "attractive or exciting" to describe their relationship.

Whenever a separation stress arises the patient is prone to lose her previously acquired insight and capacity for self-observation and to regress to the old defense which again has to be worked through. As the parents were about to leave for the trip to Canada Nancy regressed and again defended herself against the feeling of abandonment that this visit incurred by acting out. She told her parents at the very last minute that she was going to spend the time with a girl whom she knew they did not like. She hoped to provoke them into saying no; thereby relieving her feeling that they were going away because they did not care about her.

The parents, guilty about leaving, failed to perceive the test the patient had devised and passed the ball to the therapist who passed it back. After the parents left, Nancy revealed her intense dependency on the mother and her feelings of loss: "I don't like my mother being away. I thought I'd like her to go but I don't. I feel like she's left me. My mother isn't even there to see what I wear anymore. Every morning I wonder if she would like what I'm wearing. It's like that time I told you she was in my head"— as good a description of introjection as one is likely to get.

The therapist again reinforced the reality of the situation to provide a framework for the analysis of the feelings of abandonment: "Your mother has gone on a short vacation. Why do you feel this way?" The therapist elaborated: "I think you're nervous because your mother is away. It's hard for you to be on your own, you and your mother are like oil and water when together; and yet you can't stay out of the same bowl when she's gone."

Every morning the mother was away Nancy felt loss which she rationalized as a feeling of loneliness, that is, a lack of friends. The therapist again interpreted the defense: "I think you're talking about being lonely for friends to get away from talking about how badly you feel when your mother is not around."

Nancy at first resisted and then finally responded to the interpretation that her provocative acting out was an effort to deal with the feelings of loss: "Since she's been gone I've been irritable, bitchy, and upset. Pouncing on my sister. I'm not eating. I'm twisting my hair ends. I was talking to myself last night. I'm really shaky but I don't like to think it's just because my mother is gone. I did purposely mention that specific girl friend to my parents so that they would tell me I couldn't see her. So I could get them to make the decision rather than make it on my own."

In the next several weeks Nancy's clinical state again improved. However, near the end of the fourth month what eventuated in the final crisis was introduced for the first time. Nancy: "The other night my father and mother came in looking like a football team, with that 'we're going to talk' look on their face. They said we were going to move to Oregon this summer and that I should apply to a college on the West coast, not one in the East. I just can't pick up my bag and move again. I can't take all these changes. Every move I've made has been a very bad experience. The first year has always been disaster. I can't face it again. They don't realize what the move does to myself and to Linda. When I told my mother she started crying and said that she didn't realize this and wouldn't make me do anything I didn't want to do but I don't believe her. I feel eventually she'll pressure me into doing it."

When the mother disagreed with her Nancy reported that: "all my courage goes down I can't make it at all. Nobody else makes me feel like I'm anything. That I have any courage or a mind of my own. It's terrible to be that dependent on somebody. I have to depend that much on her approval, but without her approval I can't stand up"—that is, without the mother's approval she felt empty, abandoned, without emotional supplies, and could not assert herself.

Nancy had now surmounted the first crisis of the outpatient treatment, that is, the abandonment depression. She did well in school, made friends, came home on time, and was never late for an interview. She also helped her mother around the house. However, Nancy's improvement, her beginning move to autonomy as described in Chapter 16 brought into play the tie that binds: the mother began to withdraw supplies. This began with low key complaints about the cost of therapy but was to increase gradually to a crescendo, threatening the therapy itself.

CHAPTER 15

Nancy: The Second Crisis—To Termination

CONFLICT WITH THE MOTHER

At a party given by her parents Nancy overheard an intoxicated friend of the mother's tell the father: "You know your wife hates Nancy, has never liked her since the day she was born." Her own fears confirmed, Nancy said not a word to either mother or father but came to the next interview in a rage, feeling depressed, hopeless, and wanting to leave home.

It took all of the therapist's persuasive powers to get Nancy to take a look at her feelings rather than to act them out. Therapist: "Last week you were feeling fine as you had been for several weeks; things had been better between you and your mother. I think we have to figure out why this upset you so much." Nancy ignored this and returned to her rage at the mother which now had the exact same tone that it had when she was first hospitalized. Therapist: "I think you should talk to your father and your mother about it first. This doesn't prevent you from acting later." Nancy finally agreed to a joint session with the parents.

This led to a stormy but fruitful joint session in which all of the basic family pathology was again brought into the open—the mother's failure to give emotional supplies, the father's distancing, and the patient's difficulty in asserting herself with her parents. Nancy attacked her mother for not caring about her. The mother responded in a positive manner, saying: "I've been working for a year with you on my problems and then you go hear some drunken woman say that I don't care for you and off you go without talking to me about it."

Nancy: "I don't think you ever cared for me, I think you love me but I don't think you like me and it's been like that all along. I get looks from you that really kill me. You love my sister but not me."

Mother: "Maybe the fact that I run around all week for you says something about the way I care for you. If you can't accept that as the way I care for you then I'm sorry, that's the best I can do." The mother then elaborated on how upset she had been over her own father's cancer and the prospective move to Oregon.

The father, however, maintained his usual distance and said: "If Nancy feels she has to leave we have to talk about it."

The therapist interposed: "On the contrary, we have to talk about how things got this bad, not whether she leaves or not."

A discussion ensued about the father's frequent absences from the home which the father rationalized as being due to his work. The mother persisted: "You're going to have to take some of the family responsibility because I can't do it any more." Father evaded: "I don't know what you mean." Mother intervened: "I don't know how to tell you to go about it either but something has to be done because I'm falling apart. I don't know if moving to Oregon is going to be the answer or not. The big mistake was to move to New York in the first place and a bigger mistake was for me to go along with everything you said." The mother then complained about the attention the father gave to his own mother, saying: "If you put some of that effort into us things might be a little better."

At the end of the interview Nancy tested her parents again by saying she was not going home with them but instead was going to visit a friend. The parents again failed to recognize the test and the father as usual went along with Nancy. The therapist recognizing Nancy's test, and at this juncture exasperated himself, demanded that the parents declare whether they wanted her to come home with them. The parents then insisted on her coming home.

PROGRESS WITH CONFLICT: FIFTH AND SIXTH MONTHS

After the family session described above, conflict in the family again subsided this time for approximately a month. The patient felt much better and began to move further toward individuation and autonomy which again brought her fears of abandonment versus engulfment to the fore: "I feel better but I can't believe it's going to last. I'm always expecting something to happen. Sometimes I wonder why I don't bring about a bad thing just to get rid of the anxiety about this good state ending."

A few days later Nancy reported the following dream: "A circle of gray mice were staring down at me, I was in a manhole. I couldn't get out of the manhole. There was a ladder I was trying to climb up. Beyond the mice was this beautiful sunrise. Everything was bright but inside the manhole it was dark and dreary and damp. I wanted to get out but had a trapped feeling."

The therapist interpreted that the dream reflected her fear of being on her own, being trapped in the manhole meant staying a child, and the mice were her fears. She could not stay a child but was frightened of growing up, the essential fear being that if she moved toward growing up her mother would withdraw her emotional supplies.

As Christmas approached Nancy's progress was reflected in her doing well in school, in her desire to get a driver's license and a Christmas job —more individuation. The mother's withdrawal of approval prompted by this progress was reflected in her constant objections to Nancy getting a job. The therapist again interpreted these efforts as due to the mother's difficulty in letting go. At the same time Nancy reported having arranged a birthday party for her mother for whom she baked a birthday cake.

After this month of quiet progress another warning of events to come presented itself in a telephone call from the mother conveying her anxiety about what activities and friends she should permit Nancy, that is, how much should she let go?

Nancy's next defense against the anxiety associated with her improvement was to want to withdraw from therapy, to cut down to once a week. The therapist suggested that this change was an effort to deal with her fear. Nancy ignored this and complained that her Christmas job would prevent her from coming more often and asked to have the interview times changed. When the therapist could not change the time, Nancy accused him of not wanting her to get well, of not wanting her to be independent, and of wanting to keep her from doing healthy things. She then threatened to tell her parents. The therapist pointed out that this was a lot of nonsense. Nancy laughed, and said: "Things are going better with my parents and I'm talking a lot with them but I still feel very lonely, I have this underlying fear of being alone and that I never will find anyone."

Nancy then revealed that she had not yet mailed any college applications and that her father, in collusion with her procrastination, objected to spending the money for several fees for application and suggested she send in only one or two.

Therapist: "Everything is going better, treatment, school, relationships with parents, work at Saks. Mother, father and you are getting anxious and want to stop the progress to get rid of the anxiety. You want to stop treatment because you feel the anxiety. Your father drags his feet on the college applications. He has difficulty in letting you go also."

Nancy then revealed the mother's holding on by saying that the mother did not want her to work in town but only at a shop across the street from the house. The therapist reinforced his interpretation: "You know it's really surprising, everybody talks about your becoming independent, including yourself; but as soon as you start everybody says: 'Hey, that's not what we want, stop that'."

The next day the therapist received the following call from the father. "I'm a man who wants to pay my bills but Nancy is costing me too much money and she has to see you only once a week. What do you think?"

Therapist: "Nancy is getting better but she really needs to come twice a week. It's a funny thing, when a patient gets better it's not always the way the parents thought it would happen."

Father: "Well, that might be true; but, listen, doctor, I'm a businessman, and I don't want to be dunned by you for not paying my bills; I don't want to bite off any more than I can chew!"

Therapist: "I told you what I think, now you have to decide whether or not you want to do it; and you ought to decide it with your wife and Nancy." The father admitted he had not talked to Nancy at all. "The three of you ought to sit down and lay out the finances and see."

Father: "That sounds like a reasonable thing to do." The father had hoped to latch on to Nancy's resistance to cut down on the therapy but when the therapist stood firm he persisted no further with the fiction that he couldn't afford it. The therapist knew that the father could afford it from the complete financial statement the father had made at the onset of treatment.

In the very next interview the therapist described the call to Nancy, interpreting the father's behavior as a manifestation of his difficulties in letting go. He recalled for Nancy her dream in the hospital when transferred to a better floor that her parents were going to sign her out, saying: "It's difficult for you and your family to accept the fact that you're improving. Your mother has cars, diamonds, fur jackets, so it's not a matter of money."

Nancy: "I don't want to talk about money, I get tired of hearing about money. My father keeps telling me I'm a financial problem. It really makes me feel bad. If he wants to make me feel guilty he's succeeding because I feel guilty."

Therapist: "Maybe he does it for another reason, maybe the problem is you're getting better."

In the next interview Nancy reported that the father had decided to go along with the therapist: "My father decided that I should come twice a week if that's what you think but I got the feeling that father is saying well if you don't get better it's not going to be my fault, we're doing what the doctor says it's going to be his fault."

The parental conflict again momentarily settled and Nancy further revealed her own anxiety about college: "You know what I did on Saturday? I was supposed to take my college boards and I threw away the admission ticket months ago. I went down to take the exams and they wouldn't let me take them."

Therapist: "I guess again it's because you're afraid to move ahead."

Nancy: "To tell you the truth I'm not too excited about going to college. I'm scared to death that something's going to happen." Nancy showed her positive feeling for her father in a creative painting she made for him for Christmas.

When she began her job at a department store, Nancy experienced her fear of being abandoned or engulfed and reported this fear along with her defenses against it. "It was really bad. I was so frightened that I wanted to leave two, three and four times. I felt that everybody was looking at me. I felt that everyone thought that crazy girl is really crazy, she's not going to make it, that she's going to bum up everything. I felt very different, very strange and of course, they all turned around and looked at me when I lit up a Gaulois."

Therapist: "Why did you light up a Gaulois?"

Nancy: "I always smoke them."

Therapist: "Nancy, you never smoke Gaulois. I don't see why you lit up a Gaulois. It brings to mind the same hassles you had with your mother. You got very anxious you really didn't know what to do and so you start doing kooky things." Nancy then said she also wore an ultra miniskirt which she never wears anymore.

Therapist: "You're anxious for many reasons. You're really not sure about yourself, you're afraid of the implications of what it is to get a job on your own. So what do you do, start acting out. You create the very thing you're afraid of—that is, rejection, so that you can say yeah, you see, they do think I'm kooky and leave. Also I think with Saks as with your mother, you're really afraid that you're going to be swallowed up and you have to do all these crazy things to be different."

Nancy: "It's really funny that you say that because when I walked in the door the big S on the window looked like a big tunnel and I felt that it was a huge tunnel that was sucking me in from the sidewalk."

Therapist: "Of course, because you think that going in there is either destroying you or you're going to get lost in the masses."

Nancy: "That's the worst scare, which I guess is the same thing as being destroyed." Nancy projected on Saks her negative maternal introject, that is, if she asserted herself the people would reject her as her mother did.

THE THIRD CRISIS: SEVENTH MONTH AFTER DISCHARGE

Father and Mother Withdraw Emotional Supplies

The third crisis was precipitated by the mother beginning to have the exact trouble with Nancy's younger sister that she had had with Nancy.

This time, however, the father supported the daughter rather than the mother. The mother, upset, called a family conference at which she said she had no complaints against Nancy except that she was becoming too dependent on her therapist and that after January 1 she could see him only once a week. The father called the therapist to inform him, again giving finances as the reason. At the same time the father's business was about to be moved to Kansas City—a place that the mother disliked. The mother put her foot down and refused to move there.

Nancy's characteristic initial reaction to these dramatic events was to deny: "I don't feel anything."

Therapist: "You know by now that when you feel this way it means you're afraid of what you might feel."

Nancy: "I don't understand my reaction. I'm pulled between you and mother and I don't know what to do. As much as I like dependency I'm afraid. I know that being dependent on you is healthier than being dependent on her but the whole thing frightens me."

The therapist asked Nancy why her father would not come in to talk this decision over with him.

Nancy: "I don't know, father says that I'm mercenary. He makes me feel like a tax deduction. If he gets sick or breaks his back with all this work it's going to be because of me." At the same time that the father was reducing treatment because of "money," he was paying $50 per week for the sister's piano lessons.

The therapist continued to try to overcome Nancy's denial: "I'm puzzled by your lack of response."

Nancy: "I feel my father has pulled the rug out from under me once again. I don't know when it's going to stop. Only when I leave home. This is very frightening."

Therapist: "All these things happening and you don't feel anything. Your father pulling you out of treatment, your parents moving and you going off to college."

Nancy (crying): "I'm very depressed. I don't want to go. I'm afraid. Even though I have a shitty home it's a home and if they would stay put I could grow up and leave them more easily but they're threatening to move away and they want me to come with them and that means leaving you. That means I ought to be just one of them again [back in the symbiotic bind]. I don't think it's fair of them to ask me to be unhappy so they can be happy. They don't care if it makes a difference to me. I told them what I think. They're still going to do it anyway."

In the next session, the first one at the new schedule of once a week, the patient's denial was total. She talked very little. Reduction of the treatment to once a week caused the patient to be unable to open her emotions to the therapist. She had to split and deny (just as when she was discharged from the hospital) because she had no other alternatives. She could not use her therapist as an outlet.

Alarmed by this chain of events the therapist sent the father a letter attempting to raise his anxiety by emphasizing the destructive potential of his action. In response the father finally came to see the therapist. The therapist interpreted the family's anxiety about Nancy growing up, and the father reluctantly agreed to allow her to continue. In her next interview Nancy did not mention the interview with the father but when the therapist brought it up, her denial broke down. She started crying and said: "I'm so glad because I've been nervous all week. I haven't been able to concentrate in school, have had an upset stomach and headaches, I've been biting my fingernails and haven't been able to sleep."

The procrastination over the college applications again came to the fore, but this time it was finally settled. The patient applied to colleges on both coasts.

She then spoke about sex, noting that she used it to relieve anxiety: "There's this guy my age who is very infantile, really like a little puppy, always running after me and buying me cokes and whatnot. I really think he's cute but I don't feel anything for him. Last week all of a sudden I was anxious all day. All of a sudden, I wanted to ball him. I didn't know why. Just for that afternoon I found him very attractive. I was very anxious. It was like I just wanted to have sex as I would like to have a drink. Why don't I have sexual feelings for anybody except when I'm anxious." Exploring further she says: "Another guy I went out with was below me, not socially; but he was really just too freaked out, too helpless, too childish and messed up. I didn't have any respect for him. With Bernie, the guy I'm going out with now I don't really know why I don't have any sexual feelings for him. We're really the best of friends. I guess I'm going to be one of those girls who winds up marrying her best friend. My husband will just stay my best friend all of my life. He'll be my husband as long as he doesn't want to have sex with me."

PROGRESS BEGINS TO SURMOUNT CONFLICT— EIGHTH, NINTH, AND TENTH MONTHS

The theme of the next three months was one of steady progress towards separation-individuation and autonomy despite the unsettled nature of the living situation and the steady harassment of the mother whose efforts Nancy begins to manage with considerably less internal turmoil. The college applications were sent and she was finally accepted at an eastern college.

Her functioning continued to improve and her interest in boys heightened. She became interested in one boy, Bernie, started to date him regularly, and then decided to take the Pill and have sexual intercourse with him. As spring waned and summer approached, her school schedule was reduced and she started to make realistic, constructive plans for various jobs such as working in an animal hospital or department store or making hippie-style baby clothes for a local store. She also started to make and sell necklaces.

During this time her appearance and behavior in the interviews also changed. Her reality perception showed a dramatic improvement which she then turned upon her evaluation of her relationship with her parents, her schooling, and her boyfriend and dealt with them all realistically, effectively, and constructively.

The highly affect-charged intense moods moderated and there were fewer mood swings with a persistence of calmer mood states. There seemed much less need for the ventilation of intense feelings of rage, little or no need for the therapist to deal with acting out behavior, and an ongoing recognition of the continuity of good feelings from the past that could be used to resolve present impasses. In a single interview she was able for the first time to talk about a number of different areas of conflict rather than concentrating only on one because of the powerful emotions it aroused.

Nancy reported her perception of the change in her feeling state: "I don't feel like I have problems all the time. I think I want to live longer and along with this I'm giving up smoking. I don't want to die any more and maybe it's all worth while so I better take care of myself. I don't feel weighed down by my problems all day long like I used to feel. I wonder if this is going to last. This is the longest time I've ever gone in my life without being in a crisis. You know 5 months is a pretty long time. I think it's the longest time since I was 10 years old." Then laughing, she imagined all the crises she could create with her mother, for example, letting her find the pills in her pocket or putting some cigarette paper in her pocketbook to lead mother to think she was on pot.

Three themes illustrated below dominated the sessions over these months: relationship with her boyfriend Bernie, the mother's holding on, and the fear of abandonment associated with her new found independence.

Relationship with Bernie

Nancy reported her feelings about the birth control pills: "This is now the third day that I'm on the pill. I hope that my breasts will swell because the obstetrician told me that would be one of the things. But my breasts haven't been swollen at all. I really looked in the mirror all morning from the side but I still can't tell. I look at the pill about 5 minutes before I take it and I know it's really ironical. This is the last thing that my mother would expect me to be doing, taking pills, being this cautious about getting pregnant. I'm sure if my mother thought about it she would just think that I would just go out and sleep with anybody and throw caution to the winds and . . . I don't think she realizes how . . . how maturely and systematically I could handle this."

Her relationship with Bernie started out with casual contact in school, progressed to seeing each other quite steadily, and then grew to some neck- ing and petting. As the patient decided to take the pill, she ran into conflict with Bernie who did not seem interested in sex.

Her fantasies about Bernie came crashing down and she became quite realistic in her perception of the difficulty with him saying: "He didn't do his work in school. He didn't have a job, didn't bathe. He never seemed to want to take me any place. Nor, did he seem interested in having sex with me." Rather than interpreting his lack of interest as an abandonment this time, she said: "I realize I'm not beautiful but I certainly am attractive. I think I'm just as attractive as about anybody else that he could find."

At the same time she became aware of some of the reasons she may have picked Bernie out. "Except for the making out I'm always the strongest one in the relationship. I even have to decide where to go and often we can't go where I want because he doesn't have any money. He leaves everything up to me. He still doesn't have a job. There may be another reason why he's not working. Part of me doesn't want him to work. He's been out of school since the end of January and hasn't found a job. Part of me wants him not to work so he could be around me every afternoon, just like my mother wants me to come home every afternoon when I get out of school. I haven't told him but I guess he can pick this up."

Finally, she broke off the relationship with Bernie, was quite depressed, and revealed her initial motivation for starting the relationship: "I used him to avoid being alone. When I feel this emptiness or aloneness I could latch on to anyone. That's why I always avoid being alone. That's why I like sitting in Grand Central Station because I know it's always there." At the same time the patient realized that she was not ready for sexual inter- course: "I'm going to take the pills but I don't want to have sexual inter- course with anyone because I'm depressed, I don't feel like being that close to anyone. I don't know if I could tolerate it."

Mother's Holding on

As the patient continued to individuate, the mother's anxiety rose as did her efforts to hold on. For example, early in February she called the doctor again, wanting him to force Nancy to live at home when going to college. She had found a junior college 10 miles away from their prospective home in Oregon and wanted Nancy to commute to college by car. She questioned the therapist: "Don't you think Nancy's fragile state of mind indicates that she should be at home?"

Feeling equally threatened by Nancy's relationship with Bernie she sprang to the attack. She said to Nancy: "Whom do you love more your family or Bernie?"

Nancy: "I love Bernie." The mother started crying. Nancy: "Can't you see that I love Bernie in a way different than I love you?"

Mother: "I'm just upset." The mother then went into her room, came back several minutes later and said: "Don't think you're going to stay in town five nights a week to spend the time with Bernie."

Nancy reported jokingly to her therapist: "I think she wants to stop in the middle of the evening where ever she is and wonder exactly what room I'm in, where I'm sitting, what I have in my hand and who's in the room. She wants to have sort of like a telescopic lens on me at all times but I won't let her do it."

As Nancy started to make plans for a job in the city to occupy herself now that her school schedule was reduced, the mother objected: "My mother wants me to rest a lot. She doesn't want me to go to work, she wants me to just take it easy and come home at one or two o'clock in the afternoon and take a nap. She says there'll be a lot for me to do around the house to help get settled and that I only want to stay in the city because of my therapist. She says I'm going to have to give up that security blanket some day anyway."

Nancy, however, persisted in asserting herself and pursuing her own plans. The mother's anxiety mounted to the point that she finally refused to give Nancy money to buy a pair of shoes, explaining that she did not have the money until she could get it from the father. The family had never lived from payday to payday and Nancy had been wearing her winter boots for several months. Perceiving the true cause, Nancy said: "I think she's doing this 'cause she's angry that I want to work in New York City and live there. Mother says: 'I'm mad at you 'cause you think that money grows on trees and you're very mercenary and all you ever want is money from us. If you want to live outside the house, you can do it but you have to support yourself because we can't afford it'."

The patient showed her improved emotional state this time saying: "I'm mad at mother about my summer plans. She refused to budge and I asked her about my shoes and she got angry and said she couldn't buy them. I took the money out of my own bank account."

Nancy then reported another incident with the mother: "I had to go to the doctor to get a shot. Mother insisted on accompanying me into the treatment room. I told her I didn't need her there. Finally, when the doctor was about to give the shot mother just sat there. I said: 'I don't want you around.' Mother started laughing saying: 'Oh you're growing up.' Finally the doctor said I had grown up. Afterward mother broke down and cried saying that she felt she'd lost her little girl."

In April the mother called the therapist again to express her anger at the fact that the patient was giving up smoking; and to try to get the therapist to force the patient to comply with the parents' wishes that she go to college outside the city for the summer.

She told Nancy she'd never be able to quit smoking and refused to give her money for train fare. Nancy, now going to school only 2 hours a day, wanted to get up early so she could see Bernie before school; but the mother stole the alarm clock so she could not get up and later refused to take her to the station.

Other Themes

Nancy reported her fantasy of an exclusive relationship with the therapist to deal with her separation anxiety: "I know it's silly but I just don't like the idea of you seeing anybody else in fact I don't like the idea of you seeing your family. I like to think of you existing only 2 hours a week here and that you don't do anything else but treat me 2 hours a week. It's very hard to give up that idea when I see somebody walking out of the office before I come in."

She then reported how she also clung to a place (see Chapter 2) to assuage her feelings of abandonment: "You know what I like about the East coast is that the hospital is here and it can't move. You might go. You might get drafted. All the residents over there are going to go. My family, I don't know where they're ever going to be. Boyfriends I have will leave me until I meet the right one and then I'm not sure he won't leave me. The hospital will always be there." Then she quoted the date it was founded. "If it's there that long it will be there until I die. I'm quite serious about this you know. I know you think that's crazy but that's really the way I feel. I don't like to say this to people because they will tell me that I'm crazy."

FINAL CRISIS—ELEVENTH, TWELFTH, AND THIRTEENTH MONTHS

The summer plans were still indefinite and Nancy was not discussing the possibility that treatment might end. The therapist brought it up and

Nancy initially responded with denial and withdrawal. Nancy: "I don't want to think about it."

Therapist: "You know this is exactly like it was in the hospital. You would not face your feelings. You would withdraw so you had nothing to talk about. This is the way you handled my leaving on vacation. What do you think it's going to be like if you leave?"

Nancy: "I won't have anything to do on Wednesday afternoon."

Therapist: "It's more than that."

Nancy: "I don't want to talk about it. On Wednesday and Friday afternoons I'll come and stand here on the street and wonder what you're doing in that building. I will really be all alone and I feel as if I can't make it."

Therapist: "You've gotten a lot out of your treatment. Things are different. There's a part of you that can really make it by yourself."

However, there was little affective response from the patient and she said at the end of the interview: "Well I guess I wasted my money today. Maybe when I come back on Wednesday I'll have enough courage to talk to you."

The next 2 weeks the patient continued to be depressed and withdrawn, handling her anxiety about separation from the doctor by denial, suppression, and withdrawal. She graduated from high school during this time; then under the doctor's prodding she reported her fantasy of a permanent relationship, another defense against separation anxiety: "I can't think of you in terms of not seeing you again. I have to think of it as something that we're going to continue. That you'll be right here in this room, ready to start up again when I have to have you. I have a very hard time ever adjusting to the fact that something is over and no longer exists. When I decide that something exists it's there for good and there's no losing it or moving away from it or using it and moving on."

The therapist interpreted these fantasies as defenses against separation and emphasized her new capacities for coping. However, there was little affective response because the patient was now in the same situation as when discharged from the hospital, that is, under the imminent threat of abandonment.

Then, like a bolt out of the blue, while the wife was now bitterly complaining about his absences for the first time, the father cancelled her treatment with the social worker, told the therapist that he had gotten a job in Oregon, and the family had to move in 3 weeks. Furthermore, he said he had no money and treatment had to stop. Nancy had to come with them for the summer but would be permitted to come back to college in the East in the fall. All of the therapist's interpretations of the father's behavior as a reaction to Nancy's improvement and very destructive to her were of no avail. The father refused to come in to discuss it.

Nancy's response again was: "I don't want to think about that because I don't know if it's really going to happen. I don't know if we're really going to move. I don't know if treatment is really going to end. Why should I be afraid and frightened? Why should I go through all that?"

At the same time the father was putting Nancy in another bind. He complained to her about her not being able to get a job, but he put so many restrictions on her it was impossible for her to get a job; for example, he would not let her work in New York, let her come to school in New York, allow her to go to the art school in town, or let her use the car to work in another nearby town; yet still he complained that she did not have a job.

Nancy reported a dream: "I was sealed up inside a pyramid and then a cave, the two images alternating. In this hole there was a dead man. He had tried to get out and couldn't and I was left there by myself with him and there was an ax and a long rope and there was also some food, light and water in the cave." She said she felt she was trapped by her father. There was an ax and rope that she wanted to use but she did not know how to use it. Her fear of making it on her own prevented her from getting out.

As the end of treatment approached Nancy withdrew more and had less to say in interviews. In the last interview, wishing to warn Nancy about her future, the therapist said: "I guess you feel that since things are ending why bother talking about them."

Nancy: "I don't know what you mean by things ending. I'm going on vacation but I'll be back in September."

Therapist: "I don't think you really believe you're coming back and you're not ready to deal with that."

Nancy: "Well why wouldn't I be back?"

Therapist: "I don't know but the way things are going with your family I wouldn't be surprised if your father changed his mind about letting you come back." The mother, however, now came to Nancy's support when she brought this up suggesting that she go to the eastern college for the summer session. The father again said he could not afford it. The mother then reassured Nancy that if the father said he could not afford to let her return East to college the mother would pay for college as well as for continued treatment. Nancy stopped treatment and went to Oregon.

In the fall Nancy called her therapist to report that she had had a good summer and had returned to college in the East. She said that at the moment she was doing well in college and wanted to try it on her own without treatment. The last phone contact with her was about 20 months after hospitalization and she was managing quite well.

The abrupt termination of therapy without consultation with the therapist is dramatic evidence of the *vital* defensive function performed by Nancy's role as family scapegoat. At the same time it also indicates the enormity of the parents' resistance to any change or progress on Nancy's part. Nancy and the parents had been in treatment for 2 years. Despite all their own labors in therapy, despite the initial rescue of Nancy from the jaws of destructive illness, and despite their relationship with the social worker gained through 2-years' work, the parents' resistance was so great that it washed over these not insignificant influences like a tidal wave, giving a startling demonstration of just how great a battle Nancy had on her hands.

Nancy's progress toward separation-individuation threatened to remove her from the role of family scapegoat, upset the family equilibrium, and turned the mother's hostility from Nancy to the father which threw the father into a panic that could only be alleviated by sacrificing Nancy. The father was the "eminence grise" behind the family pathology as well as probably acting as the mother's agent. His need for Nancy to support his defensive distance from the mother combined with the mother's need for Nancy to defend herself against her feelings of abandonment. Nevertheless, despite all these forces Nancy's return to college where she was on her own for the first time suggests that she had been strengthened enough by treatment to overcome these forces and make this very important break.

Nancy's treatment illustrates the two themes that alternately occupy the center stage of outpatient treatment and form a vicious circle. When theme one—Nancy's defenses against her own individuation—is properly handled, Nancy improves, but this threatens the parents' equilibrium; this brings on theme two—the parents' withdrawal of supplies—which when properly handled again brings back theme one.

Experiences of this sort have led me to feel that the ideal setting for posthospital therapy would be a halfway house where the parents' resistance could be minimized and therapeutic leverage maximized. A libidinal re-fueling station was needed (see Chapter 2) that could be available to maintain emotional supplies until the patient developed with the aid of his therapy to the stage of autonomy and was internally ready and able to separate. Short of that, in most instances I have tried to find local boarding schools, foster homes, or homes with relatives—all of which seem superior to advising the patient to return home to the parents.

CHAPTER 16

Bill, Helen, and Grace: Follow-Up Summary

This chapter continues the theme of follow-up outpatient treatment by presenting summaries of the outpatient treatment of the remaining three patients. The psychological testing of two is included in the Appendix. Several brief verbatim reports are presented to illustrate how a few of the patients viewed their own outpatient treatment.

BILL

After discharge Bill was seen for 6 months three times a week until his therapist had to leave at which time he was transferred to the author. Bill's home was in the West. At the time of discharge his father was ill; his 12-year-old brother was exhibiting the same symptoms that Bill had had and was receiving psychiatric treatment as was his mother. Bill was discharged to live with an uncle and aunt in the suburbs and commute to a private high school.

Bill's defenses against his first crisis—the abandonment depression that occurs with discharge—consisted of excessive activity, for example, running all over the city, going to plays, attending the opera, trying to find people to do things with, and forming brief, dependent, clinging relationships with girls. In the interviews he first handled his feelings by denial and by taking the rage out on himself: "The past is over and I don't want to talk about it. I don't have any character, I'm junk, I'm an ape, I'm subhuman."

However, as with Nancy, the underlying pressure would suddenly burst through and "he would crash" one evening and suddenly feel depressed and suicidal. This phase, which had lasted 4 or 5 months in the hospital, lasted approximately 4 weeks in outpatient treatment—a testimony to the groundwork done on interpreting and attenuating the defense of denial while he was still in the hospital.

When Bill mentioned to his therapist that he had not gone to school, the therapist confronted him with his defenses against the abandonment depression. Bill responded: "I'm pretty angry at you. I guess I'm directing it all against myself. I guess I better talk about it."

The next night the therapist got a panicky call from Bill: "I'm suicidal, I need to talk with you. Can I see you tomorrow?" Bill talked about his fear of expressing anger at the therapist and became aware that he was in the same kind of regression that he had gone through in the hospital.

Bill then moved into his second defense, which was the fantasy of an exclusive relationship with his therapist: "I want a protective relationship with you, I'm getting tinges of what it's like to have a straight head. I realize I'm terribly dependent on you and I don't like that."

He then began to work through his feelings about separation from his therapist, crying in interviews as he expressed feelings of loss and as he projected his rage in fear of violence and of being harmed. He then explored the loss of the exclusive relationship with his mother in the setting of the loss of the exclusive relationship with the therapist. At one point, glaring at the therapist, he said: "Damn it why don't you take care of me. I want you to." After an expression of this sort he would get frightened and become compliant, seeking the therapist's approval.

In the middle of a session he reported the following fantasy: he was getting very small and the therapist was getting very large with huge, long fingernails, and was standing over him—a fantasy repetition of the father's attacks on Bill. He verbalized his fear that his therapist would attack him and might call him a "punk kid" just as his father had. He then spoke of taking his rage out on himself through self-depreciation—that he was a "shmuck," subhuman. He would deny any feelings associated with this and then several days later would call the therapist: "I feel suicidal, what can I do, can I see you?" He began having fantasies of knifing a woman, that is, repetitions of the feelings he had worked through during his abandonment depression in the hospital. He would then attempt to make the therapist omnipotent: "I don't want you to be human, I don't want to have these feelings about you. I want you to be Superman, but you're telling me you're not Superman."

Bill then revealed that he had been frustrating himself by masturbating and stopping short of orgasm with a fantasy of knifing and killing. The therapist pointed out that he was frustrating himself and suggested that masturbation was a normal physical outlet. Before the next session the patient masturbated to orgasm and arrived smiling and happy; he said: "Gee it was really great."

The mother was holding on to the patient by calling on the telephone. Bill would come to a session and say: "Damn it. I want to break away from her why doesn't she understand that." Then he would turn to the therapist and say: "You don't understand me either. There are all sorts of things about me you don't know." Following this expression of anger at the therapist he would get anxious and suicidal, and later call his therapist. After several of these instances, the therapist interpreted that the calls were for reassurance. Bill then would wait out the suicidal episode until the next session when he would again express his rage and fear.

About 6 months after discharge he had sexual intercourse for the first time. Bill: "It was a very freaky feeling but somehow or another it was a big turning point in my life. It does a lot inside you, sort of a turning point from being a little boy to becoming a man. It's a really freaky feeling. I feel manly. I belong with the guys now. A very good feeling." Bill then went on to say: "I haven't been crashing lately. Because of your leaving I've been quiet, I've been depressed. I think I'm handling it quite well. I've been afraid of facing up to life but now maybe I will."

At this point in one interview, like Nancy, he could cover three areas, any one of which would have previously produced a panic, that is, anger at his therapist or mother, depression, and fear. Then near the end of his sessions with his therapist he reported a fantasy which he had first reported right after hospitalization: "A little kid in knickers, 4 years old shoved out the door. He turns around looking back at the door slammed in his face feeling very alone." The fantasy has now changed; the door has been closed behind the kid but this time he turns around and looks at the world, knows he has to go out there, and wants to, even though he is afraid.

He finished the school year with a 94 average (out of 100) and received an award for outstanding achievement.

Let us now hear how Bill viewed his 6 months of outpatient therapy.

Therapist: "How do you see yourself as compared to when you first came in the hospital?"

Bill: "When I came into the hospital all my thoughts and feelings were jumbled up so I couldn't face what was really happening to me. I feel I have greater ability to understand what's happening inside me as well as what's happening around me. I can put all this knowledge together and act on it. I think that's the biggest difference. I'm aware and I can handle my awareness. I don't know how it happened but actually I think it was a slow gaining of trust with my therapist and being able to slowly just peak around the corner of what was there. I'm going to Europe for the summer and I'm very excited about it. I feel it will be another turning point. I'd love to be free to roam the country. I don't want to be home. My whole family is in a hassle. They're all seeing psychiatrists and having a lot of problems. I'm enjoying school, both the work and socially. I'm having ups and downs with people but I'm doing quite well. I have three or four close friends I can talk to and do things with and I know a lot of other people casually. I feel fairly comfortable and when I'm there I don't think as I used to here in the Clinic. I was always thinking about whether or not I was equal or is this right or is that right but now I can be with others and be pretty comfortable and feel equal and not act impulsively. I have one girlfriend whom I like very much and she's the only one I feel close to but the relationship isn't on the romantic level I wish it to be. However, I have another girl on the sort of mistress level."

Therapist: "Where do you stand right now?"

Patient: "Well, I think one of my biggest feelings is a sort of fear. I've been getting more independent in facing the outside, doing more and more things on my own but I've always felt that my therapist has been able to understand what's been happening inside my head and I could convey my thoughts when needed and he could grasp what I'm trying to say which I never felt anybody else could do. Now that he's leaving I feel I'm going to have to deal with all these a lot more on my own and be a lot stronger and have to handle them and face the outside. I'm scared. Next year you know I will be living on my own. I'm going to school in the City and it is frightening to be alone and I have a sense of aloneness. It's very hard to say goodbye to my therapist because a lot has happened. I got very close to him."

Bill spent the summer traveling through the hostels of Europe on his bicycle. He had a brief love affair which he terminated without an abandonment depression when he found out the girl was deceiving him. He enjoyed his summer thoroughly and returned to New York City in the fall to live alone in an apartment house, attend school, and see the author three times a week in treatment. With resumption of therapy he first worked through his feelings of abandonment at leaving his previous therapist and then his clinging defenses against further individuation. Interpretation of these led to the verbalization of the rage and depression associated with his moves toward individuation. Eighteen months after hospitalization he graduated from high school at the top of his class, and was accepted at college. At that time he separated from the author, spent another summer in Europe, and then began college in the fall. Two years after discharge he is doing well in college seeing another therapist once a week. The depressive and paranoid features are gone.

GRACE

Grace was discharged 24 months ago to resume the eleventh grade at a local boarding school where she would live 5 days a week and go home on weekends. She saw her doctor three times a week. Her first defense was to project the cause of her depression on dissatisfaction at school or with the girls; but after several weeks of working on this she could say: "I started to think that it can't all be the school, the externals; part of it is me and facing up to being on my own. I do see if you take on the responsibility it means being alone, being independent means being alone. I see that it's not going to be easy. It's not going to come all at once." She now started to deal with her depressive feelings as a reflection of her difficulty in separating from the hospital and making it on her own.

All through this time an endless push-pull existed with her parents who were constantly creating situations which would encourage Grace to regress. When Grace came in with little affect and obvious depression it was an indication that something was going on at home. After several months she talked about feelings of emptiness and whether it was really worth the struggle to be on her own. Nevertheless, she functioned very well in school and at midterm made the honor roll.

The parents' "hamstringing" efforts reached a climax over the planning of a trip out West for a family wedding. At an extra family session, Grace told them she did not want to go. Her therapy was more important. The issue then went undercover for a while, but it surfaced again to become a constant theme throughout the end of the spring (shades of Nancy's parents).

The mother again used all the mechanisms she had used before. First, outright attack, then withdrawal and the silent treatment, and then angry arguments trying to provoke guilt. Grace with the aid of therapy was able to sustain her own wishes with regard to the Western trip but in early April the parents suddenly with little warning took her to Portugal for 2 weeks.

Four months after leaving the hospital she met a boy named Ted who was a drifter. He spent his time sitting around the lobby of a local girls' college. He tried hard to get Grace out of therapy. She, on the other hand, was desperately looking for some relationship that she could hold on to. He told Grace that psychiatrists were not any good; they made you very dependent on them and they took over your life, and said if she had any guts she would get out of it. Grace terrified of her own dependence recognized what was going on with her parents and was terrified that it was also going on with her therapist. Grace worked this through with her therapist and told Ted that she was going to continue in therapy and then he left her. In May after Ted left, her mood again improved and then the family brought up the Western trip again. Grace stood firm and the parents decided that the father would stay home with Grace while the mother went on the trip. This was particularly interesting because it recreated the interaction before hospitalization; the mother using Grace as the pawn to deal with her sexual conflict with the father by pairing father and daughter together. The father attributed his staying home to Grace but at the same time spent little time with her and used the week to go out with his friends. He was happy to be away from his wife.

As summer approached Grace decided to take a photography course in which she was very much interested. The parents, again threatened by this move toward individuation, sabotaged it by refusing to pay. She did, however, manage to get a job that paid her $100 a week. This money gave Grace some independence because previously she always had to go to her parents for everything. However, predictably the parents again attacked her individuation. Her allowance was dropped. She had to pay for everything she did, her train ticket, her clothes, and every phone call she made; and most glaringly one morning the father decided to drive to the city rather than take the train and informed Grace that she had to pay her share of the drive as well as for parking the car.

Throughout this period of time Grace continued to function well at school where she again finished the year on the honor roll and planned in the fall to return for her senior year and to continue treatment with her therapist.

Let us see how Grace viewed her treatment 6 months after discharge: "Well I think I got an insight into my problems with myself but then the hardest part is after you find out about the whole thing. Getting out after knowing all this and doing something with it. It's still hard because when you are in the hospital you can say this is wrong or something is the matter and you can concentrate just on that but when you get outside and there's all this stuff going on it's much harder."

After a traumatic summer with her parents which she managed without too much inner turmoil, Grace moved into her own apartment in the city and returned to boarding school where she was elected President of her senior class after a very successful junior year.

HELEN

Helen had been discharged to live at home, attend a local tutoring school, and see her therapist three times a week.

Helen's initial defense against the first crisis was to repress feelings in order to function. She went to school every day where she did quite well. She denied any feelings of depression or conflicts at home. The issue of the conflict with the mother, that is, the mother's wish to hold on and the patient's temptation to go along with it, arose several months after discharge when the mother and her private therapist wanted the patient to join this therapist's group therapy. Helen's therapist interpreted that this meant Helen was going along with her own and her mother's wish for reunion and that the group therapy was really irrelevant. Helen had almost decided against going into the therapy when the mother's doctor and the mother made the arrangement without telling Helen's therapist. This issue occupied therapy for the next 4 weeks. Helen reported that the kids in the group had no idea what was going on and she was getting nothing out of it for herself. This clarified for her that she was doing it strictly to comply with her mother's wishes. She stopped and her mother became very upset.

Concurrently she was planning to leave home and look for a place to stay in the city and, quite depressed, spoke about the fact that although this was the best thing for her to do, the idea of being on her own and not having her mother to care for her was very depressing and perhaps she would not bring herself to do it. This was illustrated by her going through the motions of finding a place to live rather than actually following through. During this time she began to take driving lessons and went out with a boy several times who then broke up with her; this initiated a depression. She also did fairly well in school, finishing the year with a B+ average.

Let us turn briefly to Helen's report of the mother's reaction to the planned move. Helen: "I don't know why my whole family is just a mess. They've gone the wrong way and they're a bunch of sick people. I don't know how my mother feels about it. She has gone along with it. I think she's trying to hold me back. I was supposed to move earlier and she seemed very pleased that I didn't. I guess she's just like a mother. She wants her little girl around." When asked how she felt about herself, Helen replied: "I feel like a person. That is the only way I can sum it up. I have things to do and places to go. I care about people. People care about me. I don't know when I decided I wanted to grow up, that I wanted to be a person and wanted to work in every area but it was at some point in the hospital."

Helen graduated from the tutoring school and moved into her own apartment. She then worked for a year before leaving her original therapist to attend college. Two years after discharge she is doing well, seeing a therapist once a week.

SUMMARY

Nancy, Bill, and Helen are all on their own in college, seeing a therapist at most once a week. Grace is doing well as a senior in high school living away from home. Although they still need treatment for their symptoms, these symptoms are a product of the move toward individuation. Hopefully the treament will attenuate these symptoms progressively so that individuation can proceed to its natural endpoint. Although continued follow-up is necessary, the future looks promising.

PART FOUR

Other Therapeutic Factors

CHAPTER 17

Differential Diagnosis, Indications, and Contraindications: Countertransference

The difficulty in differentiating the Borderline, from Schizophrenia and sociopathic personality, springs from the fact that these three disorders probably originate in closely related developmental phases and therefore have similar—though not the-same—levels of ego fixation. This is reflected clinically in the Borderline's psychopathology which often contains traces that simulate one or both of the other disorders. For example, fluid ego boundaries, paranoid ideation, or transient psychotic episodes (usually under separation stress) raise the possibility of schizophrenia, while the ever-present acting out of the Borderline brings the diagnosis of sociopath to mind.

At the same time separation problems are a recurrent theme in patients with schizophrenia. For example, Rinsley [15], classifying schizophrenic adolescents into a presymbiotic and a symbiotic group, recommends that the treatment for each be based on the level of ego development. His program allows for the very long period of time which is necessary to treat presymbiotic schizophrenic patients. The treatment program described in this book, however, is structured on the assumption that the patient has enough ego strength to benefit from the therapeutic stress to which he is subjected within about 18 months. Therefore, to avoid placing patients under a stress they cannot handle, I feel it is important to try to differentiate and eliminate those patients with schizophrenia who usually require longer term treatment and sociopaths who cannot respond.

A DEVELOPMENTAL VIEWPOINT

To aid diagnostic differentiation it is helpful to construct a theoretical continuum (Table 2) that indicates at what level of ego development the

Table 2. Developmental Continuum

Age	Phase of Ego Development	Diagnosis of Disorder
Up to 3 months	Autistic	Infantile autism
3 to 18 months	Symbiotic	Infantile psychosis
18 months	Separation	Schizophrenia
18 to 36 months	Separation-individuation	Sociopathic personality, Borderline

problem arises, what type of psychopathology can be expected, and what type of treatment is necessary.

Patients with infantile autism are fixated at this first critical phase of development while those with infantile psychosis remain fixated at the symbiotic phase. They are unable to progress through this phase because, according to Mahler [77], they are unable to utilize the maternal supplies. Patients with schizophrenia can progress through the symbiotic phase but are unable to separate. Patients with a Borderline Syndrome can separate but become fixated in one of the subphases of separation-individuation. I have included the sociopath here because I think much of his psychopathology can be explained as a manifestation of the use of the defense of detachment to deal with separation from the mother. The sociopath behaves in adult life much as the infants described by Bowlby (see p. 34) who progressed to this last and most desperate defense against separation.

CLINICAL

It is far easier to construct the hypothetical continuum than to apply it to the clinical case. When it is not possible to clearly differentiate in advance one must submit the patient to the clinical test of therapy—for example, whether a patient can control his acting out can sometimes only be found out by treatment.

POSITIVE INDICATIONS

Work with these patients has given me a "feel" or intuition about diagnosis that is difficult to articulate. First of all one should be able to identify the abandonment depression and the narcissistic-oral fixation in the history. Invariably, as in the cases presented, there is a history of a separation experience followed by the defenses against the depression. The past history of ego defects reveals the ego fixation. Although there may be paranoid ideation, there are no paranoid delusions, and although there may be fluid ego boundaries, there is substantial contact with reality. There is rarely, as in the sociopath, a consistent history of antisocial acting out from childhood. The serious acting out tends to occur only in the present illness. The history given by the mother as well as observation of the mother should reveal the tie that binds.

The defense of clinging and reunion fantasies are important positive indications for treatment since they suggest the patient will form a clinging transference that can then be subjected to analysis. The defense of detachment, however, as seen in many sociopaths mitigates against treatment since the patient will not permit a transference relationship to develop.

Each level of evidence—that is, history of present illness, past history, personality of mother, and relationship of patient to mother—tends to reinforce the other and to build a network of diagnosis that can then be confirmed by observing how the patient relates to his therapist in the interview.

It is as important to look at the health or potential health of the patient's ego structure as at the psychopathology. Has he had relationships with other adults in his early childhood who may have been sources of nurture and introjection who could form a platform of security upon which the therapist can build? How much abandonment trauma has he had to defend against? How much must he work through?

A key indicator of the degree of health of the patient's ego structure is whether he has sublimations. Has he had hobbies or outside interests—particularly during the latency period? Did he develop appropriate social skills? Did he engage in group activities, such as team games, clubs, or boy or girl scouts? Was he able to maintain adequate grades in his school work? The assets of the family must also be considered. An intact family with a mother and father who are not only present but willing to participate seems essential.

The mother's past history should be carefully reviewed, particularly her relationship with her own mother to evaluate how deep her need is for a symbiotic relationship with the patient. This gives a clue to how much resistance she will show both at the time of hospital separation and later at the time of confrontation in the joint interviews. It may also give a hint as to whether she will react so adversely as to take the patient out of treatment at this crucial time.

The father's history should be reviewed with equal care to determine how much potential he has for changing his passivity into self-assertion. For example, is he too dependent on his wife to tolerate the anxiety involved in such a change?

These positive indications reveal to the therapist the tools available for the work that must be done.

CONTRAINDICATIONS

At the moment there are only three clear contraindications: presymbiotic Schizophrenia, paranoid schizophrenia, and sociopathic personality; in the first, the time necessary to establish an object relationship that brings the patient up to and through the symbiotic developmental phase is more than we have available. The same consideration of time applies to the treatment of the separation problem of the paranoid schizophrenic. The detachment defense of the sociopath makes the development of a symbiotic transference relationship impossible.

On occasion the clinical history will not establish the diagnosis and it is necessary to consult the finer details of the Rorschach for contraindications as indicated in the two examples below.

Schizophrenia, Paranoid

A 17-year-old boy gave a 2-year history of extreme conflict with his parents, along with depression, drinking, stealing, and taking drugs. A principal clue to his diagnosis was revealed in the Rorschach as follows: the patient was too absorbed with his inner world to respond appropriately to the environment and tended to interpret situations as the intrusion of forces from without. He was relatively good at assessing and anticipating social situations. These were capacities not inconsistent with psychotherapy since he used them to manipulate and exploit people. His perceptual organization was relatively poor with a tendency to reverse figures and to perseverate. The overall unevenness and concreteness of his descriptions and his obvious eccentricity and lapses in logic suggested a schizophrenic thinking disorder. His impulses were expressed in vivid oral imagery such as seeing animals devouring each other. Denial, projection, and covering-up operations were his most viable defenses as was a psychopathic veneer. A pervasive paranoid distrust and suspicion were covered up by a smoke-screen of hardness. The diagnostic impression was of a paranoid schizophrenic development with a psychopathic overlay.

Sociopathic Personality

Although all these patients have some psychopathic trends, it is important to distinguish patients with mere trends from those in whom psychopathic traits constitute the basic character structure. A 15-year-old boy was referred for truancy, rebellion against his parents, and drinking. One could not detect the psychopathic strain in the history, but the Rorschach revealed the following. The patient was an impulsive, unreflective, and rather thoughtless boy who was lacking in serious interest as well as long-range aims and ambitions. He was cynical about his family, bored with himself, and did not seem to have any real friendships, commitments, or thought-out values. Minor frustrations and instructions to do something and slight criticism become magnified in his mind as if they represent assaults. His limited self-centered and day-to-day approach to his life gave his character a strong psychopathic strain. It was not so much that he actively rejected conventional moral standards or that he was simply unaware of them, but that he implicitly felt that they were not relevant to his case. For example, he said: "People refrain from murder only because you can get life for it."

EGO DEVELOPMENT AND COPING WITH LOSS

We conclude this section on differential diagnosis by further pinpointing that the Borderline's vulnerability to a later life separation experience is related to his developmental separation failure. We now contrast George and Anne with another adolescent, Frank, age 17, who successfully mastered this earlier developmental task of separation from the mother, and then in his adolescence suffered not only separation but also the actual loss through death of both mother and father.

Frank was a 17-year-old high school senior, seen for the first time 2 months after his mother's death. His father had died when he was 14 and he had known that his mother was going to die when she developed cancer of the breast when he was 15. His father was domineering, a heavy drinker, and critical of the patient who never felt close to him. On the other hand, he felt he was always quite close to his mother whom he described as being warm, affectionate, and supportive.

Following the father's death, when he was 14, he recalled being sad and depressed over his loss which, however, did not seem to impair his functioning. His mourning was successfully achieved and his depression subsided in a few months. With the death of the father, he had to take on a more responsible position in the family, and with worsening health and increasing disability of the mother, he assumed practically complete responsibility for the running of the home and supervision of his 14-year-old brother.

In spite of the emotional burdens inherent in the situation, he applied himself more and more to his school work, maintained the home, and had an outside job. Finally his mother had to be hospitalized. She lingered for a month and a half in the hospital and then died. He stated that he could recall no feeling about her death, that for the most part he felt "numb." However, he came for evaluation because of his exhaustion, loss of energy, and occasional episodes of depression, which would last for days.

In addition, he would have sudden unexplained and unfocused outbursts of rage, difficulty in sleeping, and frequently recurring headaches.

About 6 months prior to his mother's death, he began "going steady" with a girl upon whom he became quite dependent, feeling "a great need for her." However, at times he would become unexplainably angry with her and turning away from her would say: "I don't need anybody." He was at the top of his class in school, had received a scholarship to college, was in the honor society, had top college board marks, and played in the band. Although he had been able to maintain these activities during his mother's illness and following her death, he found that he would sit and stare for longer and longer periods or read for hours at a time and listen alone to records and that his mind became preoccupied with "macabre thoughts" about death.

Past History of Frank

From his first year of school he had always been at the top of his class. As a child he had a number of friends and outside activities, although he was overweight. There is no other evidence throughout his childhood of significant emotional difficulties. He reported that he began to date late in high school. His mother constantly put pressure on him to do well in school and he felt she discouraged him from dating, which, however, he started at the age of 16.

Comments

Frank's history and condition of depression differ from the Borderline Syndrome of George and Anne in the following ways: his past history of functioning is relatively free of emotional difficulty, indicating that he was able to separate from his mother and that he developed what appears to be an obsessive compulsive character structure. Thus he experienced real loss of his mother, not in terms of loss of the symbiotic mother who is essential to his survival, but in all probability as a loss of an "oedipal mother" or love object.

He defended himself against the grief and mourning occasioned by this loss, not by regressive acting out, but by suppressing his feeling and by intermittent clinging to and rejecting his girl friend. To avoid mourning he substituted his girl friend for the mother. However, this was only partially successful as he developed severe headaches and unexplainable outbursts of rage.

It is important here to note, however, that despite the intensity of his feelings over his loss he was able to contain them without the marked impairment in his functioning and without recourse to acting out that occurred in George and Anne. He was able to continue at school, to maintain a social life, and although not without some despair, he did not fall prey to the devastating despair associated with the separation experiences for George and Anne. Frank's loss, although real and painful, did not deprive him of vital needs. Having passed that very early developmental level with a successful separation from the symbiotic relationship of infancy with his mother, his ego structure had strength, resilience, and resources to deal with the later trauma.

COUNTERTRANSFERENCE*

The doctor involved in the treatment process described in this book must encounter feelings in his patients which are the most intense and the most fundamental in the human vernacular—homicidal anger, incestuous wishes, dependency, helplessness, fears of abandonment, suicidal depression, despair, and hopelessness, all of which are eventually unveiled with all their naked elemental force. It is little wonder then that confronting the violence of their expression upsets not only the patient but also the therapist.

The therapist often only becomes aware of this upset through its effect on his behavior with his patient. It is crucial for the success of the psychotherapy that he contain the conflict within himself and allow as little as possible to affect his behavior with his patient. When these reactions are successfully contained, not only does the psychotherapy proceed at an optimal pace, but also the therapist receives the added dividend of personal insight and growth—that is, the treatment becomes a vehicle for the growth of the therapist as well as the patient. On the other hand, if the therapist cannot deal with the upset and cannot recognize or accept the conflicts aroused by his patient's often violently expressed emotions, he may become so preoccupied by his need to protect himself against his own emotions that he is unable either to recognize or to explore his patient's conflicts. A countertransference then ensues that effectively blocks or at least impedes further progress of the therapy.

Some of the countertransference blocks found in all young therapists in

---

* The term countertransference is being used in a broader than usual sense to mean all of the therapist's feelings about the patient that interfere with the progress of therapy rather than only those that are repetitions of feelings he has had toward significant people in his childhood.

training are indigenous to this time of life and yield rather readily to experience and supervision. For example, having rather recently emerged from his own adolescent conflicts, the young therapist's ego structure is in a rather fragile state of equilibrium based most often on repression of his conflicts. As a result, he tends to be frightened by any intense affect which he instinctively handles by avoidance. Confrontation with the mercurial emotions of his adolescent patients actually mobilizes his own latent conflicts, unresolved dependency needs and difficulties with tolerating hostility. The therapist responds with his characteristic defenses. It is impressive, however, to see as the therapist gains insight into himself, how quickly he learns to reorient and adjust himself to the new state of affairs so that the treatment can proceed.

Occasionally more serious and more intransigent countertransference blocks arise, not from factors related to this time of life and training, but rather from those unresolved conflicts deriving from a therapist's own childhood which are now deeply buried in his unconscious and must be defended against at almost all costs. Unfortunately these do not respond readily to supervision and one of the resultant costs is the slow progress of therapy. These conflicts in the therapist resemble to an astonishing degree those of his patient's and probably personal psychotherapy is the only agent that helps the therapist solve his dilemma. Sometimes, in a rather severe countertransference block, the patient, if he is not completely interfered with, will more or less conduct the therapy on his own and thereby unwittingly help the therapist to surmount his block.

Each phase of treatment poses unique countertransference problems depending on the therapeutic tasks required by the phase and the conflicts and the character structure of the therapist. In the testing phase, the countertransference problems revolve about the task of being firm, consistent, and assertive in setting limits to the patient's acting out. This poses problems for those therapists who tend to express their feelings in actions rather than in words. They have great difficulty in perceiving the significance of, and in consistently controlling, the patient's acting out. They also have difficulty in relating the acting out to expression of feeling, since this happens to be their own way of managing conflict.

Another difficulty is experienced by those therapists whose character structures are passive-aggressive and who have great difficulty in asserting themselves, tending to express their own aggression by provoking others to act out. They will be anxious and indecisive in setting limits since it is difficult for them to assert themselves and they may also get unconscious satisfaction from the patient's acting out. A third difficulty is posed by the therapist who handles his anger by withdrawal. He will then attempt to relieve his guilt about withdrawing by "doing things" for the patient which then repeats and reinforces the parental pattern.

An example of the latter occurred in the testing phase of Anne's case. The doctor, annoyed at the patient's constant provocations, expressed this annoyance by withdrawing. She then relieved her guilt by overindulging the patient and by not being firm in setting limits. For example, she permitted the patient to use an amber light in her room, rather than a red light—a "giving" to the patient to make up for her angry withholding. To say "no" to the patient is to be confronted with one's anger at the patient.

In the working through phase the most common countertransference problem is the inability of the therapist to tolerate the intense affect of the patient, either his hostility, his anger, or his depression. This is crucial since the patient, his acting out controlled, is seething within like a tight pressure cooker and must have another outlet for his feelings. If he does not get it he almost inevitably reverts back to the acting out.

As illustrated in the case of Anne, she was expressing her anger at the doctor indirectly on the floor and to the nurse while attempting to verbalize it with the doctor. However, this raised the doctor's anxiety to such a level that to defend herself she would constantly change the subject, and she would easily get seduced into an argument with the patient to justify limit setting, overlooking the clues of thinly veiled hostility in the patient's behavior. Not only did Anne's doctor have difficulty in allowing Anne to verbalize her hostility toward her, but also she had similar difficulty in allowing the patient to verbalize her hostility toward her mother. Finally, Anne, unable to express hostility to her doctor as she had been unable to express it with her mother, regressed in all her behavior and resorted to the acting out of smoking marijuana. Insight on the part of the doctor into her problem of countertransference allowed her to encourage Anne to give vent to her hostilities toward the doctor, mother, hospital, and nurses. Almost concurrently she was also able to exert the necessary controls on Anne's acting out and the therapy then moved constructively.

In the separation phase of treatment, when the focus shifts to the patient's separation anxiety, two principal countertransference problems arise: (1) the doctor fearing that the patient's dependency may be interminable may push too fast, thinking prematurely that the patient is ready for autonomy; and (2) the doctor may have a separation problem himself and difficulty in letting go his hold on the patient—thus repeating the evils of the symbiotic relationship with the parents.

The countertransference problem in this phase for the therapist in George's case was similar to that described for the second phase since the

doctor had great difficulty in perceiving that the imminent separation revived the patient's feelings of abandonment. The doctor perhaps because
of his own separation was unable to tolerate the intense feelings of anxiety
it aroused in himself as well as in his patient. Rather than holding on or
pushing the patient too fast, he made it difficult for the patient to verbalize
his feelings of abandonment by being quite matter-of-fact and directive
about the separation.

In Anne's case, the doctor, as has been mentioned in Chapter 6, was
reassuring the patient too much in her effort to deal with her own anxiety
about letting the patient go.

CHAPTER 18

Outpatient Treatment Alone

The weakness of the ego structure of the Borderline adolescent makes it very difficult for him to control his destructive acting out. Furthermore, the persistent stimulation of his conflicts and therefore of his acting out by the parent's pathologic behavior, and the basic therapeutic need for separation from the parent suggest that most of these patients require hospitalization to be treated adequately. Rinsley [108] doubts that initial outpatient treatment without hospitalization can ever be feasible.

Because the treatment described in this book has been evolved primarily through the study of inpatients, I decided to put the matter of outpatient treatment to the test and found that comparable results were possible with carefully selected patients.

The criteria of selection that seemed to be crucial were that the patient have the capacity to control his acting out once a relationship was established with the therapist, that he also be able to stabilize his function in school, and that he not be addicted to heroin. Similarly, the parents in their treatment with the social worker would have to demonstrate their capacity to control their behavior. With careful and intensive work on the part of both the psychiatrist and the social worker it was possible to keep the therapeutic process in motion. Under these conditions the outpatient therapy takes the exact same course as that described for inpatients.

The principal difference between the inpatient and outpatient treatment and the key to the success of outpatient treatment was in the therapeutic management of the acting out in the initial phase of treatment. With inpatients the principal tool for the control of acting out is the use of hospital limitations on behavior that are not available to the outpatient therapist. He must work, without the aid of an environment, to set limits; therefore, his only tool is the alliance he establishes with the patient. Once he does this and the patient begins to control his acting out, the rest of the treatment is identical to that described for our two inpatients, Anne and George. This chapter describes the treatment of two out-

237

patients: the first to illustrate the techniques used to establish the therapeutic alliance and the second to illustrate one type of outcome.

ESTABLISHING A THERAPEUTIC ALLIANCE

Customarily it has been thought that one must "establish a relationship" before one can begin to set limits with an outpatient. In other words one must deal quite gingerly with the issue of the patient's behavior, avoiding direct confrontations until enough time has elapsed for the patient to develop a positive transference. For Borderline adolescents the converse is true. Not only is it impossible to wait for a relationship to be established before starting to set limits to their acting out, but the setting of limits as early as possible is the unique means of establishing the therapeutic alliance and, indeed, as has been discussed, is the very gesture of caring that the patient hungers for.

There are perhaps two reasons why this technique is successful. The patient, riotously out of control and at the mercy of his impulses, must deny his perception of how destructive his behavior really is. Therefore, the therapist proceeds on the assumption that this perception is latent in the patient's split ego structure but kept from awareness because he is overwhelmed by his impulses and unable to act in any other way. When the therapist bluntly introduces in so many words the reality percept the patient is denying he is actually speaking to and for this silent and denied part of the patient's split ego.

An alliance develops between the patient and the doctor because of the latter's bold penetration of this latent part of the patient's ego, which action, by a feedback process, both strengthens the patient's ego and encourages him to exert the necessary control of his behavior.

The second probable reason this technique of setting limits immediately is effective is that the patient has interpreted parental inability to set limits as a lack of interest and rejection and he now experiences the doctor's efforts as a longed for expression of interest and caring. A case is presented describing the first phase which illustrates the actual verbal exchange of the technique.

Frank, age 16, a high school junior, rebelled against his mother and father for 1 year, performed poorly in school, and took drugs such as marijuana, methedrine, and LSD. He got into violent fights with his mother, would not come home until the early hours of the morning, was truant from school 80 percent of the time, and was loitering in Greenwich Village. On one occasion he was arrested by the police for having marijuana in his possession.

In the initial interview in my outpatient office the patient immediately verbalized his feeling: "My mother is smothering me." She was not letting him grow up; she was controlling him, his friends, his interests, and whatever he did. He asserted that he could take care of himself and be on his own. He said: "I want to leave home, I can't stand her domineering pressure and all the time her nagging. I am disappointed in my father too. He does nothing to help me." (On the contrary these parents had given up their efforts to control their son because anything they said or did worsened his reactions and behavior.)

Frank described his relationship with his mother as a holy war and flippantly said: "If she gets hurt, I wouldn't care less." Beneath his combative façade Frank, a short, slender boy dressed in blue jeans and a blue shirt with unkempt long hair down to his neck appeared to be bitter, depressed, and hopeless.

In suggesting treatment I agreed with his definition of his conflict with his mother. But the holy war with her, as he described it, I told him was nothing but the expression of his anger about this conflict in his behavior, and that problems existed for his mother as well as for himself. I emphasized that both would require treatment. I did suggest, however, that since his problems were with his parents that he should stay at home to work them out rather than leave to live elsewhere. After this interview, the patient twisted the therapist's words to justify further vilification of his mother. He screamed obscenities at her and pushed her out of his room. In the next interview, Frank described his behavior, chuckling with glee over his success in repulsing his mother. Beneath the glee was the unmistakable hint of masked depression.

Four interviews with the patient had taken place and one with the mother and father when, in his fifth interview, in which the patient was regaling me with glee about attacking his mother, I immediately began the task of limit setting by casting grave doubts on the patient's happy mood, saying: "It certainly looks as if you are enjoying this but I cannot believe that you could possibly be enjoying it that much. Nobody in so much conflict with his mother could be so happy." I went on further to challenge him with the statement that underneath his superficial glee, he was basically very unhappy but unable to admit it.

I continued: "Perhaps you are expressing your anger at your mother this way not only to get back at her but perhaps also to keep yourself from feeling depressed." I elaborated that this kept his feelings from coming to the surface in the interview; as a result their meaning was not discussed. I ventured to say that such expression might give him transitory relief but certainly seemed to me to do him much more harm than good; it might be to his interest to air his feelings in his interviews and to make a start toward controlling his anger. Actually, I added, if his thesis was correct that it was all his mother's fault, then he should move away from home and that he and I really had no business together; but I suspected there was a good deal more to it.

Frank then described how poorly he did in school saying: "It's to get back at my mother." He followed this with the grim assertion: "I don't care."

I responded: "That's too bad."

Frank was taken back by this and said, "What do you mean?"

I replied: "It's always very sad to see a smart person's potential for satisfaction and achievement thrown out the window in the service of a battle from which he cannot escape unwounded."

The patient then said if ever he should control his anger he would feel so badly he would have to see the therapist right away. I responded: "In addition you have to be able to maintain control over a certain period of time until you can get to the interview. This is a long-term problem and emergency measures are not going to solve it."

Each time the patient verbalized his self-destructive acting out and attempted to make of it a virtue, I quickly countered by pointing out the reality that he had harmed himself and wondered why.

In the sixth interview, after we had already agreed that the patient would pay out of his own money $15 a week for treatment, he stomped into the interview saying he refused to pay: "Why should *I* give money to you? I need it for clothes. These are my savings and I am not going to be pushed around by you. My friends think I am a patsy to pay you."

I said: "It seems to me you want to have your cake and eat it too, and that's not possible. You say you want to be on your own, but you don't seem to want to support yourself as much as you are able to do. You want the results of the treatment, but you just don't want to do what it requires." The latter statement was a potent one because it also related to another of Frank's resentful comments about the doctor's not asking questions. In other words, he wanted the doctor to make it easy for him to talk so he would not have to do any work himself.

I then elaborated that his payment of the fee was not forced on him but was proposed as one of the requirements of treatment to which he had agreed; that in refusing to pay he was distorting his relationship with me in terms of his mother, that is, the $15 fee was imposed upon him as my wish to push him around, therefore he must rebel against me as he rebelled against his mother. However, in so doing I pointed out to him, he was perhaps "throwing out the baby with the bathwater." He repeated that his friends consider him a sucker to pay the doctor this way and his own money should be used for things like drugs or records. I said: "Let us see if I get your theory correctly. The only useful purpose for money is immediate pleasure."

Patient said: "That's right, Doc."

I responded with: "Well, what that means is that such people end up nowhere, doesn't it?"

Patient responded: "Yes, but they have fun doing it."

The patient then threatened that he would try to "push drugs" to get the extra money. When he pushed drugs he defiantly told me he got money and prestige. To which I commented: "Yes, everything but self-respect. Rather than find pleasure in being on your own and supporting yourself you take the easy way out and prey on other people's weaknesses in order to make it easier for yourself. Now, what kind of self-respect do you think this builds?"

The patient brought his $15 to the seventh interview, slumped into a chair, looked at the therapist angrily and suspiciously, and demanded that he ask him questions. To which I responded: "I am afraid you've got it all wrong Frank. I can help you out of this but I can't do it for you. We will have to work together. Maybe we should look into the origin of some of these difficulties?"

This led to the question of why he felt that he was a carbon copy of his mother's wishes. For example, he went to an expensive camp of his mother's choosing. He disliked it intensely but refrained from telling his parents because they had spent so much money on it. He recalled how he asked for a musical instrument, not because he wanted it but because his mother wanted him to have it. Then he mentioned his feeling that his father was disappointed in him because he was not an athlete.

Following this interview he went home and erupted in a rage, seeing his room as a visible symbol of his childhood compliance to his mother. Determined that his room should be an expression of himself he wrote obscenities on the wall in chalk. This set off another battle with his parents in which he again twisted the content of my remarks to use them against his parents, saying: "The doctor says that my problems are all your fault."

In the next interview he told me what he had said and I reminded him that his way of expressing his anger was harmful to him. For example, he might actually provoke his mother and father into taking him out of treatment if he kept using what transpired in treatment against them, and this could not possibly be in his best interest. Nor could I believe that writing obscenities in chalk on the wall was an expression of his real self. Somewhere between his old way of compliance and this way of rebellion was an appropriate expression for himself, but he was unable to find it because he was devoting himself to being a sacrificial victim in the holy war against his mother. I mentioned incidentally that in the previous interview he had talked more about why he had complied so readily and easily to his parents' wishes. I wondered if his angry outburst could have been a response to this awareness.

He then related in some detail memories of events showing his parents' lack of interest. For example, they would throw his toys out because they felt they were too old for him without consulting him, while, on the other hand, he felt: "I like to keep things around even if I don't use them, in case I might want to someday." At this point, he spontaneously mentioned that he had decided to "go straight" for a couple of weeks. He opined: "This is very hard to do because all my friends are on drugs and drugs give you such a status!"

I responded with "good for you" and then said of his status with the drug users: "In the country of the blind, even the one-eyed is king."

In the next interview the patient commented that he had been "straight" for a week and then told how, dressed in the most outlandish outfit possible, he visited his conservative and outspoken grandfather who disliked outlandish clothes. He enjoyed the grandfather's outburst at seeing his apparel. I interpreted to Frank that he expressed his anger by provoking outbursts of disapproval from others. I wondered if there weren't a more constructive way of expressing his feelings. The patient then talked about how he was going to use heroin, giving as his reason that he intended to show his peers that he was not afraid of it.

Challenging him again, I said that it was paradoxical to see this paragon of independence so afraid of, and dependent on, the opinion of his drug taking peers and his pusher. I then emphasized that I could not understand why being afraid of heroin made him a coward. There was a very good reason to be afraid of heroin because its addiction properties were much more dangerous than other drugs.

The patient responded that there seemed to be no alternative to taking drugs. Otherwise he would be doing nothing; he would be "out of it" and bored. All his friends took drugs, and their lives were wrapped up in drugs. I said that this was a very sad state of affairs, that one either has to be on drugs or have nothing to do! I then asked him what had happened to the potential he had shown only a couple of years ago when he had a number of interests and hobbies from which he had derived a lot of satisfaction.

I also asked if these potentials had been drowned by the drugs. I then drew a contrast between the immediacy of the pleasure of the drug experience which is destructive, and other satisfactions which, however, require time, effort, and self-discipline but offer a different, more abiding kind of pleasure and are not destructive.

The patient fully understood what I was saying and finished the interview with a sigh, saying: "I feel trapped between seeing the destructiveness of this urge to act-out, and being unable to control it."

I responded: "Perhaps at the moment you may feel trapped but you don't have to remain so."

Frank started the next interview by saying he did not take the heroin but became a mugger instead and he bragged about how he and another Negro boy went around scaring younger boys, threatening them, and taking money from them. I responded: "It's curious that someone who objects so much to being bullied himself, doesn't seem to object to bullying others nor think there is anything wrong with preying on the helpless." I was answered by silence. I asked him to review our previous interview and he denied that he had talked about feeling trapped. When asked to focus on it he recalled that he was depressed after the interview. He was bitter, trapped, and full of self-pity. The choice I was suggesting to him was unattractive. The other way was attractive but harmful. He said this gave him a feeling of anger and that he was looking for a fight. I suggested perhaps the mugging was an outlet for his anger, with which he agreed.

Returning to the difficulty involved in his choice he elaborated on the fact that he was angry because there was no easy way and that he could not stand his feelings and blocked them out by taking dope. My answer to him was to repeat that there was really no easy way out for him, that taking dope could end only in disaster, and that he might be better off to control his behavior and bring the feelings that arise to discussion in the interviews. He said that he was afraid that if he let himself think about things it would "tear him up."

At the next interview, he allowed that he was not "straight" yet, but that he gave away his works for shooting drugs intravenously. He reported that he had taken mescaline for the first time and that it made him very depressed. He spontaneously then picked up the threads of the last interview, saying that he felt depressed afterwards. Frank then revealed for the first time what was bothering him about himself, the first indication that his testing of the therapist was diminishing. He was beginning to develop confidence in me. "I think something is missing inside me. I feel emasculated. I don't seem to be able to feel mad or strong or anything else, and a drive to do things is missing. I know I should feel it, but I don't. I have no interest in girls and I have no competitive feeling. I can't say no and there doesn't seem to be anything I can do about it. It makes me feel awful."

To which I responded with: "I can see how these feelings would upset you and the purpose of the treatment is to resolve these very problems."

The patient responded angrily: "Well, you don't do anything about it."

I said: "You mean if it's not an instant cure it's doing nothing?" I wondered aloud if this was why he was so tied up in drugs—it took his mind off how badly he felt and I wondered also if he was not being so daring and courageous with his gang to conceal the feelings of inadequacies he had about himself, and that he was actually creating a smokescreen to conceal his lack of fire.

To which the patient responded: "It's really trying to force fire." Then he asked me what conflicts I saw in him, and said: "I tried to fix the situation by acting independent and dominant, but it doesn't make me feel that way."

I mentioned that acting and feeling are two different things and that his efforts to act independent have so far been very destructive. I wondered why he could not be independent in a constructive way, and if perhaps part of the reason for his failure to do so had to do with the close relationship with his mother. To which he responded: "Yes, she has forced her way, her plan, her desires on me. I feel trapped with her and disappointed in my father. I have the strong inner urge to beat the insides out of her, but I am afraid I wouldn't succeed and then I have thoughts about suicide as a way out, as a way to solve the whole problem." In other words, in this interview we were not now talking so much about acting out but had begun to get beneath the symptom to the cause—the conflict with the mother.

In the next interview, Frank was silent for a number of minutes after which he finally said: "It's marvelous to get an opportunity to sleep in an air-conditioned room for thirty minutes." I wondered why he was silent and then sarcastic, and wondered if he was upset about what we talked about in the last interview and was protecting himself against resuming the topic. He said he could not remember the previous interview and I recalled it for him—his feeling of being trapped with the mother, his disappointment in the father, and his thoughts of suicide. To which he responded: "Well, I am awfully glad I didn't remember all of that. It's very upsetting." At which point for the first time in treatment he went deeper into his difficulties with his mother: "I flare up at her, but I still want to talk to her a lot and that bothers me. I am frightened of some power she has over me. As a kid, my father told me that he was weak physically, I guess he was sickly and they both make me feel guilty that I am such a terrible person and am killing them with my behavior. It makes me angry to have to feel guilty and I think of the nastiest things I can say, like 'screw you'."

I interpreted that the parents were expressing their anger and disappointment at the patient for not fulfilling their expectations. The patient then recalled how badly he felt when the parents attacked him, saying:

"They never stood up for me as a child. Help is the last thing in the world I could expect from them. For example, they would bail me out of jail, but never think I was right. Always made me feel wrong. I felt cheated." I then interpreted that he was disappointed in his expectations that his parents would support him and that he was expressing his anger at this disappointment, retaliating for it by deliberately defeating the last vestige of expectation they might have left for him. Unfortunately, at the same time he was defeating himself.

He upheld this interpretation by describing an incident in which the mother told him he must ask me if it would be feasible for him to get a driver's license. He said: "She never thinks I can do anything right. She always expects the worst and when she does I carry out her expectations. If I do get a car, I'll drive recklessly, just because she always predicts disaster." When his mother did not support him, then he carried out her direst expectations, to his own defeat.

This résumé of Frank's experiences as an outpatient illustrates that after a bare twelve interviews, the quick setting of limits to his behavior through reality interpretation of its destructive effect had established a therapeutic alliance in the short time of approximately 1 month. The content of the interviews then rapidly shifted to the underlying conflicts in his relationship with his mother.

It is important to keep in mind that at the same time as I was seeing Frank, the social worker was seeing the parents, to give them an opportunity to express and relieve their anger and disappointment about their son in their sessions with her. She interpreted the more pathologic aspects of their behavior and their attitudes toward their son. In addition, she also guided them to more appropriate methods to control their son's behavior.

From this point the therapy proceeded exactly as already illustrated for George and Anne. Frank finished his senior year, graduated from high school, and left home and entered a local college as a boarding student. After his second year of treatment he had finished his first year of college, managing to pass all but one subject—and went off to Europe to spend the entire summer—surely a signal achievement for one who had so much conflict about being on his own.

The second case, that of Jane Brown, illustrates a somewhat different outcome.

When I first saw Jane I seriously considered hospitalization because her problems were so similar to those of George and Anne. However, wanting to see if the treatment could work on an outpatient basis, I gave her a trial of outpatient psychotherapy which succeeded so well that hospitalization became unnecessary. Perhaps she was actually less sick despite the fact that her difficulties were so much like the other two. Nevertheless, in the first 12 months of treatment she went through the same stages as Anne and George. Let us take a closer look at Jane Brown's history and her second year of treatment to illustrate an outcome that differed from Frank's.

Jane, age 18½, the youngest of three children, complained of depression, obesity, and, admitting promiscuity, said that she "would do anything for affection." The history of present illness actually goes back to age 11 when her mother, with whom she always was in conflict, returned to her teaching job. At that time Jane's weight problem, previously under control, got out of hand and she became obese. Her menses had begun early at the age of ten, and by the age of 12, an extremely attractive girl in spite of being overweight, she found the attention of boys in her class a helpful substitute for the lack of affection from her mother. She had little sexual activity until her senior year in high school when she began "going steady" with an older boy and had sexual intercourse with him; she was afraid she was pregnant and told her parents who were outraged and referred her to a psychiatrist.

The psychiatrist saw Jane for several months throughout the spring of her senior year, but she did not improve. At her parent's insistence and despite her intense objections, she went away from home to college.

This separation proved too much for her. She was terrified at living alone and often would pick up a boy to relieve her fear of loneliness. Living alone, she became fearful at night, felt depressed, began to eat more, gained weight, and fell into rampant promiscuity ending up in a "ménage à trois." Sexually frigid she preferred fellatio to sexual intercourse.

Jane's past history reads just like Anne's or George's. For example, the mother did not want her, tried to have an abortion before she was born, and felt she demanded excessive attention from very early in life. She was born with a rectal stricture which required digital manipulation by the mother for the first 6 months. She had asthma from age 2 to age 7. The youngest of three children, she was in almost continuous battle with her older sister. From about age 12 until the time of treatment she was engaged in a submissive incestuous sexual relationship with her brother in which she would perform fellatio upon him on request. However, unlike George and Anne, throughout grammar school she was a good student, and interested in writing and painting, she wrote a play at the age of 11. She acted in various school plays and was a cheer leader and something of an athlete.

When I first saw her, she had returned from college and was overeating, socially withdrawn, and spending most of her time at home alone in her room. Although now markedly over weight (163 pounds) Jane still had an attractive face but was depressed, despairing, and in a rage at her mother.

I saw Jane three times-a-week for a year and as mentioned she went through the same phases as have already been described for George and Anne ending up finally by leaving home to live in an apartment of her own. At this point she had completed her sophomore year at a local college where she had made the dean's list and had lost 35 pounds in weight and had begun dating again. Leaving home for her own apartment was comparable to George or Anne's leaving the hospital to go home or to school.

When she left home her separation anxiety mounted and she had great trouble in sleeping or staying in her new apartment alone. In her dating, rather than have a slowly evolving relationship with a boy, she would plunge into "instant intimacy." She was functioning better at school but she ran into a number of difficulties related to her still unrepaired ego defects. For example, she tended to view her paintings as projections of herself and when they were criticized her feelings were hurt to the extent that she dropped out of painting class for awhile. She would rely heavily on fantasy rather than reality for satisfaction. For example, when embarking on a writing project she would fancy it as a masterpiece. But when we examined it together we would find that she had hastily written the piece once, had done no rewriting, and had expended very little effort to polish her skills so that she could express her desire to write.

She did, however, respond to the suggestion that effort and discipline in rewriting and improving her work were necessary for realistic gratification, as opposed to gratification in fantasy.

She would frequently attempt to act out her hostility toward her sister. For example, envious and resentful of her sister's stay in Europe, she refused to send a book her sister requested. In an effort to get her to neutralize this hostility so that she might be able to sublimate it, I questioned why she would do this, suggesting that it must leave her with feelings of guilt. I also posed the question of what kind of sister she wanted to be as opposed to just acting the way she felt. I furthermore suggested that if she wished to be an appropriate sister she would have to act appropriately and talk about the conflicts this created in her feelings in the treatment session.

Despite the fact that Jane's mother had helped her to move into her own apartment, her mother's difficulty in letting her go was indicated by her frequent telephone calls. The change in the relationship with the mother was no better indicated than by the fact that instead of getting angry, passively turning her mother off, and getting depressed, Jane asserted herself with her mother by telling her that she might call no more than once-a-week.

However, as she achieved this separation from her mother, her anxiety came into focus in the therapy and she was under greater and greater pressure to deal with it by acting out. While she was debating whether to live with a certain boy the therapist had to go on vacation, another separation which served to throw her "over the line." The degree of her improvement can be noted in the fact that the boy she chose differed from her previous sadistic partners in that he seemed actually to love her and his attitude toward her was very constructive. He encouraged her, supported her, and seemed to be acting in her best interest.

However, this attempt at a close relationship with a boy, the first close relationship with anyone she had ever tried in her life, immediately confronted her with her desire for fusion on the one hand and sexual conflicts on the other. It depressed her that she was not able to commit herself to love this boy and she attempted to deal with her depressed feelings by frantic sexual activity with him without much success. As her relationship progressed and the boy became more committed to her and in love with her, she became more aware that she was using him to deal with her fear of loneliness and this further deepened her depression.

She described her feelings for him, especially when in bed, as those of warmth, closeness, she liked the security of a body next to her: "It's like sleeping with my teddy bear." She became aware that she was really unable to share her feelings with him and that she did things for him not out of love, but out of fear of losing him.

In another distinct change from the past she not only was aware of this discrepancy between the wish for fusion and the desire to love him but also she tried to act in a loving way toward him even though she could not feel it. When she recognized this state of affairs, her depression deepened and she began again to overeat and put on weight. In other words as she became aware of the defensive function of her relationship with the boy, the effectiveness of that defense began to decline.

A COMPROMISE SOLUTION TERMINATES TREATMENT

Nevertheless, in the midst of Jane's vacillation between separation anxiety and the defense of clinging to this boy, the two of them decided to experiment by living together. This physical proximity so cemented Jane's clinging defense that it all but eliminated her separation anxiety and she began to feel that the psychotherapy was a threat to her relationship with the boy. Interpretations fell on deaf ears and despite all of my efforts Jane decided to stop treatment to preserve the relationship. One year later the defense was formalized by marriage. Two years after treatment I received a card from Jane saying that she was happily married and was studying for a masters degree in Nursing.

In essence treatment helped Jane to reach a better compromise with her separation-individuation problem. The extraordinarily conflictual and destructive dependency on her mother was replaced by a dependency on a husband who was very supportive. She functioned better than she ever had in her life and seemingly was content. However, unless the future is kind to her we can anticipate further trouble—such as if anything happens to her husband or when her children start their separation-individuation.

Treatment on an outpatient basis offers several advantages. Since the patient is not hospitalized his dependency needs are less stimulated and he is allowed more autonomy which automatically presses him in the right direction toward growth rather than regression. In addition, after achieving the initial objectives of treatment he can continue with the same therapist. Experience will tell us more about just what kind of patients are suitable for outpatient treatment, but even at this early stage of the game my impression is that not only is it possible to treat these adolescents as outpatients but also one can move in earlier and earlier with the limit setting—beginning, as I do now, with the very first contact in the initial consultation. These efforts hasten rather than harm the therapeutic process.

CHAPTER 19

The Psychiatric Dilemma of Adolescence Revisited

This chapter discusses some questions about the findings and reevaluates the patients seen 15 years ago who were presented in Chapter 1 from the perspective of separation-individuation.

QUESTIONS

Does the treatment always work? To maximize the prospects of success we selected only those patients who showed potential for improvement. Our rate of success (80 percent) with this selected sample is probably higher than if we had treated every Borderline adolescent who applied at the Clinic. Once the treatment had been shown to be effective it was our plan to try a wider spectrum of cases.

There were two salient clinical features to the remaining 20 percent for whom treatment seemed to be appropriate but insufficient: (1) they appeared to progress while in the hospital but relapsed on discharge; and (2) they were addicted to heroin before hospitalization. Heroin addiction seems to be a diagnostic sign of both a more serious abandonment problem and weaker ego resources.

Most of the successful 80 percent of our patients, despite the fact that they were daily under the influence of drugs varying from speed to pot to LSD before hospitalization, had *never* taken heroin and those few who had taken it were not addicted. Their ability to keep intact their perception of the utter destructiveness of heroin suggests that those who must deny this perception to "service their illness" have a more serious illness which requires more prolonged inpatient treatment than described in this book.

The patients who relapsed went through the same symptomatic changes in the hospital as those who did not relapse—that is, control of behavior, depression, and separation anxiety—and did this with insight. Although symptomatic change was relatively easy to evaluate, it was much more difficult to determine the degree to which symptomatic change was a result of adequate working through of conflicts. There were three key criteria: (1) (Phase II) working through of the trough of the depression with its attendant suicidal and homicidal feelings; (2) a clear affective confrontation with the parents; and (3) (Phase III) adequate working through of separation anxiety.

Despite the dramatic quality of Phase II, it was sometimes difficult to evaluate whether the patient had fully worked through the suicidal and homicidal feelings. If the patient had not, his defenses continued to hamper the confrontation with the parents and the working through of the separation anxiety.

GROUP THERAPY

Since group therapy could not be included in the study, the question arises as to how much it contributed to the results? The group therapy was conducted along psychoanalytic lines. It was very effective in reinforcing control of behavior and focusing the patient's consideration of therapy as an instrument to deal with his problems. It also was a synergistic and potentiating agent—the patients confronting each other with their behavior which would then be reflected back to the individual interviews for further analysis. It is difficult to say just how much working through was achieved in the group therapy.

GENERALIZATION OF FINDINGS

The small number of cases including in- and outpatients as well as private patients raises the question of how widely can these findings be generalized? Although the answer to this question must come from studies by others that verify these findings, it has been my own clinical experience that the better I understood the theory the more widely it has seemed to apply.

CONTROLS

Although there were no controls—patients who received no treatment or had another kind of treatment—the patients seen 10 years ago and presented in Chapter 1 can serve as a comparison group who were untreated or who received minimum treatment.

LENGTH OF FOLLOW-UP

The length of the follow-up is still not adequate. We have followed some of these patients in treatment for as long as 2 years after hospitalization, but they must be followed into and through college to establish that they are able to take up life on their own. However, their current records of adaptation, coping with stress, and achievement are sufficient reasons for optimism about their futures.

ROLE OF SUGGESTION

The treatment is a combination of suggestion and analysis which often makes the therapist feel as if he is walking a tightrope—trying to decide when to use the former and when the latter. The question arises as to how big a role suggestion plays? To what extent has the patient's improvement been due to the fact that he has incorporated suggestions into his defensive system which have brought about the symptomatic improvement, at the cost of greater resistance to deeper analysis [35]?

Not only as Borderline patients with ego defects, but also as adolescents, these patients need an authority with whom to identify to learn control. We quite consciously use our authority to reinforce the setting of limits; to make suggestions that are more-or-less "antithetic to the nature of the patient's pathogenic interest" [44]. The suggestion is made, and reinforced by restrictions, that it is better to handle destructive behavior by checking the impulse and analyzing it rather than by acting it out. We try to limit this suggestion to behavior. Once behavior has been controlled the working through process takes a course of its own powered by the patient's feelings and associations and the therapist limits himself to interpreting the defenses and the conflicts.

PSYCHIATRIC DILEMMA OF ADOLESCENCE REVISITED

Let us now review the histories of the patients described in Chapter 1 from the perspective of the psychodynamics of separation-individuation.

The 15½-year-old girl described on p. 8 of Chapter 1 gave a characteristic past history of narcissistic oral fixation—that is, developmental failures and ego defects, feeding problem, soiling, asthma, and temper tantrums. Her presenting illness was most likely an abandonment depression, with the rejection by her boyfriend being only a precipitating factor. Later, at age 18, when she tried to attend college her separation-individuation problem again came to the fore. Unable to separate and function on her own away from home, she became depressed and put on a lot of weight, overeating probably to satisfy her need for emotional supplies. Her depression later drove her to use narcotics and finally to form a clinging relationship with an older man. Unable to resolve her separation-individuation problem she was shackled to a life of symptomatic expressions.

The 14-year-old boy described on p. 9 developed anxiety and depression when the growth spurt of adolescence interrupted the clinging relationship with his immature Borderline mother who was holding on to him. He came into increasing conflict with her, and his need for emotional supplies drove him to obesity and excessive concern with money. When interviewed 6 years later his separation anxiety was seen in his difficulty in studying, his academic failures, his passive-aggressive defenses against his anxiety—that is, oversleeping—as well as in his continued dependency, obesity, and problems with money.

The next case, on p. 9, a 16-year-old boy, is an excellent example of one type of a relatively stable resolution of a separation-individuation problem, that is, the establishment of a symbiotic relationship with an institution. This boy was unable to graduate from high school—a crucial experience for those patients with separation anxiety because of the implications of helplessness and rejection in separation. He joined the Baptist Church and developed a dependent relationship with the minister which fulfilled his symbiotic needs and he was able to function. However, he had to employ "distancing" to avoid anxiety over emotional involvement with girls.

The patient described on p. 12, was a 17-year-old girl. In treatment it was not apparent at the time that her anger was not at rejection as much as at the mother's constant discouragement of the patient's moves toward individuation. This frustration led to her inability to separate and to her efforts to deal with her resultant depression by acting out in relationship with boys.

The contrast between the almost universally sad outcome for these earlier patients and the optimistic prognosis for our currently treated patients is clear.

CONCLUSION

In retrospect it is certain that many of the patients studied 15 years ago had a Borderline Syndrome. Ignorance at that time led us to fall back on the heterogenous and vague category of Personality Disorder and caused us to view the condition in terms of generalizations such as developmental defects and unresolved dependency needs. Understanding was limited since we did not know the right questions to ask, for example, about separation experiences, about the mother's holding on, and even how to evaluate some of the relevant information we already possessed.

There is a great contrast between the vagueness of the APA's definition of Personality Disorder and the exactness of the concept of the Borderline Syndrome. The concept of developmental defect in Personality Disorder, though basically accurate, is so broad and all inclusive that it is of very little use to the clinician. The psychoanalytic concepts of what it is all about, that is, separation-individuation, abandonment depression, and oral fixation describe this condition much more accurately by means of the tangible aspects of the level of developmental failure, the symptoms, the defenses, and the ego defects, as well as object relations. These concepts truly open the doors to the mysteries of the Borderline Syndrome.

For those who feel that the treatment does not bring about enough improvement, let us consider for a moment the alternative. What happens if there is no treatment?

The intimacy, warmth, closeness, and tenderness that are such a vital part of a mature, adult heterosexual relationship remain forever contaminated by the tie that binds. The patient experiences normal adult "closeness" as a forbidden entrapment—since it brings with it fears of either abandonment or engulfment. Fear of commitment, distrust of human relationships, and aloofness result.

Without treatment, symbiotic involvement and love and hate become a fixed pattern of interaction or a defensive structure of distance develops to prevent such an involvement. Love relationships must be avoided. Fear of commitment, distrust of human relationships, and aloofness result. Profound complications in relationships with the opposite sex arise, up to and including homosexuality.

Also without psychotherapy men tend to see marriageable women as awesome, unapproachable Madonnas, and are able to relate lustfully only to impersonal sex objects. Intimacy with the opposite sex is possible only if there is an escape hatch.

In some cases, marriage can only be tolerated providing it is not an exclusive relationship and some loopholes remain open. Women find built-in situations where occupations take men away from home for long periods such as military men, seamen, or salesmen. Men find prostitutes, divorced women, and "one night stands." On the other side of the coin clinging, dependent relationships with the opposite sex are found which are destined from the outset to severe conflict.

Such men and women cannot trust intimacy because they get caught up with it in the same symbiotic way they first experienced it in childhood. Their inordinate demands are on a primitive oral level and they display gross intolerance of any frustration. Deeply disappointed, hurt, and infuriated they withdraw from a relationship and vacillate between attraction to symbiotic or fusion states, and separation struggles to get out of them. Clearly without treatment, the legacy of childhood for these patients is awesome indeed.

FRINGE BENEFITS OF THE STUDY OF SEPARATION-INDIVIDUATION

Study of the psychodynamics of separation-individuation has some important fringe benefits or byproducts. I began in an effort to understand the Borderline Syndrome in adolescents. However, the separation-individuation theory applied as well to adults as to adolescents. This renewed my interest in the adult Borderline and impelled me to begin a study of intensive outpatient psychotherapy of adults with the Borderline Syndrome. This study already is showing promising results. Furthermore, since a successful symbiotic and separation-individuation stage of development are essential to the development of the potentials for creativity, individuality, and intimacy in adult life I became particularly interested in these qualities. Finally, the fact that separation-individuation is a universal developmental experience led me to an interest in the more minor separation-individuation pathology that characterizes the personality structure of every person. It has been a rather circuitous journey: from adolescent to Borderline, to separation-individuation, to adult Borderline, and to the separation-individuation psychopathology of every day life.

Epilogue*

But his grip was firm, yet gentle, and slowly,
I gave him my trust—a gift I thought I did
no longer possess. Following behind him, I came to the ruins,
closing my eyes for I could not bear to look,

and blindly, I stumbled to the wall, refusing to face
what I, in my own image, had created. He took my hand and placed
it on the sandy wall, instructing me to dig, and I obeyed
joyfully, for he allowed me to do it myself—yet soon I tired,
for I could not understand why, and the answer, "to help you"

was not familiar to my moulding ears.
I cried out in the darkness, "help me dig!",
and he replied that it was I who must help myself.
My fingernails were caked with sand, and I continued

to claw away at the cold wet sand, damp from a million tears,
and a decade of winter winds. Then through the blackness,
I screamed with pain, for oaken splinters had pierced my
fingers, and then with joy as I realized what I had reached.
I whispered in awe, "what now?", and the voice calmly answered,

"climb over."
The wind began to howl, the wall began to rise,
and I faltered with indecisions. I moan with my inadequacy,
and with his aid, slowly pull apart the boards,

scraping my fingers on the nails I had once so proudly
driven. And beneath the boards, corroding with disease,
I found all human attributes thought so long ago

* The second section of the poem presented in the Prologue.

to be missing and presumed dead, and the realization surprised
yet frightened me. Time passed, and with the passage,

> I accepted and no longer withdrew from
> the world, pulling toward my soul
> both the good and evil, so that I might
> distinguish between them. I no longer wished to

return to the world I had once created, now it seemed
so long ago . . . I embraced the world totally and felt capable
to contribute to it while achieving what I wished from it.
Within it, I find all that was missing from the others—
mutual love, tolerance, understanding . . . caring.
I stir with the realization of the dawn.
Time's libation has accomplished its desired effect
and I hear within myself satisfaction's sigh.
I rise, filled with the new-found freedom that was once
only tangible in dreams.

> Beyond domestic panes of glass,
> I viewed the golden crescent
> and feel its warmth caressing my cheek;
> blinding my eye with the strength of its love,

In the silence of the early morn,
I walked the deserted streets, rushing to keep my rendezvous
with my newest love—the joy of living.
How many others share my love? I am not selfish . . .
if only all might incorporate with my emotions!

> Is it fair that I envision myself
> as a free spirit, removed from the
> human maladjustments that were once present within me?
> It is fair to myself and fairer than I have ever been

. . . for I care.
My soul soars; I feel personally involved with others.

> I stand alone now, yet am unafraid. No hand is held in mine;
> I stand alone, independent . . . alive.
> Viewing the dawn, I feel the blood surge through my body,
> and laugh, grateful for the rebirth of my spirit.

But through the brightness of the dawn, memories still return.
There is a difference—they do not plague, but help to form
the future.

L. C. M.

Appendix   Initial and Follow-Up Psychological Testing*: Nancy and Bill

The developmental arrest in the Borderline, which occurs in early childhood (1½ to 3 years), forms the substrate for and gives a special meaning to later adolescent development. However, as the clinician may be misled by the patient's chronologic age (Chapter 3) into focusing on adolescence as the problem, so the psychologist may be misled into stressing the adolescent developmental aspects of the tests—that is, what he sees as the oedipal conflict and castration anxiety.

Therefore, it is important to delineate the early childhood arrest first. I have edited the full psychological reports sacrificing some complexity and depth to emphasize those themes that illustrate the early childhood arrest in the Borderline.

The psychoanalytic term orality is a convenient umbrella under which can be grouped the characteristic evidence to be looked for in the Borderline patient—both his needs and his defenses against those needs. For example, dependency, rage, and depression emerge with defenses such as avoidance, denial, distancing, and projection. Although according to our theory the oral emphasis is always there, it manifests itself in different degrees in each patient. This depends on many factors: the personality of the mother, the quality of the patient's relationship with her, and the kind of abandonment experiences the patient has had. Similarly, each patient's defense mechanisms against the feelings of abandonment are unique. Two individual reports are presented to capture these variations within the overall psychodynamic concept of abandonment.

Before reporting the tests let us briefly review the theory to predict what we might expect to find. The conflict between the push for separation-individuation and the withdrawal of supplies produces both the abandonment depression and the oral fixation. We would expect to find the following consequences of this conflict on the tests.

---

* The testing was performed and reported by the Adolescent Program Psychologist, Mrs. Edna Lerner.

NEEDS AND FEELINGS

Dependency, need for exclusive symbiotic relationship.
Need for supplies, fear of loss of supplies.
Fear of engulfment or abandonment.
Depression, feelings of loss of self, of starvation, of death, along with despair, suicide, suicidal impulses.
Homicidal rage.

DEFENSE MECHANISMS

Wish for reunion.
Projection.
Denial.
Avoidance.
Isolation.
Detachment.
Passivity.
Passive-aggressiveness.
Acting out.
Projection to the point of paranoid thinking.

EGO DEFECTS

Fluid ego boundaries leading to poor reality testing.
Poor impulse control.
Low frustration tolerance.

GENDER IDENTITY CONFUSION

Since a sense of identity as a person precedes the development of gender identity, the latter inevitably falls victim when the former is lacking. The male patients feel their lack of assertiveness and autonomy as a severe sense of masculine inadequacy. The lack of assertiveness plays such a key role in the conflict with the mother that the adolescent feels dominated and castrated as a male. Indeed, it is his very maleness that is discouraged by the mother since it is such a quintessential sign of individuation. This situation frequently gives rise to a fear of being homosexual on the part of the adolescent. Nonetheless, the problem is not homosexuality but anxiety over self-assertion. Females also have a feeling of feminine inadequacy though this seems somewhat less acute since passivity is not only a part of femininity but also is in our culture more tolerated in the female than the male.

Nancy

TEST BATTERY

The following battery of tests were given: Rorschach, WAIS, Bender Gestalt, Sentence Completion, and Figure Drawings. The WAIS and Rorschach are presented for each patient. Since cognition was not a focus of this work, a full discussion of its role is presented for only one patient. To evaluate their progress the patients were retested 8 months after admission—in the latter part of the working-through phase.

Nancy

Wechsler Adult Intelligence Scale

Information	12	Digit Symbol	12
Comprehension	14	Picture Completion	11
Arithmetic	11	Block Design	10
Similarities	14	Picture Arrangement	11
Digit Span	9	Object Assembly	15

Verbal Scale	I.Q.	119
Performance	I.Q.	113
Full Scale	I.Q.	118

The full WAIS reflects a Full Scale I.Q. of 118, with a Verbal I.Q. of 119 and a Performance I.Q. of 113, with moderate scatter. The essential Verbal I.Q. level is 143 indicating an excellent academic potential.

Rorschach

She is a less creative person than her vivacity and colorful vocabulary would lead one to expect, and the Rorschach is by and large unremarkable, except for a series of recurring images of *abysses* and chasms. These appear related to a fear of *engulfment* or a basic instability, and are consistent with the *depression* noted and the suicidal ruminations. Her reality testing is firm and good.

The girl's overt rebellion is explicit and uncontained. She enjoys the release of ventilation and even casual interactions are marked by explosive irritability. But much of this is façade and bravado: she fails to carry through, the expression of anger appears to suffice, and she then moves on to work cooperatively, even seriously and earnestly, protesting, and spluttering as she works.

The father emerges as hero and the mother as villain. But beneath the explicit anger against the mother, elements of a positive feminine identification emerge reflected in her beginning interest in pregnancy and motherhood and suggest some progress toward acceptance of an adult feminine role. Unfortunately the hostility to the mother has resulted in a fusing of a healthy drive toward autonomy with self-destructive aggressive rebellion and a negative personal identity.

She is extremely apprehensive about her developing sexuality and her feminine fate. The tough talk appears a means of postponing and covering the ambivalent acceptance of womanhood. It also affords her time for testing of limits. The underlying dependency needs are so prominent as to threaten her progress toward individuation, though as noted above the hidden positive aspects of the tie to the mother support the movement ahead.

The acting out appears to be less real impulsivity than a deliberate choice—an ability usually to let fly and then pull together at will. Her obsessive-compulsive defenses are probably potentially adequate if she can learn to use them. The brash, slap-dash quality covers anxiety, fear, and sharp depression and is as yet the only means she knows of reacting to others.

The following aspects of this test support the basic theme: the conflict with the mother, the underlying strong dependency, the fear of engulfment which is defended against by acting out, and the anxiety about femininity. It also indicates her assets, her good intelligence, good reality testing, and obsessive-compulsive defenses.

Follow-Up Test: Figure Drawings, Rorschach, and Sentence Completion

The change in this patient occurs within a fairly fixed characterological set of provocative passive aggressive maneuvers and pervasive distrust. Nevertheless, there appears to be an overall movement toward a strengthening of ego function in the sense of greater self-acceptance and awareness, the ability to accept some responsibility for herself and her future, more competent if not conflict free cognition, improved planning capacity, and integration.

A comparison of the tree drawn on admission and that produced after 8 months of therapy reflects the change in Nancy. Her first tree (Fig. 1) has no environment, its boundaries are broken and poorly reinforced and the core of the trunk is open, reflecting the unexpected flow of the unconscious and the poor control over the instinctual and the primitive psychic organization. The roots are not embedded in the environment, and that which should be covered is exposed, suggesting her failing repressions. The branches are unsealed and the stalk, without leaf or fruit, is a barren, "old" depressive representation for a 15-year-old girl. In the second tree (Fig. 2) the environment is massively represented by two supportive holders, suggesting an increased relationship to the environment and an acceptance of her dependency needs. The tree has begun to grow leaves: it is alive and growing. Depression is still there, as in the fuzzy boundaries in the leaf area. But the improvement is real; this is a viable tree.

More significant in the Rorschach and Sentence Completion tests is the tentative but courageous reaching out toward growth experiences and relationships to others. The substrate of the patient's problems as earlier noted is her sense of inadequate support which has been overlaid by what she experiences as engulfing, unreasonable parental behavior on one level, but on a more basic

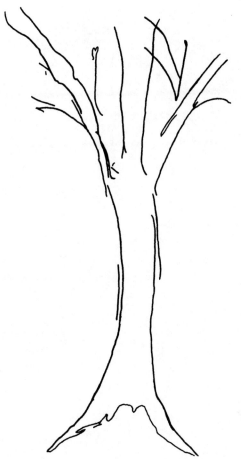

Figure 1. Nancy's stick tree—initial.

level as arising from her own failures and inadequacies, being unloved, un-lovable, and, in some global sense, guilty.

She appears, however, in a period of transition with some of her problems unevenly exacerbated: perhaps temporarily more open to insight and perspective, particularly in the area of the interpersonal. She tries to control her reactions, to move off, to be objective, and to modify her initial impulsive hostile rejections. And she retains the psychic bounce and vigor which is so appealing and which serves to cancel out a good deal of the off-putting anger she so persistently displays. The amount of depression, even now skirting the suicidal, should not be underestimated. There appears to be a seesaw movement toward and away, up and down, as if whole-hearted commitment to life and belief were still impossible.

Figure 2.   Nancy's growing tree—Follow-up.

Bill

Bill's clinical history has been given in Chapter 3.

Wechsler Intelligence Scale for Children

Information	17	Picture Completion	10
Comprehension	14	Picture Arrangement	10
Arithmetic	13	Block Design	13
Similarities	16	Object Assembly	12
Digit Span	11	Coding	20
Vocabulary	13		

Verbal Scale	I.Q.	125
Performance	I.Q.	121
Full Scale	I.Q.	125

The intellectual functioning reflects a very superior endowment, and even now, with evidence of an ongoing mild thinking disorder, his WISC scores are superior with a Full Scale WISC I.Q. of 125, a Verbal I.Q. of 125 and a Performance I.Q. of 121. His arithmetic and Digit Span scores are depressed by his inability to concentrate and his Picture Completion and Picture Arrangement reflects his poor judgment and anticipation and a general decathexis from the environment. Qualitatively the performance is that of a decompensating obsessive-compulsive. His answers are multiform—he adds detail after detail, unable to stop himself or to discriminate. He persistently spoils answers by the additions of irrelevant or absurd details. A schizophrenic flooding is reflected, with lucid association, inability to sustain an orderly logical sequence. One of his "wishes" demonstrates the logical lapse—"immortality in the physical and mental state I am in."

Rorschach

The patient is an expansive, tense adolescent who is functioning unevenly—at times adequately and adaptively, but decompensating easily under the slightest pressure. His self-esteem is low and he attempts to compensate by a Nietzschean grandiosity, standing accepted values on their heads, espousing eccentric causes for which he claims special significance—and finding in selected authority or aspects of hippy philosophy support for his views and a sense of superiority and uniqueness.

He is extremely fluid, with ill-defined boundaries—unable to discriminate easily between self and environment, inner and outer stimuli. On the Rorschach this is reflected in his figure-ground confusion, in a series of porous or shifting percepts and in his preoccupation with "insides." A precipitous, uncontrolled flight forward is expressed in his elliptical writing and his pressured speech.

His central problem is the maintenance of integrity. Specifically he is concerned with control both of his inner confusion and especially of his violence. This is reflected throughout the projectives: in his slashing, scrawling "dirty" handwriting, in the sudden expansion of the aggression laden arrrow figure on the Bender, in the oral aggressive responses which pervade the Rorschach, and especially in his animal figure drawing—a "nurse shark." (See Fig. 3.) He

Figure 3. Bill's nursing shark.

expresses—and attempts to control—his aggressive impulses by displacement to intellectual activities pursued with ferocious avidity, and intrapunitively in depression. Nevertheless these impulses take over periodically, but so ego alien is anger against the parental figures—that he experiences his rage in an almost depersonalized way, as a visitation from without.

The violence is expressed in relation to, and precipitated by the intense push-pull relationship with the parents and especially the mother, and is enhanced by a quite conscious competition with the brother. It is experienced on a primitive level as a life-death struggle for supplies and is reflected in the oral aggressivity displayed throughout the projectives—which alternates with and is a reaction formation against the underlying oral demanding orientation.

He fights a symbiotic pull to the mother which is well expressed in his response to the vaginal area of Rorschach Card VII: "This looks like little magnets—trying to cling to each other going out to grab it." "Not magnets— *things* trying to get together, pulling each other—the stretching toward each other." "Then—you're not going to believe this—an avalanche in a bay—a landslide covering a bay. The landslide spreads out—cuts off the bay and soon its going to make it into a lake." The mother is experienced as central, crucial, and irresistible and at the same time as destructive and engulfing. His "nurse-shark" animal figure drawing (decorated in much the same way as his female figure drawing, see Chapter 11) well expressed the combination of nurturance and primitive oral threat he struggles to disentangle. The preoccupation with the masculine and feminine differentiation is reflected in two bizarre, idiosyncratic responses to phallic areas which contain the shark theme: "Claspers— the claspers of a shark" which he explains are a male shark's genital organs. The patient is psychosexually underdeveloped and his sex role image is complex and confusing.

The intensity of his preoccupation with the parental figures, and with his controls leaves little psychic energy available for peer relationships. He shows little capacity for empathy, and though he feels isolated and lonely is probably not capable of complex interaction with his peers except when it is confined to the intellectual sphere. His response to affective stimuli is not integrated into the rest of his functioning, and on the Rorschach, when it occurs, is usually regressive and maladaptive.

As his repression weakens he is absorbed in wider and wider defensive operations. He is pervasively paranoid, suspicious, and covert, constantly orienting himself and scoring his own efforts in relation to others. He rationalizes, avoids, denies, endlessly projects, isolates, and indulges in frantic doing and undoing rituals.

My clinical diagnosis was that of a Borderline Syndrome on the verge of a psychotic break. This patient illustrates the following aspects of the basic theme: the severe conflict with the mother, the need for supplies, the rage, and the need to defend himself against the rage with such defenses as intellectualization, denial, avoidance, projection, reaction formation, rationalization, isolation, doing, and undoing. The fluid ego boundaries, severe depression and the fight against the symbiotic pull, are also illustrated. This patient's defense mechanisms against the symbiotic pull to the mother are of the schizoid obsessive-compulsive variety. They are in marked contrast to the previous patient who defended herself primarily by acting out. Though they both suffer from an abandonment depression their clinical pictures differ because their defenses differ.

Follow-Up Test: Rorschach, Sentence Completion, Figure Drawing, and Bender Gestalt

This gifted but disturbed boy has made modest but significant progress during his hospitalization. There is an overall modification of his pathology

Figure 4. Bill. Female—initial.

with some increase in control—in the capacity to sustain anxiety and delay impulse expression, and to achieve a little distance through his ability to give himself an account of his experience and feeling. He is also able to sustain a less erratic pattern of function though this breaks down under stress. Yet he retains his core fluidity, and the Rorschach protocols now as previously are studded with bizarre figure-ground confusions and combinations, as well as with responses describing the relentless inroad on one part of the blot by another (flowing lava, flooding water, etc). This expresses his sense of being invaded, overwhelmed by forces from within and without, and as well as revealing his porous boundaries and difficulty in distinguishing between internal

Figure 5. Bill. Male—initial.

and external stimuli. And this in turn is related to his problem in individuation, relinquishing the symbiotic tie to the parents.

The figure and animal sequence of this patient dramatically illustrates progress achieved through therapy within the limits of basic pathology. The first series (Fig. 4 and 5) is eccentric. The figures are lifeless, with stereotyped grieving faces and skewed lopsided distorted bodies. Compulsivity is reflected in the decorative detailing. Depression is seen in the darkened areas especially of the woman whose hands are useless for coping. Eye and ear detailing on the male (Fig. 5) have a paranoid emphasis. The instinctual representation is of

Figure 6. Bill. Female—Follow-up.

a "nurse shark," (Fig. 3) fusing the oral aggression and demanding and demonstrating verbal conceptual overlap as well. This overlap (of the maternal and destructive) is evident also in the decorative detailing on both the shark and the mother figure.

The second set of figures (Fig. 6, 7 and 8) have improved. The pencil line is less tense and aggressive and they are less lifeless. But they retain the executed strangeness of the first—the barrel-hipped bodies, the useless curled arms (Fig. 6 and 7). Oral needs are expressed in the over emphasized mouth and pockets and paranoid watchfulness in the wide open, pupiled eyes. The compulsive defenses are exhibited more in relation to chest and shoulders (power and

Figure 7.   Bill. Male—Follow-up.

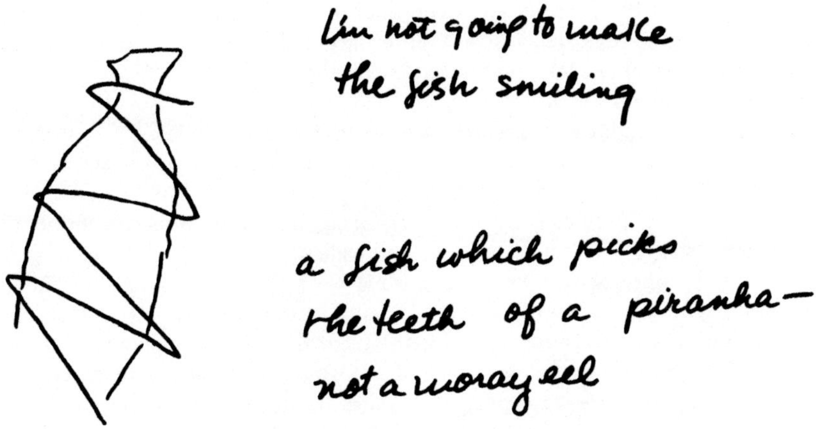

I'm not going to make the fish smiling

a fish which picks the teeth of a piranha—not a moray eel

Figure 8.   Bill. Animal—Follow-up.

coping) than in the instinctual area. The animal (Fig. 8) is still a regressive choice of a fish; but it is no longer the destructive shark, but even more bizarre: the servant fish who picks the teeth of a man-eating piranha or lethal moray eel. The patient controls his destructive urge by isolation—accepts the crumbs from the table (teeth) of the predator, controls by denial and a kind of regression.

A strenuous reinforcement of the defenses is now in process with a pattern characteristic of obsessive/compulsiveness; heavily invested in efforts to cope, though not consistently able to marshall resources effectively. Thus on the Bender Gestalt in spite of counting and recounting he gets the wrong number of dots on a simple sequence, and in his multiple doing and undoing of the dependency figures he ends with a figure indistinguishable from his first effort. Nevertheless, the emphasis now is on the defenses. The paranoid projection is still prominent. But the repressive barriers are reinforced, even if unreliably, and the breakthroughs from the unconscious have now an ego alien quality. Some growth in observing ego is evident. For example, the bizarre "claspers of a shark" given on Rorschach I is repeated on II—but the patient pauses to make explicit his discomfort with the response and his awareness of what it means to him. Other flagrantly bizarre responses and confusions are now modified or omitted. (Note the general improvement in the feminine figure (Fig. 6) drawing, the loss of the fusion of the shark/mother, and generally greater competence in coping with the idea of the feminine.)

The defensive pattern is strikingly polar, with doing and undoing and re-action formations so automatic that each impulse appears to trigger its opposite. On the Rorschach he demonstrates his compulsivity in his preoccupation with tiny details, which proliferate even as he ignores the whole—a flight to the periphery by which he escapes the essential. His intellectualizations also serve to protect him, to keep threatening ideas and emotions at a distance, to serve as an impersonal bridge to others. The intensity of the push from the unconscious and intermittent repressive failures are reflected in the disparities in size on the Bender Recall particularly with the dependency figures, and in judgmental lapses on the Rorschach. The strength of the impulses, the pattern of flight forward and loss of control once he gets under way is expressed in his handwriting in his peculiar perseverative M's and W's—where he simply cannot stop.

The underlying problems remain unchanged. The patient is caught in an excruciating struggle to separate from ambivalently experienced parents—and his increased ability to see them objectively, to describe the destructive interaction, does little to modify the essential nature of the primitive bind. A change in the quality of the relationship is noted—from the simple symbiotic pull and need to hang on, to the sad and fearful recognition that the parents are not capable of real support—as expressed in the Rorschach responses in Card VII, the "feminine card": in Test I: "magnets trying to attract each other"; in Test II: "they look insecure, as if they'd break and fall apart." And as well, the affective change—the center of Card VII previously "an engulfing landslide"—is now resistant "ice."

The patient has no basic trust, feels permanently at odds with himself and the world. He is suspicious and fearful of others, of the danger of interaction and intimacy. He is unable to wring from others emotional supplies on a level and in the quantity his insatiable needs demand. The Rorschach is studded with oral imagery—a breast, pigs, bears, beaks of birds, crocodiles, wolves and other oral aggressive imagery. And his animal drawing has simply moved from a "nurse shark" to a "fish" which cleans the teeth of a piranha fish—no, "a moray eel." (See Fig. 6.) He is unable to be spontaneous—must control by planning ahead, attempting to tamp down the unacceptable fears, and ward off dangers by anticipating all eventualities.

As the effort to police his ideas, confront his feelings, and control his impulses builds, his depression has mounted, and a long range suicidal potential is noted. In the Rorschach, in a small detail in a colored (affective) area he sees "a dead figure toppling." In a large space detail he sees "a gate, with insufficient fortifications" (gates often represent the passageway between life and death). And the Sentence Completions contain not only death completions "closer and closer there comes death," but also the final completion often considered pathognomonic of suicide: "if one cannot own his own life, he is not living." The general context is one of helpless hopelessness and doubt about the future. It is mitigated by the wistful recognition of love, the wish to relate in spite of his fears, and a brave and ephemeral impulse to opt for life.

References

1. Atkins, N. B. Comments on Severe and Psychotic Regressions in Analysis. *J. Amer. Psychoanal. Ass.*, 1967, **15**, 584–605.
2. Bateson, C. F., Mishler, E. G., & Waxler, N. E. *Family Processes and Schizophrenia.* New York: Science House, Inc., 1968.
3. Benedek, T. Adaptation of Reality in Early Infancy. *Psychoanal. Quart.*, 1938, **7**, 200–215.
4. Benedek, T. The Psychosomatic Implications of the Primary Unit: Mother-Child. *Amer. J. Orthopsychiat.*, 1949, **19**, 642–654.
5. Benedek, T. Psychobiological Aspects of Mothering. *Amer. J. Orthopsychiat.*, 1956, **26**, 272–278.
6. Benedek, T. Parenthood as a Developmental Phase. *J. Amer. Psychoanal. Ass.*, 1959, **7**, 389–417.
7. Blanck, G. Some Technical Implications of Ego Psychology. *Int. J. Psychoanal.*, 1966, **47**, 6–13.
8. Blos, P. *On Adolescence.* New York: The Free Press of Glencoe, 1962.
9. Bonnard, A. Primary Process Phenomena in the Case of a Borderline Psychotic Child. *Int. J. Psychoanal.*, 1967, **48**, 221–236.
10. Bowlby, J. Separation Anxiety. *Int. J. Psychoanal.*, 1960, **41**, 89–113.
11. Bowlby, J. Grief and Mourning in Infancy and Early Childhood. *Psychoanal. Study Child*, 1960, **15**, 9–52.
12. Bowlby, J. *Attachment and Loss,* Volume I. New York: Basic Books, Inc., 1969.
13. Bowlby, J. The Nature of the Child's Tie to His Mother. *Int. J. Psychoanal.*, 1958, **39**, 350–371.
14. Bowlby, J. Process of Mourning. *Int. J. Psychoanal.*, 1961, **42**, 317–340.
15. Boyer, L. B., & Giovacchini, P. L. *Psychoanalytic Treatment of Characterological and Schizophrenic Disorders.* New York: Science House, 1967.
16. Brodey, W. M. On the Dynamics of Narcissism: I Externalization and Early Ego Deviation. *Psychoanal. Study Child*, 1965, **20**, 165–193.
17. Chess, T. A., & Birch, H. *Temperament and Behavior Disorders in Children.* New York: New York University Press, 1969. Pp. 27–82.
18. Clark, L. P. Some Practical Remarks Upon the Use of Modified Psycho-

analysis in the Treatment of Borderline (Borderland) Neuroses and Psychoses. *Psychoanal. Rev.*, 1919, **6**, 306–315.

19. Deutsch, H. Some Forms of Emotional Disturbances and Their Relationship to Schizophrenia. *Psychoanal. Quart.*, 1942, **11**, 301–321. Also (Rev.) in H. Deutsch, *Neuroses and Character Types*. New York: International Universities Press, 1965. Pp. 262–281.

20. Deutsch, H. *The Psychology of Woman*, Volume 1. New York: Grune and Stratton, 1944. Pp. 3–23.

21. Dickes, R. Severe Regressive Disruptions of the Therapeutic Alliance. *J. Amer. Psychoanal. Ass.*, 1967, **15**, 508–533.

22. Eisenstein, W. W. Differential Psychotherapy of Borderline States. In G. Bychowski and J. L. Despert (Eds), *Specialized Techniques in Psychotherapy*. New York: Basic Books, 1952.

23. Ekstein, R., & Rangell, L. Reconstruction and Theory Formation. *J. Amer. Psychoanal. Ass.*, 1961, **9**, 684–697.

24. Ekstein, R., & Wallerstein, J. Observations on the Psychology of Borderline and Psychotic Children. *Psychoanal. Study Child*, 1954, **9**, 344–469.

25. Ersnitz, A. J. Narcissistic Object Choice and Self-Representation. *Int. J. Psychoanal.*, 1969, **50**, 15–25. Discussed in *Int. J. Psychoanal.*, 1970, **51**, 151–157.

26. Fairbairn, W. R. D. A Revised Psychopathology of the Psychoses and Psychoneuroses. In *Psychoanalytic Studies of the Personality*. London: Tavistock, 1952; New York: Basic Books (*An Object-Relations Theory of the Personality*), 1954.

27. Fraiberg, S. Libidinal Object Constancy and Mental Representation. *Psychoanal. Study Child*, 1969, **24**, 9–47.

28. Freeman, T. Some Aspects of Pathological Narcissism. *J. Amer. Psychoanal. Ass.*, 1964, **12**, 340–561.

29. Freud, S. Fetishism (1927). In *Collected Papers*, Volume V. J. Strachey (Ed.). London: Hogarth Press, 1950. Pp. 198–204.

30. Freud, S. Splitting of the Ego in the Defensive Process (1938). In *Collected Papers*, Volume V. J. Strachey (Ed.). London: Hogarth Press, 1950. Pp. 372–375.

31. Freud, S. On Narcissism: An Introduction (1914). In *Collected Papers*, Volume IV. J. Riviere (Ed.). London: Hogarth Press, 1948. Pp. 30–59.

32. Frosch, J. Severe Regressive States During Analysis. *J. Amer. Psychoanal. Ass.*, 1967, **15**, 491–507.

33. Frosch, J. The Psychotic Character Clinical Psychiatric Consideration. *Psychiat. Quart.*, 1964, **38**, 81–96.

34. Frosch, H. Severe Regressive States During Analysis Summary. *J. Amer. Psychoanal. Ass.*, 1967, **15**, 606–625.

35. Fryling-Schreuder, E. C. M. Borderline States in Children. *Psychoanal. Study Child*, 1969, **24**, 307–327.

36. Geleerd, E. R. Borderline States in Childhood and Adolescence. *Psychoanal. Study Child*, 1956, **11**, 336–351.

37. Giovacchini, P. L. The Submerged Ego. *J. Amer. Acad. Child Psychiatry*, July 1964, **3** (3).

38. Giovacchini, P. L. Maternal Introjection and Ego Defect. *J. Amer. Acad. Child Psychiat.*, April 1965, **4** (2).

39. Giovacchini, P. L. Transference, Incorporation and Synthesis. *Int. J. Psychoanal.*, 1965, **46** (Part 3).

40. Giovacchini, P. L. Frustration and Externalization. *Psychoanal. Quart.*, 1967, **36**, 571–583.

41. Giovacchini, P. L. The Frozen Introject. *Int. J. Psychoanal.*, 1967, **48** (Part 1).

42. Giovacchini, P. L., et al. On Regression: A Workshop. J. A. Lindon (Ed.). *The Psychoanalytic Forum*, Winter 1967, **2** (4).

43. Giovacchini, P. L. Effects of Adaptive and Disruptive Aspects of Early Object Relationships and Later Parental Functioning. In E. Anthony and T. Benedek (Ed.). *Parenthood*. Boston: Little Brown, 1970.

44. Glover, E. A Psycho-Analytical Approach to the Classification of Mental Disorders. *J. Mental Sci.*, 1932, **78**, 819–842.

45. Glover, E. *The Technique of Psychoanalysis*. New York: International Universities Press, 1955. Pp. 353–367.

46. Greenacre, P. Regression and Fixation. *J. Amer. Psychoanal. Ass.*, 1960, **8**, 703–723.

47. Greenacre, P. The Predisposition to Anxiety. In *Trauma Growth and Personality*. New York: International Universities Press, 1952, pp. 27–82.

48. Grinker, R., Werble, B., & Drye, R. *The Borderline Syndrome*. New York: Basic Books, 1968.

49. Guntrip, H. *Personality Structure and Human Interaction*. London: Hogarth; New York, International Universities Press, 1964.

50. Hammerman, S. Conception of Superego Development. *J. Amer. Psychoanal. Ass.*, 1965, **13**, 320–355.

50a. Hendrickson, W. J., & Holmes, D. J. Control of Behavior As A Crucial Factor in Intensive Psychiatric Treatment In An All Adolescent Ward. *Amer. J. Psychiat.*, 1959, **115**, 11.

50b. Hendrickson, W. J., Holmes, D. J., & Waggoner, R. W. Psychotherapy of the Hospitalized Adolescent. *Amer. J. Psychiat.*, 1959, **116**, 6.

50c. Hendrickson, W. J., & Holmes, D. J. Institutional Psychotherapy of the Delinquent. *Progress in Psychotherapy*, V. New York, Grune & Stratton, Inc., 1960.

50d. Holmes, D. J. *The Adolescent in Psychotherapy*, Boston: Little Brown & Co., 1964.

51. Hunter, R. C. A. *The Analysis of Episodes of Depersonalization in Borderline Patients. Int. J. Psychoanal.*, 1966, **47**, 32–41.

52. Jacobson, E. Denial and Repression. *J. Amer. Psychoanal. Ass.*, 1957, **5**, 61–92.

53. Jacobson, E. *The Self and the Object World*, New York: International Universities Press, 1964.

54. Kalina, E. Aspects of a Clinical Case Transferential Relations in Face of Separations. Presented April 19, 1966 to the Argentina Psychoanalytical Association.

55. Kalina, E. The Analytical Process of an Adolescent with an "As If" State: Diagnostic Problems and Psychopathology. Presented November 11, 1969 to the Argentina Psychoanalytical Association.

56. Kernberg, O. Borderline Personality Organization. *J. Amer. Psychoanal. Ass.*, 1967, **15**, 641–685.

57. Kernberg, O. A Psychoanalytic Classification of Character Pathology. *J. Amer. Psychoanal. Ass.*, 1970, **18**, 800–822.

58. Kernberg, O. Factors in the Psychoanalytic Treatment of Narcissistic Personalities. *J. Amer. Psychoanal. Ass.*, 1970, **18**, 51–85.

59. Kernberg, O. The Treatment of Patients with Borderline Personality Organization. *Int. J. Psychoanal.*, 1968, **49**, 600–619.

60. Kernberg, O. Structural Derivatives of Object Relationships. *Int. J. Psychoanal.*, 1966, **47**, 236–253.

61. Kernberg, O. Notes on Countertransference. *J. Amer. Psychoanal. Ass.*, 1965, **13**, 38–56.

62. Klaus, A. On Symbiosis and Pseudosymbiosis. *J. Amer. Psychoanal. Ass.*, 1967, **15**, 294–316.

63. Klaus, A. Loss of Identity and Acting Out. *J. Amer. Psychoanal. Ass.*, 1965, **13**, 79–84.

64. Klein, M. *The Psychoanalysis of Children.* London: Hogarth, 1932.

65. Klein, M. Contribution to the Psychogenesis of Manic Depressive States. In *Contributions to Psychoanalysis 1921–1945.* London: Hogarth, 1948.

66. Klein, M. Mourning and its Relation to Manic Depressive States. In *Contributions to Psychoanalysis 1921–1945.* London: Hogarth, 1948.

67. Klein, M. Notes on Some Schizoid Mechanisms. In J. Riviere, (Ed.) *Developments in Psychoanalysis.* London: Hogarth, 1946.

68. Knight, R. P. (Ed). Borderline States. In *Psychoanalytic Psychiatry and Psychology.* New York: International Universities Press, 1954.

69. Kohut, H. The Psychoanalytic Treatment of Narcissistic Personality Disorder: Outline of a Systematic Approach. *Psychoanal. Study Child,* 1968, **23**, 86–113.

70. Kohut, H. Autonomy and Integration. *J. Amer. Psychoanal. Ass.*, 1965, **13**, 851–856.

71. Kohut, H. Forms and Transformations of Narcissism. *J. Amer. Psychoanal. Ass.*, 1966, **14**, 243–272.

72. Kohut, H. Panel on Narcissistic Resistance (N.P. Segal Reporter). *J. Amer. Psychoanal. Ass.*, 1969, **17**, 941–954.

73. Kut (Rosenfeld), S. Some Thoughts on the Technical Handling of Borderline Children. *Psychoanal. Study Child,* 1965, **20**, 494–517.

74. Lichtenstein, H. Identity and Sexuality: A Study of Their Interrelationship in Man. *J. Amer. Psychoanal. Ass.*, 1961, **9**:179–260.

75. Litowitz, N. S. & Newman, K. M. The Borderline Personality and the Theatre of the Absurd. *Arch. Gen. Psychiat.*, 1967, **16**, 268–281.

76. Little, M. Transference in Borderline States. *Int. J. Psychoanal.*, 1966, **47**, 476–485.

77. Mahler, M. S. *On Human Symbiosis and the Vicissitudes of Individuation.* New York: International Universities Press, 1968.

78. Mahler, M. S. Thoughts About Development and Individuation. *Psychoanal. Study Child*, 1963, **18**, 307–324.
79. Mahler, M. S. Autism and Symbiosis—Two Extreme Disturbances of Identity. *Int. J. Psychoanal.*, 1958, **39**, 77–83.
80. Mahler, M. S. On the Significance of the Normal Separation-Individuation Phase. In M. Schur (Ed), *Drives, Affects and Behavior*, Vol. 2. New York: International Universities Press, 1965, pp. 161–169.
81. Mahler, M. S. & Furer, M. Certain Aspects of the Separation-Individuation Phase. *Psychoanal. Quart.*, 1963, **32**, 1–14.
82. Mahler, M. S. and LaPerriere, R. Mother-Child Interactions During Separation-Individuation. *Psychoanal. Quart.*, 1965, **34**:483–489.
83. Mahler, M. S. & McDevitt, J. Observations on Adaptation and Defense in Statu Nascendi. *Psychoanal. Quart.*, 1968, **37**, 1–21.
84. Mahler, M. S. Pine, F., & Bergman, A. The Mother's Reaction to her Toddler's Drive for Individuation. E. Anthony and T. Benedek (Eds.), *Parenthood*. Boston: Little Brown, 1970.
85. Masterson, J. F. *Psychiatric Dilemma of Adolescence.* Boston: Little Brown, 1967.
86. Masterson, J. F. The Psychiatric Significance of Adolescent Turmoil. *Amer. J. Psychiat., May* 1968, **124**, 11.
87. Masterson, J. F. Intensive Psychotherapy of the Adolescent With A Borderline Syndrome. To be published in *American Handbook of Psychiatry* (Special Edition on Adolescence, G. Caplan (Ed.)), 1972.
88. Masterson, J. F. Intensive Psychotherapy of the Borderline Adolescent. To be published in *Annals of Adolescent Psychiatry*, Vol. II, 1972.
89. Masterson, J. F. Treatment of the Adolescent With Borderline Syndrome (A Problem in Separation-Individuation). *Bull. Menninger Clinic*, 1971, **35**, 5–18.
90. Modell, A. H. Primitive Object Relationships and the Predisposition to Schizophrenia. *Int. J. Psychoanal.* 1963, **44**, 282–292.
91. Modell, A. H. Denial and the Sense of Separateness. *J. Amer. Psychoanal. Ass.*, 1961, **9**, 533–547.
92. Novey, S., The Principle of "Working Through" in Psychoanalysis. *J. Amer. Psychoanal. Ass.*, 1962, **10**, 658–676.
93. Offer, D. *The Psychological World of the Teenager.* New York: Basic Books 1969.
94. Olinick, S. Negative Therapeutic Reaction. *J. Amer. Psychoanal. Ass.*, 1970, **18**, 655–672.
95. Parens, H. A Contribution of Separation-Individuation to the Development of Psychic Structure. In J. McDevitt and C. Settlage, (Eds.) *Separation-Individuation* New York: International Universities Press, 1971, pp. 100–112.
96. Perrault, C. *Cinderella.* New York: Scribner, 1954.
97. Peto, A. Dedifferentiations of the Therapeutic Alliance. *J. Amer. Psychoanal. Ass.*, 1967, **15**, 534–550.
98. Piaget, J. *The Construction of Reality in the Child.* New York: Basic Books, 1954.

99. Piaget, J. *Play, Dream and Imitation in Childhood.* New York: Norton, 1951.
100. Piaget, J. *The Psychology of Intelligence.* London: Routledge and Kegan Paul, 1950.
101. Pine, F. & Furer, M. Studies of the Separation-Individuation Phase: A Methodological Overview. *Psychoanal. Study Child*, 1963, **18**, 325–342.
102. Pollack, G. H. On Symbiosis and Symbiotic Neurosis. *Int. J. Psychoanal.*, 1964, **45**, 1–30.
103. Provence, S. Some Aspects of Early Ego Development:Data From a Longitudinal Study. In R. M. Loewenstein, L. M. Newman, M. Schur, and A. J. Solnit (Eds), *Psychoanalysis—A General Psychology* New York: International Universities Press, 1966, pp. 107–122.
104. Puzo, M. *The Godfather.* Greenwich, Conn.: Fawcett Publications Inc., 1969.
105. Rangell, L. The Role of Early Psychic Functioning in Psychoanalysis. *J. Amer. Psychoanal. Ass.*, 1962, **9**, 595–609.
106. Rickman, J. The Development of the Psycho-Analytic Theory of the Psychoses 1893–1926. London: Bailliere, Tindall & Cox for the Institute of Psychoanalysis, 1928.
107. Rinsley, D. B. Economic Aspects of the Object Relations. *Int. J. Psychoanal.* 1968, **49**, Part I 44–45.
108. Rinsley, D. B. Theory and Practice of Intensive Residential Treatment of Adolescents. *Psychiatric Quart.* 1968, 611–638. Also (Rev) in *Ann. Amer. Soc. Adolesc. Psychiat.*, **1**, 1971, 479–509.
109. Rinsley, D. B. Psychiatric Hospital Treatment with Special Reference to Children. *Archives Gen. Psychiat.*, 1963, **9**, 489–496.
110. Rinsley, D. B. The Adolescent in Residential Treatment:Some Critical Reflections. *Adolescence*, Spring 1967, **2**(5), 83–95.
111. Rinsley, D. B. Intensive Psychiatric Hospital Treatment of Adolescents: An Object-Relations View. *Psychiat. Quart.*, July 1965.
112. Rinsley, D. B. & Hall, D. D. Psychiatric Hospital Treatment of Adolescents:Parental Resistances as Expressed in Casework Metaphor. *Archives Gen. Psychiat.* 1962, **7**, 286–294.
113. Rinsley, D. B. Special Education for Adolescents in Residential Psychiatric Treatment: A Contribution to the Theory and Technique of Residential School. *Ann. Amer. Soc. Adolesc. Psychiat.*, to be published.
114. Rinsley, D. B. Residential Treatment of the Adolescent. In G. Caplan (Ed.), *American Handbook of Psychiatry*, 2nd ed., to be published.
115. Rinsley, D. B. The Adolescent Inpatient:Patterns of Depersonification. *Psychiat. Quart.*, 1971, **45**, 1–20.
116. Ritvo, S. (Reporter). Object Relations. *J. Amer. Psychoanal. Ass.*, 1962, **10**, 102–117.
117. Rogers, R. The Unmotivated Adolescent Patient Who Wants Psychotherapy. *Amer. J. Psychother.*, July 1970, **24**, 411–418.
118. Roshco, M. Perception, Denial and Depersonalization. *J. Amer. Psychoanal. Ass.*, 1967, **15**, 243–260.

119. Ross, N. An Examination of Nosology, According to Psychoanalytic Concept. *J. Amer. Psychoanal. Ass.*, 1960, **8**:535–551.

120. Sandler, J. and Joffe, W. G. Notes on Childhood Depression. *Int. J. Psychoanal.*, 1965, **46**, 88–95.

121. Savitt, R. A. Transference Somatization & Symbiotic Need. *J. Amer. Psychoanal. Ass.*, 1969, **17**, 1030–1054.

122. Scher, J. M. II:Primary Gain: The Game of Illness and the Communicative Compact in the Borderline Patient. *Psychoanal. Quart.*, 1961, 532–543.

123. Segel, N. P. (Reporter). Narcissistic Resistance. *J. Amer. Psychoanal. Ass.*, 1969, **18**, 941–954.

124. Singer, M. B. Fantasies of a Borderline Patient. *Psychoanal. Study Child*, 1960, **15**, 310–356.

125. *Snow White and the Seven Dwarfs*, translated and illustrated by Wanda Gag. New York: Coward, 1938.

126. Spitz, R. A. Anaclitic Depression. *Psychoanal. Study Child*. 1946, **2**, 313–341.

127. Spitz, R. A. *The First Year of Life (A Psychoanalytic Study of Normal and Deviant Development of Object Relations)*. New York: International Universities Press, 1965.

128. Spitz, R. A. The Smiling Response: A Contribution to the Ontogenesis of Social Relations. *Genet. Psychol. Mongr.*, Vol. 34. Provincetown, Mass.: Journal Press, 1946.

129. Spitz, R. A. *No and Yes*. New York: International Universities Press, 1957.

130. Spitz, R. A. The Evolution of Dialogue. In M. Schur (Ed.), *Drives, Affects, Behavior*, 2nd ed., New York: International Universities Press, 1965, pp. 170–190.

131. Spitz, R. A. Relevancy of Direct Infant Observations. *Psychoanal. Study Child*, 1950, **5**:66–75.

132. Stein, A. Psychoanalytic Investigation of and Therapy in the Borderline Group of Neuroses. *Psychoanal. Quart.*, 1938, **7**:467–489.

133. Stewart, W. A. The Split Ego and the Mechanism of Disavowal. *Psychoanal. Quart.* 1970, **39**(1), 1–16.

134. Wallerstein, R. S. Reconstruction and Mastery in the Transference Psychosis. *J. Amer. Psychoanal. Ass.*, 1967, **15**, 551–583.

135. Weiss, J. (Reporter). Clinical and Theoretical Aspects of the "As If" Characters (Participants:Atkin, Tarakoff, Ross, Greenson, Katan, Deutsch, Chase, Bychowski, Kaywin). *J. Amer. Psychoanal. Ass.*, 1966, **14**, 569–591.

136. Winnicott, D. W. The Capacity to be Alone. In *The Maturational Processes and the Facilitating Environment*. New York: International Universities Press, 1965, pp. 29–36.

137. Winnicott, D. W. The Theory of the Parent-Infant Relationship. In *The Maturational Process and the Facilitating Environment*. New York: International Universities Press, 1965, pp. 37–55.

138. Winnicott, D. W. Ego Integration in Child Development. In *The Maturational Process and the Facilitating Environment* New York: International Universities Press, 1965, pp. 56–63.

139. Winnicott, D. W. The Development of the Capacity for Concern. In *The Maturational Processes and the Facilitating Environment.* New York: International Universities Press, 1965, pp. 73–82.

140. Winnicott, D. W. From Dependence Towards Independence in the Development of the Individual. In *The Maturational Processes and the Facilitating Environment.* New York: International Universities Press, 1965, pp. 83–92.

141. Winnicott, D. W. Psychotherapy of Character Disorders. In *The Maturational Processes and the Facilitating Environment.* New York: International Universities Press, 1965, pp. 203–216.

142. Winnicott, D. W. Hospital Care Supplementing Intensive Psychotherapy in Adolescence. In *The Maturational Processes and the Facilitating Environment.* New York: International Universities Press, 1965, pp. 242–248.

143. Wolberg, A. R. The Borderline Patient. *Amer. J. Psychother.* 1952, **6**, 694–710.

144. Wolberg, A. R. The Psychoanalytic Treatment of the Borderline Patient in the Individual and Group Setting. *Topical Probl. Psychotherapy,* 1960, **2**, 174–197.

145. Zentner, E. B. & Aponte, H. J. The Amorphous Family Nexus. *Psychiat. Quart.,* 1970, **44**, 91–113.

146. Zetzel, E. R. A Developmental Approach to the Borderline Patient. *Amer. J. Psychiatry,* 1971, **7**, 127.

147. Zilboorg, G. Ambulatory Schizophrenias. *Psychiatry,* 1941, **4**, 149–155.

Index